BEST OF THE BEST
from
MISSISSIPPI

Selected Recipes from Mississippi's
FAVORITE COOKBOOKS

REVISED EDITION

BEST
of the BEST
from
MISSISSIPPI

Selected Recipes from Mississippi's
FAVORITE COOKBOOKS

REVISED EDITION

EDITED BY

Gwen McKee

AND

Barbara Moseley

Illustrated by Tupper England

QUAIL RIDGE PRESS
Brandon, Mississippi

Recipe Collection© 1987 Quail Ridge Press, Inc.

Reprinted with permission and all rights reserved under the name of the cookbooks or organizations or individuals listed below.

Copyright © 1987 by QUAIL RIDGE PRESS, INC.

ISBN 0-937552-19-4

Manufactured in the United States of America

First printing, October 1987 • Second, July 1989 • Third, March 1992 • Fourth, January 1994
Fifth, January 1997 • Sixth, March 1997 • Seventh, May 1998 • Eighth, August 1998 • Ninth, January 2001

Chapter opening photos courtesy of Mississippi Department of Economic Development

QUAIL RIDGE PRESS

P. O. Box 123 • Brandon, MS 39043 • 1-800-343-1583 • Email: info@quailridge.com • www.quailridge.com

CONTENTS

Scenic Mynelle Gardens. Jackson.

PREFACE

Best of the Best from Mississippi was published in 1982 as the first book in QRP's growing "Best of the Best" series (which now includes a number of southern states—see back page for listing). Because so many new cookbooks have been published since that time, we felt it necessary to completely revise the book. Of the 53 cookbooks represented here, only 20 are from the original edition. We are very proud to present this greatly expanded collection of specially selected recipes from the leading cookbooks in the state.

Because Mississippi is blessed with a near-perfect balance of mild climate and abundant rainfall, it is wrapped in a lush greenery of trees, flowers and plants. From the mighty river that forms most of its western border, through the flat Delta land, the gentle rolling hills, the piney woods, to the coastal shores, Mississippi is a place that inspires affection in people who come to know and appreciate its special charm. It is also a place that offers genuine southern hospitality and a superb culinary heritage. The cookbooks that have developed in this region reflect a rural past unhurried by hustle and bustle. They contain recipes created by Mississippians who have taken the time to give careful attention to the preparation and perfection of delicious food.

This book is meant to be a diversified sampling—from the simple to the simply elegant. It is a peek at Mississippi food perfection prepared by accomplished cooks from all over the state. Each recipe is identified beneath by its contributing book, a picture of which can be found in the catalog section of the book along with ordering information. What cannot be conveyed in this book are the uniqueness and originality that make each cookbook included so special. Besides elegant recipes, many have historical sketches, original photographs and artwork, helpful kitchen hints, and humorous anecdotes—good reading as well as good cooking.

Our special thanks to Betsy McKee who worked so diligently in the search for new books and for contacting the original ones for revised information. And we salute Tupper England, whose delightful illustrations have added so much to all of our "Best" books, for yet another superb job. And we are grateful to the Mississippi Department of Economic Development for access to their photographs. And, as always, the work goes smoothly when our great office staff lends their good words, good work and good spirits.

We are extremely pleased to share a significant part of Mississippi's heritage through the foods of her past and present. We thank the many authors, chairmen, and publishers represented here for their gracious cooperation in helping us gather together *The Best of the Best from Mississippi.*

Gwen McKee and Barbara Moseley

CONTRIBUTING COOKBOOKS

Accent One
Answering the Call to Duck Cookery
Aunt Freddie's Pantry
Bayou Cuisine
Bell's Best
Bell's Best 2
Bouquet Garni
Come and Dine
The Cook's Book
Cook with a Natchez Native
The Country Gourmet (Miriam Cohn)
The Country Gourmet (Mississippi Animal Rescue League)
The Country Mouse
DAR Cookbook
Dixie Dining
Down Here Men Don't Cook
Family Secrets
Festival
Gardeners' Gourmet II
Giant Houseparty Cookbook
Gourmet of the Delta
Great American Politicians' Cookbook
Great American Writers' Cookbook
Great Flavors of Mississippi
The Gulf Gourmet
Hors D'Oeuvres Everybody Loves
Hospitality Heirlooms

CONTRIBUTING COOKBOOKS

Into the Second Century
Inverness Cook Book
I Promised A Cookbook
Just a Spoonful
Madison County Cookery
The Mississippi Cookbook
Mississippi Memories II
My Mother Cooked My Way Through Harvard
Natchez Notebook of Cooking
The Pick of the Crop
Pilgrimage Antiques Forum Cookbook
Pineapple Gold
A Salad A Day
Seasoned With Love
The Seven Chocolate Sins
Special Menus for Very Special Occasions
Southern Legacies
Southern Sideboards
Standing Room Only
Taste of the South
Tasting Tea Treasures
Temptations
Top Rankin Recipes
Twelve Days of Christmas Cookbook
Vintage Vicksburg
Waddad's Kitchen

Appetizers

Emerald Mound on Natchez Trace above Natchez.

Orange Julius

1 (6-ounce) can frozen orange
   juice concentrate
1 cup milk
1 cup water

$1/2$ cup sugar
1 teaspoon vanilla
5-6 ice cubes

Blend in blender 30 seconds. Makes 6 cups.

The Country Gourmet
(Mississippi Animal Rescue League)

Iced Tea Cooler

2 large family size tea bags
3 quarts boiling water
$1/2$ cup sugar
1 (12-ounce) can frozen
   lemonade

1 quart chilled gingerale or
   7-up

Brew tea in boiling water. Add sugar; stir and cool. Add frozen lemonade. Before serving, add chilled gingerale or 7-up. Pour over ice and add mint.

Natchez Notebook of Cooking

Hot Spiced Percolator Punch

9 cups pineapple juice
9 cups cranberry cocktail juice
$4^{1}/2$ cups water
1 cup brown sugar

$1/2$ teaspoon whole cloves
4 sticks cinnamon, broken in
   pieces
$1/4$ teaspoon salt (optional)

Mix juices, water and sugar. Put in 30-cup percolator. Place cloves, cinnamon and salt in basket. Perk as you would coffee. Makes 30 cups.

Bell's Best

Fruit Slush

4 bananas, mashed well
1 (6-ounce) can frozen
   lemonade concentrate,
   undiluted and thawed
2 cups sugar
3 cups water

1 (12-ounce) can frozen orange
   juice concentrate, undiluted
   and thawed
3 cups pineapple juice
3 quarts lemon-lime
   carbonated beverage

Mix bananas with lemonade until smooth. Combine sugar and water in a saucepan. Bring to a boil, stirring until sugar dissolves. Combine sugar mixture with banana mixture. Add orange juice, pineapple juice, and the lemon-lime beverage. Mix well and pour into freezer trays. Freeze until firm. Remove mixture from freezer several hours before serving and let thaw until it is slushy. Ladle into punch cups or juice glasses and serve with a spoon. Yield: 1 gallon.

Come and Dine

Coke, Good Food, Hot Coffee, and Lunch...names of communities in Mississippi.

Special Company Coffee

Have ready on a silver tray:

Bowl of semi-sweet chocolate
   chips
Small pitcher fine brandy

Bowl of fresh whipped cream
Pot of freshly made hot coffee

Each guest prepares his own coffee, according to taste. It is recommended that a little of each of the above ingredients be used. This is wonderful after a good dinner. It is also a fun thing to do at a morning meeting.

Pineapple Gold

Amaretto Freeze
Delicious as an after dinner drink or as a frozen dessert.

Serves 6 as an after dinner drink. Double recipe to serve 6 for a parfait.

1/3 cup Amaretto liqueur
1 tablespoon dark brown
  sugar

1 quart vanilla ice cream
Whipped cream
Maraschino cherries

Mix Amaretto and brown sugar together and stir until the sugar is dissolved.

Combine the Amaretto mixture and the ice cream in container of blender and process until smooth.

You may serve immediately in brandy snifters or pour mixture into parfait glasses. Fill 3/4 full and freeze. When ready to serve, top with a spoon of whipped cream and a cherry.

This is a grand dessert after a heavy meal.

Pineapple Gold

Coffee Rum Punch

12 tablespoons instant coffee
2 cups sugar
2 cups water
3 large cans evaporated milk
3 large cans whole milk

1/2 gallon coffee ice cream,
  softened
2 large bottles soda water
1/2 bottle light rum
Whipped cream

Add sugar and coffee to water. Stir, heat, blend, remove from heat, and chill. Add remaining ingredients. Top with whipped cream and serve. Serves 30 cups. A big hit for a brunch or luncheon.

The Gulf Gourmet

Pappy's Hot Toddy
(William Faulkner)

William Faulkner (1897-1962) was the author of *The Sound and the Fury, As I Lay Dying, Absalom, Absalom!* and *Light in August*. He won the Nobel Prize for Literature in 1950. (The following recipe was submitted by his niece, Dean Faulkner Wells.)

When grownups in the Faulkner family were sick, Pappy had an instant cure—his ever-popular Hot Toddy. It was guaranteed to cure or ease anything from the aches and pains of a bad spill from a horse to a bad cold, from a broken leg to a broken heart. Pappy alone decided when a Hot Toddy was needed, and he administered it to his patient with the best bedside manner of a country doctor.

He prepared it in the kitchen in the following way: Take one heavy glass tumbler. Fill approximately half full with Heaven Hill bourbon (the Jack Daniel's was reserved for Pappy's ailments). Add one tablespoon of sugar. Squeeze ½ lemon and drop into glass. Stir until sugar dissolves. Fill glass with boiling water. Serve with potholder to protect patient's hands from the hot glass.

Pappy always made a small ceremony out of serving his Hot Toddy, bringing it upstairs on a silver tray and admonishing his patient to drink it quickly before it cooled off.

It never failed.

The Great American Writer's Cookbook

Mississippi is the birthplace of an exceptional number of major literary figures, including Eudora Welty, William Faulkner, Walker Percy, Tennessee Williams, Richard Wright, Beth Henley, Willie Morris, and John Grisham.

Cheese Dip with Apple Slices

1 (8-ounce) package cream
  cheese
2 cups shredded Cheddar
  cheese
6 tablespoons half-and-half
1 teaspoon Worcestershire
  sauce

1/4 teaspoon dry mustard
1/4 teaspoon onion salt
3 drops Tabasco
6 slices bacon, diced and
  sautéed
3-4 large apples, sliced
Lemon juice

In a heavy saucepan combine first 7 ingredients. Heat until cheese melts and mixture is hot. Add bacon. Sprinkle apple slices with lemon juice to prevent browning. Serve dip warm in a chafing dish with apples on the side. Serves 35.

Taste of the South

Six Layer Dip

2 large avocados
1/8 teaspoon garlic powder
1/8 teaspoon garlic salt
1 tablespoon lemon juice
2 tablespoons mayonnaise

2 (8-ounce) jars picante sauce
3/4 cup chopped ripe olives
3 cups peeled and chopped
  tomatoes
1 1/2 cups shredded Cheddar

Peel, seed and mash avocados. Stir in garlic powder, garlic salt, lemon juice and mayonnaise. Spread evenly in 12 x 8 x 2-inch baking dish. Carefully spread sour cream over avocado mixture. Drain picante sauce well. Spoon over sour cream. Top with layers of olives and tomatoes. Sprinkle with cheese. Serve with large corn chips. Yield: 6 cups.

*The Country Gourmet
(Mississippi Animal Rescue League)*

Hot Mushroom Dip

4 tablespoons butter
1 clove garlic
1 pound mushrooms, sliced
2 tablespoons dried parsley

½ teaspoon salt
¼ teaspoon pepper
1 cup sour cream

Melt butter in chafing dish. Add garlic which has been minced, mushrooms, parsley, salt, pepper. Cook until mushrooms are tender. Fold in sour cream. Serve on melba toast.

Best of Bayou Cuisine

Jane's Broccoli Dip

1 stick oleo
1 cup chopped onion
2 packages frozen, chopped
    broccoli
1 (4-ounce) can sliced
    mushrooms

1½ rolls (9-ounce) garlic
    cheese
1 cup slivered almonds
2 cans mushroom soup
Tabasco sauce and
    Worcestershire sauce to taste

Sauté onions in oleo. Add broccoli and simmer until tender. Add remainder of ingredients and serve hot with corn chips. Makes 4 cups.

Bell's Best

Delicious Dip

1 (8-ounce) package cream
    cheese, room temperature
1 (4-ounce) can chopped black
    olives

1 can smoked oysters, chopped
¾ pint mayonnaise
5 dashes Tabasco
3 teaspoons lemon juice

Mix thoroughly. Serve with cocktail crackers.

The Cook's Book

Spinach Dip Bread

1 (10-ounce) package frozen
chopped spinach, cooked,
drained and squeezed dry
1 cup mayonnaise

1 bunch green onions,
including tops, chopped
1 large round rye or French
loaf of bread

Mix spinach with mayonnaise and onions. Cut center out of a big, round loaf of French or rye bread, leaving ¾ to 1-inch bottom and around sides. Cut the bread removed from the center into 1-inch chunks. Pour dip mixture into center of hollowed out bread and place loaf on serving dish. Arrange bread cubes around bread with toothpicks for dipping. Yield: 12 or more servings.

Note: One loaf will usually hold a double recipe of this dip. You may need to have additional bread cubes handy for extra dipping.

Mississippi Memories

Vegetable Mousse

2 tomatoes, chopped
1 small white onion, chopped
1 cup celery, finely chopped
1 bell pepper, finely chopped
1 cucumber, finely chopped
1 envelope plain gelatin

¼ cup cold water
¼ cup boiling water
1 pint Kraft mayonnaise
1 teaspoon salt
Tabasco to taste
Lemon juice to taste

Finely chop all vegetables. Drain well on paper towels. Soften gelatin in cold water, then add hot water. Let cool. Fold in mayonnaise and seasonings. Add vegetables last. Refrigerate overnight. Serve as a dip with Melba rounds. Can also be used to stuff tomatoes. Serves 20 to 30 as a dip.

The Gulf Gourmet

Delightful Fruit Dip

¹/₂ cup sugar
2 tablespoons all-purpose flour
1 cup pineapple juice
1 egg, beaten

1 tablespoon butter or
   margarine
1 cup whipping cream,
   whipped

Combine first 5 ingredients in a heavy saucepan; cook over medium heat, stirring constantly, until smooth and thickened. Let cool completely, fold in whipped cream. Serve with fresh fruit. Yield: about 2 cups.

Into the Second Century

Hot Spinach and Crab Dip

1 bunch green onions and tops, minced
1 clove garlic, crushed
1/2 cup margarine
2 (10-ounce) packages frozen, chopped spinach
1 tablespoon Parmesan cheese

2 (6-ounce) cans crabmeat
4 tablespoons margarine
4 tablespoons flour
2 cups milk
2 (6-ounce) rolls jalapeño cheese

Sauté onions and garlic in margarine. Cook spinach and drain. Add sautéed onions and garlic, Parmesan cheese, and crabmeat to spinach. Make a medium white sauce with margarine, flour, and milk. Melt jalapeño cheese in white sauce. Add spinach mixture to the cheese sauce. Serve warm in a chafing dish.

Festival

Hot Cheese and Crabmeat Canapes

1 (4-ounce) jar Old English cheese (sharp)
1 (6-ounce) can crabmeat
2 tablespoons mayonnaise
1 teaspoon onion juice

1/4 teaspoon white pepper
1 teaspoon Worcestershire sauce
1/4 teaspoon Tabasco sauce
Small rounds of bread

Mix cheese and drained crabmeat. Add mayonnaise, onion juice, white pepper and both sauces and blend well. Spread on small rounds of bread and bake at 400° for about 15 minutes or until brown. Makes 56 (1 1/2-inch) rounds.

Gourmet of the Delta

Scrumptious Shrimp Appetizer

12 ounces cream cheese, softened
1 tablespoon mayonnaise
1 teaspoon curry powder
Salt and pepper to taste

1 (7-ounce) can whole baby shrimp, drained
4 green onions minced
2 hard-boiled eggs, chopped

Combine cream cheese, mayonnaise, curry powder, salt and pepper. Place on a flat dish or platter and sprinkle on top the shrimp, then green onions, and chopped eggs. Serve with assorted crackers. Serves 12. Can double.

Standing Room Only

Escargot

3 tablespoons butter
2 teaspoons soy sauce
1 teaspoon Worcestershire
1 pod minced garlic
4 chopped green onions

1-2 teaspoons chopped parsley
2 teaspoons lemon juice
1 can escargot or snails
Salt and pepper

Melt butter in a small skillet or pan. Add soy sauce, Worcestershire, garlic, green onions, parsley, lemon juice, salt and pepper. Add escargot or snails. Simmer 10 minutes or so. Serve with toothpicks and crackers. Delicious!

Down Here Men Don't Cook

Mushroom Turnovers

½ cup butter
1 (8-ounce) package cream
  cheese

1 ½ cups flour

Blend butter and cream cheese together. Add flour slowly until a soft ball of dough forms. Refrigerate in waxed paper for about 1 hour. Roll out dough and cut with a biscuit cutter.

FILLING:
1 onion, finely chopped
1 tablespoon chopped parsley
½ teaspoon thyme
½ pound mushrooms, frozen
  or fresh, chopped

4 tablespoons butter
1 teaspoon salt
½ cup sour cream

Cook onion, parsley, thyme, and mushrooms in butter until a very light brown. Add salt and sour cream. Remove from heat and cool. Put a spoonful of this mixture on center of each pastry round. Fold over and seal edges. Bake at 425° for 5 to 6 minutes. Yield: 40.
    Note: These freeze well unbaked.

Bouquet Garni

Shrimp Mold

1 can tomato soup
1 ½ packages unflavored
  gelatin
½ cup cold water
¾ cup finely chopped celery
¾ cup finely chopped onions

1 ½ pounds cooked shrimp,
  chopped
1 (8-ounce) package cream
  cheese, softened
1 cup mayonnaise

Heat soup. Dissolve gelatin in water and stir into soup until mixed. Add remaining ingredients, mixing slowly. Pour into greased mold and chill 4 hours before serving. Serve with Ritz Crackers. Yields 1 ½ quarts.
    Tuna or crab may be substituted for shrimp.

Madison County Cookery

Chopped Chicken Liver
(Pâté de Foie Gras)

3 pounds onions, sliced
$^1/_2$ stick oleo or 2 tablespoons
  chicken fat
2 pounds chicken livers,
  cleaned

1 dozen eggs
Salt and pepper to taste

Sauté sliced onions in oleo until wilted (about 5 to 10 minutes). Boil chicken livers until tender. (Add just enough water to cover livers.) Hard boil eggs and peel. When all is cold, put livers, eggs and onions through a meat grinder. Mix well and add salt and pepper. Refrigerate. This can be molded when cold. Take the top off a fresh pineapple. Put on top of molded chicken liver. Down the sides of molded chicken liver, slice pimiento olives and it makes a unique looking hors d'oeuvre.

The Country Gourmet (Miriam G. Cohn)

French Fried Pickles

1 quart dill pickles, thinly
  sliced
1 $^3/_4$ cups all-purpose flour,
  divided
2 teaspoons red pepper
2 teaspoons paprika

2 teaspoons pepper
2 teaspoons garlic salt
1 teaspoon salt
3 dashes hot sauce
1 cup beer
Vegetable oil

Dredge sliced pickles in 1 cup flour; set aside. Combine remaining $^3/_4$ cup flour and dry ingredients. Add hot sauce and beer, mixing well. Dip dredged pickles into batter. Deep-fry in hot oil (375°) until pickles float to surface and are golden brown. Drain on paper towels; serve immediately. Yield: About 2$^1/_2$ dozen appetizer servings.

Editor's Note: This recipe appeared in the April, 1982 issue of *Southern Living.* With Janice Jones' permission, we are proud to reprint it here.

**The Country Gourmet
(Mississippi Animal Rescue League)**

Egg Rolls

1 pound uncooked shrimp,
  peeled
1 pound boneless lean pork,
  uncooked
4 ounces fresh mushrooms
8 green onions
1 red pepper, seeded
1 (8-ounce) can water
  chestnuts, drained
8 ounces Chinese cabbage
  (about 1/2 head)

3 tablespoons sherry
1 1/2 tablespoons soy sauce
2 teaspoons fresh grated ginger
1 teaspoon sugar
1/2 teaspoon salt
1/4 cup water
1 1/2 tablespoons cornstarch
24 egg roll wrappers

Finely chop shrimp, pork, mushrooms, onions, pepper, cabbage, and water chestnuts. May use food processor. Place in large bowl and add sherry, soy sauce, ginger, sugar and salt. Mix well. Mix water and cornstarch. Place 1/4 cup of meat mixture evenly across corner of wrapper. Brush cornstarch mixture around edges. Carefully roll wrappers around filling; fold in corners. Fry egg rolls in hot oil until golden brown, about 5 minutes. Drain and serve warm. 2 dozen

Temptations

Bacon Roll Ups

1/4 cup butter or margarine
1/2 cup water
1 1/2 cups package herb
  seasoned stuffing

1 egg slightly beaten
1/4 pound hot bulk pork
  sausage
1/2-2/3 pound sliced bacon

Melt butter in water in saucepan. Remove from heat; stir into stuffing then add egg and sausage. Blend thoroughly. Chill for one hour for easier handling. Shape into small oblongs about the size of pecans. Cut bacon strips into thirds crosswise; wrap one piece around dressing mixture and fasten with wooden pick. Place on rack in shallow pan and bake 375° for 35 minutes until brown and crisply turning halfway. These may be made the day before baking. Also freezes well before baking. Yield: 36 appetizers.

The Pilgrimage Garden Club
Antiques Forum Cookbook

Hot and Spicy Cocktail Meatballs

MEATBALLS:

3/4 pound ground beef
1 1/2 teaspoons minced onion
3 drops Tabasco sauce
3/4 teaspoon salt
3/4 cup fine dry bread crumbs

1/2 teaspoon prepared
  horseradish
2 eggs, beaten
1/2 teaspoon pepper

Mix all ingredients for meatballs and shape into balls 3/4-inch in diameter. Melt 1 tablespoon butter in electric skillet set at 340°. Add meatballs and brown. Shake frequently for even browning and to keep balls round. When meatballs are browned and done, pour off any fat and add sauce.

SAUCE:

3/4 cup catsup
1/4 cup cider vinegar
1 tablespoon minced onion
1/4 teaspoon pepper

1/2 cup water
2 tablespoons brown sugar
2 teaspoons dry mustard
3 drops Tabasco sauce

Combine sauce ingredients. Add to browned meatballs, cover, and continue to cook about 10 minutes, shaking occasionally. Can be made the day ahead or frozen.

   To serve, put in chafing dish and keep hot. Makes about 4 1/2 dozen meatballs.

The Pick of the Crop

Jezebel Sauce

18 ounces pineapple preserves
18 ounces apple jelly
1 small can dry mustard

3/4-1 jar horseradish
Approximately 1 teaspoon
  coarse black pepper

Serve over cream cheese, ham or with small slices of Cheddar cheese and crackers.

Top Rankin Recipes

Spinach Balls

2 (10-ounce) boxes frozen
  chopped spinach, cooked
  and drained well
2 cups herb bread stuffing mix
2 onions, finely chopped
6 eggs, beaten
3/4 cup butter, melted

1/2 cup grated Parmesan cheese
1 tablespoon garlic salt
1/2 teaspoon thyme
1 teaspoon monosodium
  glutamate

Mix ingredients well. Form balls, using 1 teaspoon mixture for each, and bake on lightly greased baking sheet 20 minutes at 350°. May be frozen either before or after baking. Yields 4-5 dozen.

Southern Sideboards

Orange Balls

1 (12-ounce) package vanilla
  wafers, crushed
1 cup confectioners' sugar
1/4 cup soft butter, softened to
  room temperature

1/2 cup frozen orange juice
  concentrate, thawed
1/2 teaspoon vanilla
1 cup chopped pecans

Combine crumbs and sugar; blend in butter. Stir in orange concentrate; add vanilla and nuts. Shape mixture into bite-sized balls; shake in plastic bag with additional confectioners' sugar. Arrange orange balls in single layer on tray; store uncovered overnight in refrigerator. Yield: 36-40 balls. Roll in coconut, if desired.

Bell's Best

In the 1830's a ten dollar note was issued by a New Orleans bank which read "Dix" (which is French for ten). Riverboat workers returning to the north boasted that they had "a pocketful of Dixies" or ten dollar notes. With the help of a minstrel tune, the Deep South soon became known as "Dixie."

Snappy Chicken Balls
So pretty piled high in a glass dish, decorated with little yellow flowers

2 cups cooked chicken, chopped finely
1 ½ cups almonds, chopped finely
1 tablespoon finely chopped green onion
4 tablespoons Major Grey's chutney, chopped

1 (8-ounce) package cream cheese, softened
¼ cup mayonnaise
2 teaspoons curry powder
Salt to taste
1 cup coconut

Combine chicken, almonds, green onion and chutney. In a separate bowl, blend cream cheese, mayonnaise and curry powder. Combine chicken mixture and cream cheese mixture. Chill. Shape into bite-size balls. Roll each ball in grated coconut. Refrigerate, covered, until ready to serve. Garnish with tiny yellow and white flowers or candied orange peel. Makes 80-90 balls and will keep 3 days.

Hors D'Oeuvres Everybody Loves

Spinach Cheese Pastries

PASTRY:

1/2 pound soft cream cheese   2 cups plain flour
1 cup soft salted butter

Combine cream cheese and butter, using pastry blender. Cut in flour. Use hands to work dough until it holds together. Place on wax paper. Form into a ball and chill overnight. Roll dough to 1/3-inch thickness with floured rolling pin on a generously floured surface. Cut into 2-inch rounds with cutter.

FILLING:

1 medium onion, finely
    chopped
1/4 cup olive oil
1 1/4 teaspoons salt
1/4 teaspoon white pepper
1 (10-ounce) package frozen
    spinach, thawed and drained

1 cup feta cheese
1/2 cup pot cheese or cottage
    cheese
1 egg, beaten

Sauté onion in olive oil. Add seasonings and spinach, while cooking. Mix cheeses and egg. Combine spinach with egg mixture. Be sure to mix thoroughly. Cool to lukewarm. Place teaspoonful of filling in center of each round of pastry. Fold over to make crescent shape. Edges may be pressed with fork. Place on ungreased cookie sheet. Bake at 425° for 15 to 20 minutes. May be served warm or at room temperature. This is a great make-ahead-freeze-bake as needed.

Waddad's Kitchen

Grace's Spinach Sandwiches
A real trendsetter—equally good as a dip

1 (10-ounce) package frozen chopped spinach
1/2 (8-ounce) can water chestnuts, finely chopped
1/4 cup sour cream
1/2 teaspoon lemon pepper
1/2 teaspoon Tony's Creole Seasoning (or seasoned salt and Cayenne)

3 green onions with stems, chopped
2 tablespoons mayonnaise
1 loaf thin sliced bread (28 slices)

Thaw and squeeze water from spinach. Place it between paper towels and pat dry. Do *not* cook. Mix with other ingredients. Add more sour cream for a spreadable consistency, if needed. Amount of onion and spice may also be increased to taste.

Trim crust from bread and spread spinach mixture on half the slices. Top with other half of slices. Cut sandwiches diagonally, making 4 tiny triangles. Makes 112 sandwiches.

Hors D'Oeuvres Everybody Loves

Cucumber Sandwiches

1 large package ranch style dressing mix
1 1/2 cups mayonnaise
3/4 cup buttermilk

Bread rounds
2 large cucumbers, sliced thinly

Combine the dressing mix, mayonnaise, and buttermilk. Blend until smooth and of good spreading consistency. Spread each bread round with dressing mixture. Top with a slice of cucumber and finish with a dollop of dressing. Chill before serving.

Bouquet Garni

Hot Buttered Brie

1 (4¹/₂-ounce) round ripened
  Brie
1 tablespoon butter, softened

¹/₄ cup slivered almonds,
  lightly toasted

Carefully cut top crust of Brie off with knife. Place cheese in an oven-proof serving dish. Spread top of cheese with softened butter. Add slivered almonds on top. Cover and bake at 325° 15 minutes or until cheese is soft and creamy. Serve with assorted crackers, preferably bland, and green grapes or slices of pear. (Crust is edible.)

The Country Mouse

Cheese Fondue

1 pound imported Swiss cheese
2 tablespoons flour
1 clove fresh garlic
2 cups dry white wine

1 tablespoon lemon juice
3 tablespoons kirsch or brandy
French bread

Shred cheese and dredge lightly with flour. Rub cooking pot with garlic, pour in wine, set on low heat. When air bubbles rise to surface add lemon juice—then add cheese by handsful, stirring constantly with wooded spoon until cheese is melted, add kirsch and blend well. Serve bubbling hot from chafing dish. Break bread into pieces, stick with fork and swirl in fondue. Keep fondue at simmer.

According to Swiss tradition, if the bread falls off the fork in the fondue, ladies pay a kiss to the nearest man, who pays for the next round of wine.

Inverness Cook Book

Homemade Boursin

1 (8-ounce) package cream
   cheese, softened
1 clove garlic, crushed
1 teaspoon basil

1 teaspoon caraway seed
1 teaspoon dill weed
1 teaspoon chives, chopped
Cracked black or lemon pepper

Blend cream cheese with garlic, caraway, basil, dill weed and chives. Pat into a round flat shape. Roll on all sides (lightly) in lemon pepper or cracked black pepper. Make a few days ahead. Serve with assorted crackers.

The Country Mouse

Dunleith Cheese Ring

2 pounds Cheddar cheese
2 cups chopped nuts
2 cups mayonnaise
2 small onions, grated
4 tablespoons Worcestershire
   sauce

Salt
Pepper
Cayenne

Mix all ingredients, mold with hands into desired shape (preferably a ring). Refrigerate or freeze. When ready to serve, fill center with strawberry preserves.

The Pilgrimage Garden Club
Antiques Forum Cookbook

Sweet and Spicy Pecans

1 egg white, slightly beaten
1 teaspoon water
3/4 cup sugar
1 teaspoon salt
1 1/2 teaspoons ground
    cinnamon

1/2 teaspoon ground cloves
1/2 teaspoon ground nutmeg
2 cups shelled pecan halves

Combine egg white with water and beat lightly. Set aside. Combine sugar, salt, and spices. Dip pecan halves in egg white mixture, then in sugar mixture. Spread on a greased baking sheet. Bake at 300° for 20 minutes, turning at least once. Let the pecans cool, and store in a tightly covered container, or in the refrigerator.

Come and Dine

Cheese Straws

1 (8-ounce) package sharp
    Cheddar cheese
1 stick margarine
1/4 teaspoon cayenne pepper
    (this is mild)

1 level teaspoon sugar
1/2 teaspoon salt
1 1/4 cups plain flour

Cheese and margarine should be at room temperature. Shred cheese and mix well with margarine. Add cayenne, sugar and salt. Stir in flour, half at a time. Mix thoroughly. Pipe through cookie press or cake decorator using star tip onto cookie sheets. Bake at 350°for 8 to 10 minutes. Makes about 80 finger-length straws.

Note: For party-size cheese patties, add about 1/4 cup more flour and knead dough a bit longer. Roll out and cut with small round cookie or biscuit cutter. Makes about 100 patties.

I Promised A Cookbook

Soups

Cypress Swamp. Natchez Trace Parkway.

Asparagus Soup

2 pounds fresh asparagus
Salt, black pepper
2 cups milk
1 teaspoon tarragon
1 cup white wine

1 extra teaspoon dried
   tarragon
6 tablespoons unsalted butter
6 tablespoons all-purpose flour
6 cups canned chicken broth

Wash asparagus and cut off tough ends. Break in pieces and boil in salted water 12 to 15 minutes until tender. Drain and purée. Return purée to saucepan with milk and simmer, stirring until smooth. Put tarragon into a saucepan with the white wine and add some pepper, bring to simmer and cook until it reduces to about one tablespoon. Set aside. In a saucepan melt 4 tablespoons butter. Stir in flour and continue cooking and stirring a few seconds. Add chicken broth and simmer several minutes, then add asparagus purée. Pour a cup of soup into the saucepan which contains reduced wine and tarragon. Sitr over heat, then pour back into asparagus mixture. Bring to a boil. Taste and correct seasoning. Stir the remaining butter and tarragon into the soup. 6 servings.

Temptations

Down Home Cheddar Cheese Soup

1/2 cup margarine
1/2 cup each finely chopped:
   celery, green pepper, onion,
   carrot, cauliflower
1 tablespoon granulated
   chicken bouillon or 2 cubes

2 cups water
1/2 cup margarine
2/3 cup flour
4 cups milk
1/2 pound sharp Cheddar
   cheese, shredded

Heat margarine over medium heat. Add vegetables; cook until tender, stirring often. Add water and chicken bouillon; heat to boiling. Cover; cook over low heat 10 minutes. Meanwhile, heat remaining margarine in saucepan. Stir in flour; cook until bubbly. Remove from heat. Gradually stir in milk. Cook over medium heat, stirring often, until thickened, but do not boil. Stir in cheese till fully blended. Stir cheese mixture into vegetables and chicken broth mixture. Serves 8-10. Flavor is outstanding.

The Country Mouse

Garfield's Broccoli and Almond Soup

1 gallon water
4 chicken bouillon cubes
2 pounds fresh broccoli
1 medium carrot, grated
2 teaspoons garlic powder
1/2 cup butter
1/2 cup margarine

1 cup flour
1/2 cup sherry
Salt and pepper to taste
1 cup blanched almonds
1 tablespoon monosodium
  glutamate

In a large pan, bring water to a boil and dissolve chicken bouillon cubes in it. Add broccoli, carrot, and garlic. Cook for about 30 to 45 minutes. In a deep pan, melt butter and margarine and add flour to make a roux. Stir in broccoli mixture and cook until slightly thickened. Add sherry and salt and pepper to taste. Stir in almonds and monosodium glutamate. Yield: 12 bowls or 24 cups.

Note: This recipe from Maxwell's Restaurant has been requested by many, but never revealed until now.

Vintage Vicksburg

Broccoli Soup III

3 pounds broccoli (about 3
  bunches
3 (14 1/2-ounce) cans
  regular-strength (not
  condensed) chicken broth
1 medium-size onion, chopped
4 tablespoons butter
1/2 teaspoon salt
1 cup peeled, chopped
  potatoes

1/4 teaspoon each, marjoram
  and thyme
1 pint half and half (or
  whipping cream)
1 (15-ounce) can evaporated
  milk
Cooked, crumbled bacon for
  garnish

Cut broccoli head from stems, then peel and slice stalks. Simmer broccoli, broth, onions, butter, salt, potatoes, and herbs, covered, until vegetables are tender. Purée mixture in food processor or blender until smooth. Stir in milk products. Serve hot or cold. Serves 12.

Note: Liquids (broth and milk) can be adjusted to desired consistency without changing basic ingredients.

Gardeners' Gourmet II

Cream of Zucchini Soup

1 pound zucchini, cleaned and
   sliced thin
1 clove garlic, minced
3 tablespoons finely chopped
   green onion

2 tablespoons butter
1 teaspoon curry powder
$1/2$ teaspoon salt
$1/2$ cup whipping cream
$1 3/4$ cups chicken broth

In tightly covered pan simmer zucchini, garlic, green onion in the butter for about 10 minutes, stirring occasionally to prevent vegetables from burning. Place in blender or food processor and add remaining ingredients. Blend until smooth. Serve either very cold or hot.

Note: We think it's much better served as a cold soup. Serves 4.

Giant Houseparty Cookbook

Curried Pumpkin Soup

$1/4$ cup butter
1 large onion, sliced, or $3/4$ cup
   green onion, chopped
1 (16-ounce) can pumpkin
1 bay leaf
$1/2$ teaspoon sugar

$1/2$ teaspoon curry powder
$1/4$ teaspoon nutmeg
4 cups chicken stock
2 cups milk or light cream
$1 1/2$ teaspoons salt, or to taste
White pepper

Melt butter; sauté onion until soft, sprinkle with curry powder, add pumpkin and seasonings, except salt, and one cup stock. Simmer 15 minutes. Process to pureé. Add remaining stock and cream and adjust seasonings. Simmer 10 minutes but do not allow to boil. If the soup is to be frozen, freeze the base after it is pureéd, and add the remaining stock and the cream when the soup is to be used. Serves 6-8. Can do ahead. Can freeze.

Standing Room Only

French Onion Soup

¼ cup butter or margarine
4 cups thin-sliced onion
4 (10½-ounce) cans beef
   bouillon, undiluted
1 teaspoon salt

4-6 French bread slices, 1-inch
   thick
2 tablespoons grated Parmesan
   cheese

Heat butter in large skillet. Add onion and sauté, stirring until golden (about 8 minutes). Combine sautéed onion, bouillon, and salt in medium saucepan and bring to boil. Reduce heat and simmer, covered, for 30 minutes. Toast French bread slices under broiler until browned on both sides. Sprinkle one side of bread with grated cheese and run under broiler until cheese is bubbly. Pour soup into individual soup bowls. Float the toast, cheese side up, on top of the soup. Serves 4 to 6.

The Cook's Book

Cream of Leek Soup

¼ cup butter
2 cups chopped leeks, bottoms
   only
½ cup finely-chopped onion
4 cups thinly-sliced, raw
   potatoes
2 cups rich chicken broth

1¼ teaspoons salt
1 tablespoon freeze-dried
   chives
2 cups half-and-half
1 cup whipping cream
Crisp buttered croutons

Melt butter in saucepan over low heat; add leeks and onion; simmer until tender. Add potatoes, broth, and salt; simmer until potatoes are tender. Pour into blender or food processor; blend or process until smooth. Return to saucepan; add chives and pour in half-and-half. When very hot, not boiling, remove from heat; stir in whipping cream and serve garnished with croutons.

Accent One

Vegetable Soup

2 pounds boneless stew meat
8 cups water
1 soup bone
1 (6-ounce) can tomato paste
1 large onion, sliced thin
Salt and pepper
1/3 cup barley
1 large potato, chopped
2 (10-ounce) packages frozen
    mixed vegetables or,

2 (16-ounce) cans mixed
    vegetables
1 (32-ounce) can tomatoes
1 (16-ounce) can whole kernel
    corn
3 sprigs parsley, finely cut
1/4 teaspoon rosemary
1/4 teaspoon marjoram
1/4 teaspoon thyme
1/2 bay leaf

Cut meat into small chunks. Place in large Dutch oven. Add water, salt, pepper, tomato paste, 1/2 onion, and soup bone. Simmer, covered, for 1 1/2 hours, or until meat is tender. Remove bone; skim fat from top. Add barley; simmer for 45 minutes. Add rest of onion, tomatoes, vegetables, parsley, rosemary, marjoram, thyme and bay leaf. Simmer until vegetables are tender. Remove bay leaf. Seasonings should be omitted or adjusted, according to taste. Makes 8-10 large servings.

(This is Van Cliburn's favorite, as prepared by his aunt, Mrs. Mattye Cliburn of the Linwood Community.)

Giant Houseparty Cookbook

Carrot Pecan Soup

10 carrots, cooked
1 quart chicken stock
1/2 stalk celery, chopped
1/3 onion, chopped
1 shallot, chopped

1/4 pound butter
1/4 cup flour
1 quart heavy cream
1/2 teaspoon cinnamon
Pecans, finely chopped

Cook carrots until tender. Drain and purée, using some of the chicken stock. Cook remaining vegetables in butter until tender. Add flour to make a roux and cook about 1 minute—do not brown. Add remaining chicken stock, heavy cream, puréed carrots, and cinnamon. Simmer 10 minutes. Serve garnished with finely chopped pecans. Makes 3 quarts.

Natchez Notebook of Cooking

Black Bean Soup a la Tampa

1 1/2 quarts water	1 tablespoon salt
1/2 pound black beans	1 ounce bacon
1/2 cup olive oil	1/4 pound ham bone
2 large onions, chopped finely	3 bay leaves
1 bell pepper (green), chopped	1/2 cup vinegar
1 pod garlic	1/2 cup chopped onions

Soak beans thoroughly overnight. Fry onion, bell pepper and garlic lightly in 1/2 cup olive oil. Combine all ingredients including water in which beans were soaked except vinegar and additional onions, and cook with slow fire until beans are tender and liquid is of thick consistency. Add vinegar a few minutes before serving. Serve in a bowl with one cup cooked rice over which black beans are placed and topped with 1/2 cup chopped onions.

Variation: 1 pound black beans (washed well), placed in large pot with enough water to cover half again (approximately 3 or 4 quarts). Add 2 chopped peppers, 2 chopped onions, 4 pods garlic, 4 tablespoons salt, 6 bay leaves, 4 tablespoons oregano and 1 teaspoon baking soda. Sauté 2 peppers and 2 onions, chopped in 1/2 cup olive oil then add 1/2 cup more oil and 1/2 cup wine vinegar to the beans which have cooked on low fire until very soft. Cook a while longer.

Best of Bayou Cuisine

Soup Davila

A great treat is in store for you with this quintessential soup. The flavors draw out and compliment the goodness of skillet browned duck and provide a bonus of an unusually forgiving dish in which less flavorful diving ducks can be used with confidence. Most of us, however, enjoy this dish so much that we save breast and other meat from our best ducks for Soup Davila just as we reserve premium shot shells for use on our annual trip to Duck Heaven Lodge.

2 eggs
7 cups water
1 cup tomato sauce
1 cup consommé
1/2 teaspoon celery salt
4 cloves garlic, minced
1/2 teaspoon thyme
4 tablespoons chopped fresh
    parsley
1/4 cup Worcestershire sauce
1 small whole onion
6 cloves

1/2 cup butter or margarine
1/2 cup chopped green onions
    with tops
1/2 cup flour
3 cups duck meat taken from
    the breast and thigh and cut
    in bite-size pieces
2 bay leaves
Salt
Pepper
Lemon Juice
Sherry

Hard boil eggs in salted water for about 15 minutes; remove and set aside to cool. Remove shell, crumble yolk, and dice white in about 1/8-inch pieces. Mix yolk and white and set aside.

Heat water in a large pot and add tomato sauce, consommé, celery, salt, garlic, thyme, parsley, and Worcestershire sauce. Mix well and heat to keep warm but do not allow to boil. Remove the dried outside skin from the onion and press the sharp points of cloves into the bulb. This is done to facilitate removal of cloves before serving.

Melt butter in a Dutch oven and brown duck well. Remove duck and sauté green onions in the remaining butter until edges are brown; blend in flour and cook a few minutes with stirring; don't try to brown the flour as you would in preparing a roux. Add duck

CONTINUED

CONTINUED

and stir in the warm liquid in cup quantities; continue to mix between each addition until smooth. Add bay leaf, onion with cloves, and simmer uncovered for about 2 hours or until the meat is tender. Add a little water if necessary to maintain a creamlike consistency. Remove bay leaf, onion with cloves, and correct the seasoning with salt, pepper and a few drops of lemon juice. Rarely will more than about a teaspoon of lemon juice be required.

Serve a cup or more in large warm soup bowls. Add 1 tablespoon sherry per serving and garnish with chopped egg. This dish constitutes a marvelous herald of good things to come as a soup course, and brings the host equal accolades as a light luncheon or supper accompanied by warm French bread and a fruit salad such as cubed pineapple and fresh strawberries on a bed of lettuce leaves.

Answering the Call to Duck Cookery

She-Crab Soup

1 medium onion, chopped
4 teaspoons butter
3 teaspoons flour
1 quart whole milk
1 pound white crab meat or
   Alaskan king crab

$^1/_2$ teaspoon white pepper
Salt to taste
1 cup light cream
1 teaspoon Hungarian paprika
Dry sherry

Sauté onion in half the butter over low heat. Melt the rest of the butter in the top of a double boiler. Blend in the flour. Stir in onion and add milk gradually, stirring constantly. Add crab meat, pepper, and salt. Cook slowly for approximately 20 minutes. Add cream, paprika, and wine. Immediately remove from heat. Serve in heated bowls to which 1 teaspoon of sherry has been added. Serves 6 to 8.

The Gulf Gourmet

Shrimp and Corn Soup
Easy and Delicious

1 small onion, finely chopped
2 tablespoons butter or oleo
2 tablespoons flour
2 cups milk
1 can shoepeg corn

1 can small cleaned shrimp
   (drained)
White pepper, salt and a
   grating of nutmeg

Sauté onion in butter. Add tablespoons flour. Stir and cook for 3 minutes over low heat. Slowly add 2 cups of milk and blend—a wire whisk is handy for this. Add corn and cook for 3-5 minutes over low heat stirring constantly. Lastly add drained shrimp. Season to taste with pepper, salt and a pinch of nutmeg. Serves 4.

The Pilgrimage Garden Club
Antiques Forum Cookbook

Crabmeat Bisque

5 tablespoons butter
$1/2$ cup finely-chopped onion
$1/3$ cup finely-chopped celery
2 tablespoons shredded green
   onions
$1/3$ cup flour
3 cups half-and-half
2 cups rich chicken broth

2 tablespoons dry white wine
$1 1/2$ teaspoons salt
$1/2$ teaspoon white pepper
4 tablespoons butter
1 pound fresh claw crabmeat
Paprika and freeze-dried
   chives for garnish

Melt 5 tablespoons butter in skillet; sauté onion, celery, and green onions until tender. Add flour, stirring until well-blended. Pour in half-and-half, chicken broth, and wine, stirring until thick. Add salt and pepper; reduce heat; simmer a few minutes. Melt 4 tablespoons butter in small skillet; add crabmeat; heat and add to sauce. Cover; simmer 10 minutes; pour into blender, pureeing until smooth. Serve hot, garnished with paprika and chives.

Note: Claw crabmeat is more flavorful and is less expensive than lump crabmeat.

Accent One

Crabmeat or Crawfish Bisque

6 tablespoons butter or margarine

4 tablespoons finely chopped onion

4 tablespoons finely chopped green pepper

1 scallion (including top), coarsely chopped

2 tablespoons chopped parsley

1 cup sliced fresh mushrooms

2 tablespoon flour

1 1/2 cups milk

1 teaspoon salt

1/8 teaspoon pepper

1/4 teaspoon ground mace

Dash of Tabasco sauce

1 cup half & half milk/cream

1 1/2 cups cooked crab meat, or 2 (6-ounce) packages frozen crabmeat, thawed, or 1 1/2 cups crawfish

3 tablespoons dry sherry

In a medium skillet, heat 4 tablespoons butter. Add onion, green pepper, scallion, parsley and mushrooms. Sauté until soft, but not brown. Set aside.

In a large saucepan, heat remaining 2 tablespoons butter; remove from heat. Stir in flour. Gradually add milk. Cook, stirring constantly, until thickened and smooth. Stir in salt, pepper, mace and Tabasco sauce. Add sautéed vegetables and half-and-half cream. Bring to boiling stage, stirring. Reduce heat and add crabmeat or crawfish meat. Simmer, uncovered, 5 minutes. Just before serving, stir in sherry. Makes 4 servings.

The Country Gourmet
(Mississippi Animal Rescue League)

The world's largest manmade beach—26 miles long—is located on the Mississippi Gulf Coast.

Okra and Sea Food Gumbo

$^1/_3$ pound smoked sausage
3 tablespoons bacon or pork
   drippings
1 cup ham , diced
3 large onions, chopped
3 cloves garlic
3-4 shallots, chopped
2 pounds fresh okra (or 2
   boxes frozen okra)
3 tablespoons celery, chopped
3 tablespoons parsley
1 medium green pepper

1 tablespoon Worcestershire
1 can tomatoes
2 bay leaves
1 teaspoon black pepper
$^1/_2$ teaspoon red pepper
3 quarts hot water
$^1/_3$ cup flour
2 cups cold water
3-4 fresh crabs, cleaned
1 pound shrimp, cleaned
$^1/_2$ lemon, sliced

In large heavy pot, fry sliced smoked sausages in bacon fat or drippings. Add ham, fry few minutes longer. Remove meat. Fry onions, garlic, and shallots for a few minutes then add sliced okra and fry well. Do not burn. Add celery, parsley, green pepper and Worcestershire sauce. Add tomatoes, bay leaves, seasoning, ham and smoked sausages. Let cook few minutes; add about three quarts of hot water. Cook 30 minutes. Brown flour in bacon fat until dark brown, remove from fire and stir in two cups cold water; add to pot. Stir and cook 20 minutes. Add crabs, shrimp and lemon slices. Cook until thick as gravy. Serve with cooked rice. (More water may be added for right consistency.)

My Mother Cooked My Way Through Harvard
With These Creole Recipes

Seafood Gumbo

To the inexperienced cook, a recipe is a law; to the more experienced, it is merely a suggestion. The first reads a recipe, sighs that some minor ingredient is lacking from the pantry shelf, and eliminates the dish from the menu. The second will read, for example, this gumbo recipe; receive inspiration; then go to the kitchen, and using what ingredients are on hand, create a masterpiece. Variations of gumbo are infinite; in fact, few cooks ever prepare it the same way twice. Feel free to substitute or omit ingredients.

$^{1}/_{2}$ cup oil	Liquid from 2 pints oysters
$^{1}/_{2}$ cup flour	1 meaty ham bone
1 (16-ounce) can tomatoes	Tabasco sauce to taste
1 cup finely-chopped celery	Cayenne pepper to taste
1 cup finely-chopped green onions, tops and bottoms	1 bay leaf
1 cup finely-chopped onion	1 teaspoon powdered thyme
$^{1}/_{2}$ cup finely-chopped bell pepper	1 teaspoon powdered basil
$^{1}/_{2}$ cup finely-chopped fresh parsley	Salt and pepper to taste
3 cloves garlic, crushed	6 gumbo crabs
3 cups chopped okra	1 pound smoked link sausage
3 cups chicken broth	Hot water as needed
	1 pound fresh claw crabmeat
	2 pounds peeled, raw shrimp
	2 pints fresh oysters

Make a roux by heating oil in cast-iron Dutch oven over medium-low heat; stir in flour. Cook, stirring constantly, until flour is golden brown; stir in vegetables. Simmer until tender; pour in chicken broth and oyster liquid; add ham bone, Tabasco, cayenne, bay leaf, thyme, basil, salt, pepper, and gumbo crabs; simmer until ham can easily be removed from bone. Remove bone, taking meat off and chopping; return ham-bits to Dutch oven.

Cook sausage in heavy skillet until done; drain; slice and add to gumbo pot. Simmer at least 1 hour,* stirring occasionally; add hot water as needed. About 25 minutes before serving, add crabmeat, shrimp, and oysters. Serve over hot rice.

Note: *It is all but impossible to overcook gumbo; the longer it is cooked, the better it is; however, if not watched carefully and stirred often, it will scorch.

Accent One

A Perfect Roux

Brown 2 cups of flour in a large iron skillet in a 350° oven without any grease. Watch it carefully and mix often. It will take about 40 minutes. When cold, put into a jar and it will be available as needed for any thickening. Add only cold water to this flour so it will make a smooth paste. One-quarter cup of flour and 1 cup water is usual proportion for a perfect roux and you haven't used any grease. Add this "roux" to gumbo, soups or gravy to make it thick. Continue to cook with stock and seasonings.

The Country Gourmet (Miriam G. Cohn)

Salads

Basket weaving at Choctaw Village Indian Fair. Philadelphia.

Fantastic Potato Salad

12 medium white potatoes
2 tablespoons cider vinegar
2 tablespoons melted
   margarine
2 tablespoons sugar
2 tablespoons salt
1 whole bunch celery, chopped

12 hard-cooked eggs, sliced
1 cup minced parsley
2 (4-ounce) jars chopped
   pimentos
1/2 cup minced onion
1 (10-ounce) jar sweet pickle
   relish

Boil potatoes in skins until tender. While hot, peel, cube and toss potatoes lightly with vinegar, margarine, sugar and salt. Refrigerate until thoroughly chilled. Then add celery, eggs, parsley, pimento, onion and pickle relish. Chill until flavors blend. Moisten with chilled Mayonnaise-Horseradish Sauce 1 hour before serving. Yield: 12 to 15 servings.

MAYONNAISE-HORSERADISH SAUCE:
1 quart mayonnaise

1 (5-ounce) jar prepared
   horseradish

Mix well and refrigerate. This sauce is also very good on roast beef or corned beef.

Vintage Vicksburg

Cold Corn Salad

2 cans shoe peg corn
2 green onions, chopped
1 large bell pepper, chopped
1/2 cup chopped celery

Black pepper
Mayonnaise
2 medium tomatoes, chopped

Drain corn well; add green onions, bell pepper, celery, lots of black pepper and a little mayonnaise to hold salad together. Just before serving, add chopped tomatoes. Serves 4-6.

Bouquet Garni

My Potato Salad

Peel and cook about 2 to 2$^1/_2$ pounds red potatoes. After they are tender, drain. Take a potato masher (or you can do it with a fork) and mash potatoes. Add:

1 medium onion (diced)
1 small can drained and
  mashed pimento
2 teaspoons mustard
5 boiled eggs (I mash them, too)

$^1/_2$-$^3/_4$ cup sweet pickles, diced,
  (or use a pickle relish)
$^1/_2$ cup salad dressing or
  mayonnaise
Salt and pepper to taste

It may take more mayonnaise. You want it smooth and not dry. It is better to make this salad when potatoes are hot. Let cool and serve with lettuce cup.

Seasoned With Love

Picnic Salad

1 can shoe peg corn
1 can tiny English peas
1 can French style green beans
1 jar pimento, cut up
4 stalks celery, chopped fine

1 large bell pepper, chopped
  fine
1 purple onion, thinly sliced,
  to make rings

Combine the following ingredients:

$^1/_2$ cup vegetable oil
1 cup sugar
$^3/_4$ cup white vinegar

1 teaspoon salt
1 teaspoon pepper

Boil and then cool the above. Pour slowly over vegetables. Let marinate at least 24 hours covered in refrigerator. Drain and serve cold.
   Note: A great dish to take on a tailgate picnic.

Pineapple Gold

Broccoli Salad

3/4 cup olive oil
2/3 cup red wine vinegar
1/4 teaspoon sugar
2 teaspoons salt
1 cup onion, finely chopped
1 cup celery, finely chopped
3 small yellow squash, sliced
   thin
1 cup fresh mushrooms, sliced

1 (8-ounce) can water
   chestnuts, sliced
1 (14-ounce) can artichoke
   hearts, drained and
   quartered
6 slices bacon, fried and
   crumbled
Florets from two large heads of
   broccoli

Mix oil, vinegar, sugar and salt. Combine next 6 ingredients in a large salad bowl; add dressing (first 4 ingredients) and mix to coat. Last, add broccoli and bacon and toss. Adjust seasonings, then chill. Serves 10-12. Must do ahead. Can double.

Standing Room Only

Korean Salad

1 cup oil
1/4 cup vinegar
1/3 cup catsup
1/2 cup sugar
2 tablespoons grated onion
2 tablespoons Worcestershire
1 pound spinach
1 pound bean sprouts

1 (5-ounce) can sliced water
   chestnuts
2 hard-boiled eggs, chopped
6-8 slices cooked and crumbled
   bacon
1 avocado, cut up

Combine first six ingredients for dressing and set aside. Wash spinach, dry with towel and tear into bite-size pieces. Combine spinach with bean sprouts and water chestnuts. Toss vegetables with dressing and sprinkle salad with eggs, bacon and avocado.

Bouquet Garni

Twenty-Four Hour Spinach Salad

1 pound fresh spinach, washed, dried and torn
4 hard cooked eggs, sliced
1 pound bacon, cooked and crumbled
1 small head iceberg lettuce, shredded
1 large bag frozen English peas
2 Bermuda onions, thinly sliced
1/2 cup mayonnaise
1/2 cup Miracle Whip
Salt and pepper to taste
12 ounces baby Swiss cheese, shredded

Place spinach into a large glass salad bowl so that the layers may be seen. Sprinkle with salt and pepper. Add a layer of eggs, crumbled bacon, lettuce and another sprinkle of salt and pepper. Add a layer of onions and uncooked frozen peas. Repeat this process until the bowl is filled. Cover and refrigerate overnight. Early in the morning of the day the salad is to be used, mix mayonnaise and Miracle Whip and spoon over the top of the salad. This topping should penetrate through the salad. Sprinkle shredded Swiss cheese over top and refrigerate until serving time. Serves 12.

The Gulf Gourmet

Layered Lettuce Salad

1 head lettuce, torn apart
3 ribs celery, chopped
1 purple onion, chopped
1 bell pepper, chopped
1 (10-ounce) package frozen English peas, thawed
4 hard-boiled eggs, sliced
1 pint Hellman's mayonnaise
Parmesan cheese
8 slices bacon, cooked and drained

Put 1/2 torn lettuce into salad bowl. Layer celery, onion, bell pepper, English peas and sliced eggs in bowl, then top with remaining lettuce. Top with mayonnaise and sprinkle with Parmesan cheese. Crumble bacon on top of this. Serves 10.

Madison County Cookery

Cucumber and Onion Salad

6 cucumbers   6 large onions

Chill thoroughly, peel, and slice in alternate layers. Just before serving, mix with the following salad dressing:

DRESSING:
1/2 cup vinegar   1 teaspoon salt
1 tablespoon butter   2 whole eggs
1/2 cup sugar   Whipped or sour cream
2 tablespoons flour

Heat vinegar and butter until hot. In top of double boiler, mix well sugar, flour, salt, and eggs. Add heated vinegar and cook over boiling water until thick. When cool, add whipped cream in equal quantity, using either sweet or sour cream, and mix well.

Inverness Cook Book

Asparagus Gláce

1 tablespoon plain gelatin   1 (8 1/4-ounce) can asparagus
1/4 cup cold water   tips
1 3/4 cups beef bouillon   Lettuce and mayonnaise
3 eggs, hard cooked and sliced

Soften gelatin in cold water. Bring bouillon to a boil and stir in gelatin until dissolved. Chill until gelatin begins to thicken. Pour a thin layer of bouillon into a mold and arrange the egg slices in the bouillon. Chill until bouillon begins to set. Carefully fold in asparagus tips into the remaining thickened bouillon and pour onto egg layer. Chill until set. Serve on lettuce and garnish with mayonnaise.

A Salad A Day

Comes the Sun

1 (1-pound) can whole green
    beans, drained
Vinaigrette dressing
4 strips bacon

2 eggs, hard cooked
2 tablespoons mayonnaise
1 teaspoon lemon juice

Marinate the beans in Vinaigrette and chill. Fry bacon until crisp and crumble it. Chop the egg whites and mix with mayonnaise and lemon juice. Arrange beans like spokes around a center of egg white mixture. Sprinkle the bacon onto the beans, and sieve the egg yolks over all. Scrumptious and sunny!

A Salad A Day

Vinaigrette

1 cup salad oil
5 tablespoons vinegar or 3
    tablespoons vinegar plus 2
    tablespoons lemon juice

1 clove garlic
1 ½ teaspoons mustard
1 ½ teaspoons salt
½ teaspoon pepper

Crush garlic with salt. Add mustard and pepper. Beat in oil by tablespoons alternately with vinegar. Refrigerate overnight. Remove garlic, if milder flavor is desired.

A Salad A Day

Hilltop Farms Salad with Parsley Dressing

SALAD:

1 head Boston lettuce
1 bunch spinach
$1/2$ bunch watercress
1 small head red leaf lettuce
1 (15-ounce) can large black
   olives, drained
$1/2$ cup fresh or frozen green
   peas, blanched and cooled
1 (10-ounce) package artichoke
   hearts, preferably frozen,
   cooked

1 avocado, peeled, seeded and
   sliced
$1/4$ pound mushrooms, sliced
3 tablespoons sesame seeds
3 tablespoons unsalted
   sunflower seeds
3 tablespoons pumpkin seeds
12 raw cashew nuts, halved

Prepare greens by washing and tearing; drain and dry. On separate salad plates place mixture of greens. Divide evenly the olives, peas, artichoke hearts, avocado and mushrooms among the plates. Combine sesame seeds, sunflower seeds and pumpkin seeds; sprinkle over salads. Top each salad with 3 cashew nut halves. Serve with Parsley Dressing. Serves 8.

PARSLEY DRESSING:

1 cup parsley
1 teaspoon salt
1 teaspoon sugar
$1/2$ cup lemon juice
1-2 cloves garlic

4 tablespoons chives or 2
   tablespoons chives and 2
   tablespoons green onions
1 cup oil

Process all ingredients except oil in a blender until puréed; slowly add oil with blender running until all oil is added. Dressing is best if used the same day it is made. Yield: $1^{1}/_{2}$-2 cups.

Taste of the South

Wild Rice Salad

2 small boxes wild rice
1 small can tiny English peas,
  drained
2 jars marinated artichoke
  hearts, drained and slightly
  chopped
Green onions and tops,
  chopped

Cherry tomatoes, cut in fourths
  (reserve about 10 for
  decoration)
French dressing, just enough to
  moisten

Cook rice according to directions. Cool and drain. Toss with remainder of ingredients and put into a glass bowl. Shape into a mound. Cut cherry tomatoes in half and place in a circle around the mound. Refrigerate.

Cherry tomatoes are better if marinated in Italian dressing beforehand.

Special Menus for Very Special Occasions

Rice Salad

2 packages chicken-flavored
  rice
3/4 cup green pepper, chopped
8 green onions, chopped (use
  tops, if not too strong)
16 pimiento-stuffed olives,
  sliced

2 (6-ounce) jars marinated
  artichoke hearts, sliced
2/3 cup mayonnaise
1 teaspoon curry powder

Cook rice as directed on package, omitting butter. Cool. Add pepper, olives, and onions. Drain artichoke hearts and save marinade. Add sliced artichokes. Mix marinade, mayonnaise, and curry powder. Add to salad, toss, and chill. Serves 12.

The Cook's Book

Treasures

2 cups mayonnaise
1/2 cup horseradish, drained
1/2 teaspoon MSG
2 teapoons dry mustard
2 teaspoons lemon juice
1/2 teaspoon salt
1 pound medium shrimp,
   cooked and peeled

1 pint box cherry tomatoes
1 (6-ounce) can black olives,
   drained
1 (8-ounce) can water
   chestnuts, drained
1 (6-ounce) can whole
   mushrooms, drained
1/2 head cauliflower florets

Combine first 6 ingredients; mix well. In a large bowl, combine remaining ingredients, excluding cauliflower. Pour mayonnaise sauce over shrimp and vegetables, refrigerate. Before serving, add cauliflower florets. A TRUE EPICUREAN TREASURE!!

Great Flavors of Mississippi

Crab and Avocado Salad with Louis Dressing

3 large avocados
2 1/2 pounds lump crabmeat
1/2 cup finely chopped celery
1/4 cup lemon juice
4 tablespoons olive oil
1/4 cup vinegar

1/4 teaspoon cayenne
Salt to taste
3 tablespoons finely chopped
   shallots
1/2 cup thinly sliced radishes

Combine all ingredients except avocados an hour or two before serving. When ready to serve, cut the peeled avocados into medium-sized cubes and toss with crabmeat mixture. Mound the salad on a serving dish and garnish with tomato wedges, boiled eggs, or whatever you like. Serves 12. Easily halved.

LOUIS DRESSING:
1 cup mayonnaise (homemade
   or Hellman's)
2 tablespoons chopped parsley
1/4 cup heavy cream, whipped

1/4 cup chili sauce
1 tablespoon finely chopped
   chives
Dash of cayenne

Add other ingredients to mayonnaise. Fold in whipped cream last and serve with crabmeat.

The Gulf Gourmet

Hot Crab Salad

1 pound white crab meat
1 package (6-ounce) Swiss
   cheese (cut in strips)
1 cup sour cream
1 cup mayonnaise

1 cup celery
1 cup grapes (halves)
1 package slivered almonds
White pepper, celery salt, salt
   (to taste)

Mix ingredients; heat at 325° until cheese melts (15 or 20 minutes). Serve hot with Melba rounds. (Can be used as an appetizer.) Serves 4 to 6.

Gardeners' Gourmet II

Chicken and Pasta Salad

1/2 pound vermicelli
1/2 cup lemon garlic dressing
2 cups cooked chicken, cut into
    chunks
10 fresh mushrooms, sliced
1 cup broccoli florets,
    blanched
1 zucchini, cut in half
    lengthwise and then cut into
    slices

1 green pepper, chopped
12 pimento-stuffed green
    olives, sliced
3 tablespoons red wine vinegar
10 cherry tomatoes, cut into
    fourths
1/8 cup fresh basil (optional)

Cook vermicelli according to package directions until tender; drain. In a large bowl, toss the pasta with the lemon garlic dressing; cover and chill at least 3 hours. In another bowl, toss chicken, mushrooms, broccoli, zucchini, green pepper and olives with red wine vinegar; cover and chill for 3 hours. When ready to serve, add chicken and vegetable mixture to pasta; toss with tomatoes and basil. 6-8 servings.

Temptations

Ham Pastiche

1 cup cooked pasta shells
1/2 cup ham, chopped
1/2 cup Cheddar cheese, cubed
1/2 cup black olives, sliced
1/4 cup bell pepper, finely
    chopped

1 teaspoon prepared mustard
1/2 cup mayonnaise
Salt and pepper

Combine first five ingredients in a dressing made by blending the mustard into mayonnaise. Season and chill.

A Salad A Day

Avocado Ribbon Aspic

AVOCADO LAYER:

1 package gelatin (plain)
1 teaspoon salt
3 tablespoons lemon juice

Tabasco sauce (5 drops)
1 1/2 cups sieved ripe avocado
Green food coloring

Soften gelatin in 1/4 cup cold water; add 1/4 cup boiling water. Stir in salt, lemon juice, and Tabasco. Cool until thick. Stir in avocado (meat from 1 large peeled avocado). Add a little food coloring. Pour into a loaf pan 9x5, 2 1/2 inches deep. Chill until almost firm. While this is setting, prepare cheese layer.

CHEESE LAYER:

2 teaspoons gelatin
4 (3-ounce) packages cream
   cheese
1/2 cup milk

1 teaspoon salt
2/3 cup mayonnaise
1/4 teaspoon Worcestershire
   sauce

Soften gelatin in 1/4 cup cold water. Dissolve over boiling water. Gradually mix the milk with the cheese. Blend in other ingredients. Stir in dissolved gelatin. Spread over avocado layer. Chill.

TOMATO LAYER:

3 cups tomato juice
1/2 bay leaf
2 whole cloves
2 or 3 sprigs parsley
1/2 cup, finely chopped celery

3/4 teaspoon salt
Dash of cayenne
1 1/2 packages gelatin
1 1/2 tablespoons vinegar
1 1/2 teaspoons grated onion

Simmer tomato juice with bay leaf, cloves, parsley, celery, salt, and cayenne for 10 minutes. Strain; soften gelatin with 1/3 cup cold water. After a few minutes, add to hot tomato juice with vinegar and grated onion. Chill until partially thickened and pour on the cheese layer when the cheese layer is almost firm.

Chill the whole thing until firm. Turn out and slice. Garnish with tomato quarters and lettuce. Wonderful with cold meats or by itself. Russian dressing is good with this salad.

Best of Bayou Cuisine

Cheesy Congealed Salad

1 (20-ounce) can crushed
    pineapple
1 (13-ounce) can evaporated
    milk
1 1/2 cup grated cheese (mild
    Cheddar)

1 cup pecans
2 (3-ounce) package (small)
    orange jello
1 cup mayonnaise

Empty the can of pineapple into a saucepan and let it come to a boil.
Add jello; stir well. Take off heat and add cheese, pecans and mayonnaise, then add the milk. Stir well and pour in mold or square
casserole. Place in the refrigerator. Serves 16.

Top Rankin Recipes

Spiced Grape Salad

1 (17-ounce) can spiced grapes
Pineapple juice
1 package lemon flavored
    gelatine

1 teaspoon unflavored gelatine
1/2 cup stuffed olives, sliced
1 cup diced celery
1 cup chopped nuts

Drain grapes and save liquid. Add pineapple juice to grape liquid to
make 1 3/4 cups liquid and bring to a boil. Add gelatines to the hot
juice. Chill until mixture begins to thicken. Place a layer of sliced
olives in the bottom of a mold, add grapes, celery and nuts. Carefully pour the gelatin mixture into the mold. Put in refrigerator
until firm. Unmold on bed of lettuce on serving platter. Garnish
platter with celery tops and whole stuffed olives. Serves 8.

Note: This is a delicious salad to serve with meats. It can be made
with plain white grapes but is better with spiced grapes.

Southern Legacies

Hot Pepper Jelly Salad

1 (3-ounce) box lemon Jello
1 (10-ounce) jar green hot
  pepper jelly
1 small can crushed pineapple
1 small jar pimentos, chopped
1 (3-ounce) package
  Philadelphia cream cheese,
  softened

$^1/_4$ cup pecans, chopped
Half and half
Mayonnaise
Tabasco

Follow directions on Jello box, dissolving in hot water and using $^1/_2$ water called for. Dissolve hot pepper jelly in hot Jello. Add crushed pineapple, juice, and pimento. Mash cream cheese and add small amount half and half, Tabasco, mayonnaise, and pecans. Grease muffin cups with Wesson oil. Add small amount Jello mix. Put in spoonful of cream cheese mixture. Fill with remaining Jello mix. Refrigerate.

Natchez Notebook of Cooking

Cranberry-Apple Salad

2 cups whole berry cranberry
  sauce
2 cups boiling water
2 (3-ounce) packages
  strawberry gelatin

2 tablespoons lemon juice
$^1/_2$ teaspoon salt
1 cup mayonnaise
2 cups diced apples
$^1/_2$ cup chopped nuts

Melt cranberry sauce over medium heat. Drain, reserving liquid and berries. Mix together cranberry liquid, boiling water, and gelatin. Stir until gelatin is dissolved. Add lemon juice and salt. Chill until slightly jelled. Add mayonnaise and beat until smooth. Fold in cranberries, apples and nuts. Pour into two-quart mold or individual molds. Chill overnight.

Gardeners' Gourmet II

Strawberry Pretzel Salad

3/4 cup butter or margarine
3 tablespoons sugar

1 2/3 cup stick pretzels, broken
   up finely

Cream butter and sugar; add pretzels. Press dough into a 9x13-inch pan. Bake for 10 minutes at 350°. Let cool.

1 (9-ounce) carton Cool Whip
1 (8-ounce) package cream
   cheese

1 cup sugar

Mix together and spread on top of dough mixture that has cooled.

1 large package strawberry
   Jello
2 cups boiling water

1 pint frozen strawberries,
   thawed

Dissolve Jello in water. Mix with strawberries when partially set, then spread on top of other 2 layers. Refrigerate till firm.

Tasting Tea Treasures

Bing Cherry Salad

1 can pitted Bing cherries
1/2 pint sour cream
1 cup chopped pecans

1 package lemon Jello
1/2 envelope Knox gelatin

Drain cherries and reserve juice. Dissolve Jello in 1 cup hot cherry juice. If not enough juice to make 1 cup, add water. Dissolve gelatin in 1/4 cup cold water and mix with hot Jello. Chill until nearly thick and then add sour cream and blend. Add cherries and nuts and mold. Serve on lettuce with mayonnaise.

Inverness Cook Book

Helen's Melon Salad

1 (6-ounce) package strawberry
  gelatin
2 cups hot water
3 cups watermelon balls or
  cubes
1 (8¼-ounce) can crushed
  pineapple, undrained
1¼ cups chopped pecans,
  divided

1 (4-ounce) container
  non-dairy topping
¼ cup milk
¼ cup plus 2 tablespoons
  sugar
1 (8-ounce) package cream
  cheese, softened

Dissolve gelatin in hot water. Chill until slightly set, 20 minutes. Add melon balls, pineapple and 1 cup pecans; pour into a 9 x 13-inch pan. Chill until firm. Beat cream cheese until fluffy. Gradually add milk and sugar; beat until smooth. Fold in non-dairy topping and place on chilled fruit mixture. Sprinkle with remaining ¼ cup pecans. Refrigerate until serving. Serves 12.

Hospitality Heirlooms

Celery Seed Dressing for Fruit Salad

½ cup Karo
1 tablespoon cornstarch,
  heaping
½ cup vinegar
¾ cup Wesson oil

1 teaspoon salt
1 teaspoon dry mustard
1 teaspoon celery seed
1 tablespoon onion juice

Mix Karo with cornstarch until smooth. Add vinegar and cook in top of double boiler over boiling water until thick. Let cool, then add slowly, beating constantly, Wesson oil and seasonings.

Gourmet of the Delta

Butter Churn Croutons

6 slices stale bread, cubed
4 tablespoons butter

Dashes of seasoned salt, garlic
salt, red pepper, lemon
pepper

Melt butter in large skillet. Add seasonings, then add bread cubes all at once and stir to coat evenly. Spread on cookie sheet and bake 10 minutes in 325° oven, then turn it off and leave them in the oven for several hours. Children love these—a good way to introduce them to salads is to include these.

A Salad A Day

Jo's Salad Dressing

2 cloves garlic, pressed
1 tablespoon salt
1 teaspoon coarse ground
  pepper

$^1/_2$ teaspoon dry mustard
Juice of 3 or 4 lemons
Olive oil
Vegetable oil

Place first four ingredients in shallow bowl. Mash together with a fork until it resembles wet sand. Mix lemon juice and salt mixture, stirring until salt dissolves. Pour into a 16-ounce jar and add oil ($^1/_2$ olive and $^1/_2$ vegetable oil) to make the lemon mixture equal $^1/_3$ of salad dressing. Keep in refrigerator indefinitely. Remove from refrigerator at least 1 hour before using on tossed salad. 1 cup.

Temptations

Poultry

Mississippi's State Capitol. Jackson.

Chicken Las Vegas

2 jars dried beef
8 whole chicken breasts
8 slices bacon
1 1/2 cans mushroom soup

1 1/2 cups sour cream
2 tablespoons sherry
Paprika

Roll one piece dried beef inside each chicken breast. Wrap 1/2 piece bacon around each breast. Layer the remaining dried beef in the bottom of a 9x13-inch casserole. Place chicken on top. Mix soup, sour cream and sherry; pour over chicken and dried beef. Sprinkle with paprika. Cover with foil and bake at 300° for 2 1/2 hours. Remove foil and cook for 30 minutes more.

Tasting Tea Treasures

Herbed Breast of Chicken

1 medium onion
4 whole cloves
4 whole chicken breasts, skinned
3 teaspoons minced fresh lemon thyme
3 teaspoons minced fresh marjoram
1 teaspoon minced fresh rosemary, sage or tarragon

1 teaspoon low-sodium seasoning
1/2 teaspoon grated ginger root
Dash pepper
4 large mushrooms, sliced
1/3 cup dry white wine
Parsley

Cut 4 small slits in onion, and insert a clove into each slit. Set aside. Place chicken, meaty side up, on a large piece of foil. Sprinkle chicken with herbs, low-sodium seasoning, ginger root, and pepper; top with mushrooms and onion. Add wine; fold foil to seal securely. Bake at 350° for 1 hour or until done; open foil during the last 10 minutes of baking to allow browning. Cut the onion into wedges for serving. Yield: 4 servings.

Gardeners' Gourmet II

Chicken Parmesan

1 ¹/₂ cups Italian bread crumbs
   or use homemade
¹/₂ cup Parmesan cheese
1 tablespoon salt

1 teaspoon pepper
6 chicken breast halves
1 ¹/₂-2 sticks butter, melted

Combine crumbs, cheese, salt, and pepper. Dip breasts in melted butter, then in the crumb mixture, being careful to coat the breasts evenly.

Place the breasts skin side up in a buttered baking dish and bake in a 350° oven for 35 to 40 minutes. Do not turn the chicken.

Recipe may be prepared the day before and refrigerated, then baked. Also freezes well both before and after baking. To reheat after thawed, heat in a 325° oven.

Pineapple Gold

Chicken Breast in Mustard/Wine Sauce

2 chicken breasts, boned &
   pounded thin
Salt
Pepper
Peanut oil

2 shallots, chopped
¹/₂ cup white wine
2 teaspoons dry mustard
¹/₄ cup heavy cream

Sauté chicken breasts in small amount of peanut oil. Remove, cover and keep in warm oven. Add shallots and sauté in pan. Add wine and reduce by half. Add dry mustard and cream. Blend well and pour over warmed chicken breasts. Serves 2.

Natchez Notebook of Cooking

Baked Chicken and Broccoli

2 whole chicken breasts, split
2 tablespoons butter or
   margarine, melted
1 (10-ounce) package frozen
   broccoli
1 (10³/₄-ounce) can cream of
   mushroom soup, undiluted

¹/₂ cup milk
¹/₂ cup (2-ounces) shredded
   Cheddar cheese
¹/₄ cup bread crumbs
Paprika

Place chicken in a 9-inch square pan and drizzle with butter. Bake at 375° for 40 minutes. Cook broccoli according to package directions; drain. Arrange around chicken. Combine soup, milk and cheese; pour over chicken and broccoli. Sprinkle with bread crumbs and paprika. Bake an additional 20 minutes. Yield: 2 servings.

Bell's Best 2

Chicken Ambassador

6 — 8 large chicken breasts
1 tablespoon salt
1 teaspoon poultry seasoning
Paprika
¹/₂ cup melted butter
1 can beef consomme

¹/₂ cup sherry
¹/₂ pound mushrooms (fresh or
   1 large can button
   mushrooms)
2 (10-ounce) cans artichoke
   hearts

Season chicken with salt and poultry seasoning. Sprinkle with paprika to give them a good color. Spread out in roasting pan, skin side up. Baste with combined melted butter and consomme. Bake at 325° in oven for one hour, basting every 20 minutes. Add the sherry to pan drippings and keep on baking and basting ¹/₂ hour longer. Sauté the sliced fresh mushrooms when ready to serve; remove chicken breasts to heated platter and combine drippings in pan with mushrooms and artichoke hearts. Heat thoroughly and pour sauce over chicken. Serve at once.

Best of Bayou Cuisine

Chicken and Shrimp Creole with Saffron Rice
Easier than it looks, just read through before you start.

1 green pepper, cut into julienne strips	2 cloves garlic, minced
1 red pepper, cut into julienne strips	1 teaspoon chili powder
1/2 cup chopped onion	1/4 teaspoon each ground cumin, thyme and allspice
1/4 cup oil	Dash Tabasco sauce
2 (8-ounce) chicken breasts, skinned, boned and cut into 1/2-inch strips	1/2 cup Brown Sauce (see below)
	1 tomato, cut into julienne strips
12 ounces cleaned shrimp (frozen ones are fine)	2 tablespoons chili sauce
	Saffron Rice Ring (see below)

Sauté vegetables quickly in hot oil to maintain firm texture; remove from skillet with slotted spoon. Sauté chicken just until done; remove from skillet. Sauté shrimp; remove from skillet. Sauté garlic and spices; add Brown Sauce, tomato and chili sauce to skillet and stir well. Add sautéed vegetables, chicken and shrimp and heat gently until hot through.

BROWN SAUCE:

1 tablespoon margarine	1 cup beef broth
1 tablespoon flour	

Melt margarine, blend in flour. Stir over low heat until browned. Add beef broth; bring to boil and simmer 30 minutes.

SAFFRON RICE RING:

1/2 cup chopped scallions or green onions	1/4 teaspoon saffron
	1 cup rice
1/3 cup chopped onion	2 cups chicken broth
2 tablespoons margarine	Salt, pepper to taste

Sauté scallions and onions in margarine. Add saffron, then rice and mix well. Stir in chicken broth; bring to boil. Place in a covered baking dish; bake at 375° for 30 minutes. Remove from oven, season with salt and pepper. Shape about 1 cup rice into ring on each serving plate, fill ring with chicken/shrimp mixture.

Just a Spoonful

Italian Chicken Delight

6 boned and skinned breast
   halves
1 egg, beaten
3/4 cup Italian bread crumbs
1/2 cup oil
1 large can tomato sauce
Salt and pepper

1 tablespoon butter
1 tablespoon basil
Generous amount garlic
   powder
3/4 cup Parmesan cheese
Mozzarella cheese

Dip boned and skinned chicken into beaten egg, coating well. Roll breasts in bread crumbs. Brown in oil. Drain chicken and place in casserole in single layer.

To oil in skillet add: tomato sauce, salt, pepper, butter, basil and garlic powder. Simmer and pour over chicken in casserole. Sprinkle with Parmesan cheese. Seal top with foil. Bake at 350° 30 minutes. Uncover and top with triangles of Mozzarella cheese. Bake 10 more minutes. Serves 4-6.

Bouquet Garni

Chicken Island Supreme

1 broiler-fryer, cut in parts
3 tablespoons fresh grated
   ginger root
1 lemon, sliced
1 teaspoon salt
1 teaspoon Accent

1/2 teaspoon ground mace
1/4 teaspoon curry powder
1/4 teaspoon black pepper
1/4 cup Mazzola corn oil
1/4 cup water

Place chicken in shallow baking pan in single layer, skin side up. Sprinkle over all ginger root, lemon, salt, Accent, mace, curry powder and pepper. Pour over corn oil and water. Bake in 350° oven, covered, 1/2 hour. Remove cover and add more water, if necessary. Continue baking until chicken is well browned, about 1/2 hour, or until fork can be inserted with ease. Serve with rice. Serves 4.

This recipe was the Mississippi state winner and was entered in the 1977 National Chicken Cooking Contest held in Jackson in July of that year.

Southern Sideboards

Chicken and Sausage Casserole
(Freezes Well)

10-11 chicken breasts
9 cups water, boiling
3 envelopes dry Lipton
   chicken noodle soup mix
2 cups raw rice
1 pound hot sausage
1 bell pepper, chopped

1 large onion, chopped
1 cup celery, chopped
Salt to taste
Curry powder to taste
2 cans mushroom soup
$^1/_2$ cup blanched almonds,
   toasted in melted butter

Boil chicken breasts until tender. Let cool. Debone chicken and cut into small pieces; set aside.

To boiling water add soup mix and rice. Boil 9 minutes, uncovered. Fry sausage; remove from skillet and drain. In sausage drippings sauté bell pepper, onion and celery. Add this and sauage to soup mix. Season to taste with salt and curry powder. Add mushroom soup and chicken pieces.

Place mixture in casserole and bake 45 minutes at 350°. Top with blanched toasted almonds and bake an addtional 15 minutes. Serves 16. Can be prepared ahead; frozen, thawed and baked.

Hospitality Heirlooms

Chicken Pie-Pinwheel Crust

1 (3½ to 4-pound) hen
2 cups water
1 tablespoon salt
3 tablespoons flour

1½ cups milk
1½ cups chicken broth
1 tablespoon lemon juice

Boil hen in salted water. Remove from bones. Place chicken in a 3-quart casserole. Make a sauce by blending flour, milk and broth. Cook slowly until thick. Add lemon juice and pour over the chicken in the casserole. Set aside while you make crust.

CRUST:

3 tablespoons shortening
1½ cups flour
3 tablespoons baking powder
½ teaspoon salt

½ cup milk
3 pimientos, chopped
¾ cup grated cheese

Cut shortening into the flour to which the baking powder and salt has been added. Add the milk. Form a ball and chill 30 minutes. Roll out ¼-inch thick. Spread the pimiento and grated cheese over the pastry and roll up, starting at the short end. Slice. Place slices over the chicken mixture and bake at 400° for 40 minutes or until brown.

Dixie Dining

Mississippi has been one of the leaders in the poultry industry for a number of years, ranking sixth nationally in commercial broiler production.

Chicken 'N' Dumplings

1 large hen, cut up
2 ribs celery and leaves,
  chopped
1 onion, chopped
1 sprig thyme
1 bay leaf
1 sliced carrot
1 1/2 teaspoons salt
Pepper
1 small green pepper, sliced

3 cups water
3 tablespoons butter or
  chicken fat
3 tablespoons flour
1/4 cup cream
1 small can mushrooms and
  liquid
1/2 cup green peas
1 pimento, sliced

Place chicken, celery, onions, thyme, bay leaf, carrots, salt, pepper and green pepper with water in heavy covered pot and cook until tender (about 2 hours). Remove from pot. Reserve stock after straining three times. Remove bones from hen and cut meat into large pieces. Set aside. Heat shortening in large pot. Add flour, blend until smooth and golden brown. Add chicken stock, cream, mushrooms, peas, pimentoes, and chicken. Heat mixture until it reaches a low boil. Cover and steam over low heat without lifting lid for 15 minutes.

DUMPLINGS:

2 cups flour, sifted
1 tablespoon baking powder
1/2 tablespoon salt
1/4 teaspoon red or white
  pepper
1 egg, well beaten

1 tablespoon melted butter or
  oleo
1/2 cup milk
1/4 cup softened butter
1/4 cup chopped celery leaves
Chopped parsley

Sift flour, salt, baking powder, and pepper together. Combine beaten egg, milk, and melted butter. Add to dry ingredients. Stir just to moisten. Roll out 1/4-inch thick. Spread with soft butter, sprinkle with celery leaves. Roll up and slice into 1/2-inch slices. Place on top of hot chicken mixture. Cover and steam low heat without lifting lid for 15 minutes. Garnish with chopped parsley. (Six to eight servings.)

My Mother Cooked My Way Through Harvard
With These Creole Recipes

Mamie's Fried Chicken
(Willie Morris)

Willie Morris has been editor-in-chief of *The Texas Observer* and *Harper's*. Among his books are *North Toward Home, Yazoo, The Last of the Southern Girls, James Jones: A Friendship,* and *Terrains of the Heart.* He lives in Oxford, Mississippi.

My grandmother Mamie cooked me this fried chicken after our baseball games when I was a boy in Mississippi. After I grew up, she told me her recipe, which I have used many times. You may serve this chicken along with my John Birch Society Beans if you desire a feast.

1. Marinate the pieces of chicken overnight in buttermilk.
2. Take a large sack (nowadays a plastic garbage bag) and pour in much flour. Add generous portions of salt and pepper.
3. Put the chicken in the bag and shake vigorously.
4. Melt an equal mixture of butter and lard in the skillet until it is bubbling hot.
5. Place the pieces of chicken in the skillet. Turn constantly to avoid burning. When the chicken is a deep, golden brown, take it out and put on heavy paper to absorb the grease before serving.

This is a splendid fried chicken recipe for those who like ample Southern crusts. However, I once blundered on eastern Long Island, having marinated the pieces of chicken in the buttermilk for two days rather than one. The artist Saul Steinberg took a bite and said: "This is cement!"

My apologies to Mamie for that uncharacteristic mishap. Usually this chicken is very good—as good as Mamie was.

The Great American Writer's Cookbook

 Mississippi is blessed with climate and soil well suited to growing trees, America's renewable resource. Forests cover approximately 56% of the total land area and play a vital role in the state's economy.

Yorkshire Chicken

My grandmother's cook made a divine dish when I was a child called "yaksha" chicken. She never wrote the recipe down, and no one had clue as to how she made it. Years later I discovered this dish in an English country pub—exactly the same thing Pearl used to make. We had always thought that "yaksha" was an African word. Little did we know what it really was.

2²/₃ cups flour
4 teaspoons salt
3 teaspoons crumbled dried
   sage
Paper bag
2 (3-pound) chickens, cut-up
Peanut oil

3 eggs, beaten
3 cups milk
¹/₂ cup melted butter
¹/₂ tablespoon chopped parsley
2 teaspoons baking powder

Combine two-thirds cup flour, 2 teaspoons salt, and sage in a paper bag and add chicken pieces, one at a time, until they are thoroughly coated. Brown each piece in peanut oil. Place in a shallow casserole dish when browned. Mix together eggs, milk, melted butter, and parsley. Combine with 2 cups flour, 2 teaspoons salt, and baking powder. Pour over chicken and bake uncovered at 350° for 1 hour. Serves 8.

Cook with a Natchez Native

Chicken-Chestnut Souffle

9 slices white bread, crust removed
4 cups cubed, cooked chicken, seasoned to taste
1 (8-ounce) can sliced mushrooms (optional)
1/4 cup melted butter
1 (8-ounce) can sliced water chestnuts
9 slices sharp Cheddar cheese

1 envelope dry onion soup mix
1/2 cup mayonnaise
4 eggs, well beaten
2 cups milk
1 teaspoon salt
1 can cream of chicken soup
1 can celery soup
1 (2-ounce) jar pimiento
2 cups buttered bread crumbs

Line a 13x9-inch dish with bread slices and top with chicken. Sauté mushrooms in butter and spoon over chicken. Top with water chestnuts, cheese and soup mix. Combine mayonnaise, eggs, milk and salt, beating well. Pour over cheese. Combine chicken and celery soups and pimiento and spoon over casserole. Cover with foil and place in refrigerator overnight. Bake uncovered for 30 minutes at 350°. Top with crumbs and bake 15 to 20 minutes longer. Serves 12.

Dixie Dining

Quick Chicken and Broccoli Crepes

1 (10-ounce) package frozen, chopped broccoli
1 (10 1/2-ounce) can cream of chicken soup
1/2 teaspoon Worcestershire sauce
1/3 cup grated Parmesan cheese

2 cups cooked, chopped chicken
9-10 crepes
1/3 cup mayonnaise
1 tablespoon milk
1/4 cup grated Parmesan cheese

Cook broccoli according to package directions; drain thoroughly. Combine with soup, Worcestershire sauce, 1/3 cup cheese, and chicken. Fill crepes with chicken mixture; roll up and place in shallow baking pan. Combine mayonnaise with milk; spread over crepes. Sprinkle with 1/4 cup cheese. Broil until bubbly. Yield: 9 to 10 crepes.

Festival

Chicken Salad Supreme

1 (2¹/₂ to 3-pound) cooked hen
1 cup seedless white grapes or
   seedless red grapes
1 (5-ounce) can water chestnuts
   (optional)
1 cup slivered almonds
1 cup diced celery

1¹/₂ cups mayonnaise
1¹/₂ teaspoons curry powder
1 tablespoon soy sauce
1 tablespoon lemon juice
¹/₂ cup toasted slivered
   almonds

Remove chicken from bone and cut in bite-size pieces. Mix chicken, grapes, chestnuts, celery and the cup of slivered almonds. Then mix mayonnaise, curry powder, lemon juice and soy sauce, and add to the chicken. Mix well. Serve on pineapple slices or crisp lettuce leaves. Top with mayonnaise and ¹/₂ cup toasted slivered almonds. This will serve 12 to 15.

The Mississippi Cookbook

Mississippi Dirty Rice

6 tablespoons cooking oil
Finely chopped giblets from 3
  chickens
2 large onions, diced
1 cup celery, diced
2 dozen oysters, chopped
$^1/_4$ cup oyster liquid

$^1/_2$ cup parsley, diced
$^1/_2$ cup green onions, diced
2 cloves garlic, minced
1 cup raw rice, cooked
Salt, black pepper and cayenne
  pepper to taste

Pour oil into heavy skillet or Dutch oven and add chopped giblets, onion and celery. Cook on medium heat, stirring as needed, until giblets are browned and onions and celery are soft. Add oysters and liquid, parsley, green onions and garlic, cover and simmer for 10 minutes. Stir in cooked rice, salt and pepper and heat to steaming. Makes 8 to 10 servings.

Note: 1$^1/_2$ cups of ground beef, veal or pork may be substituted for the giblets. The flavor is better if the oysters, giblets and vegetables are ground and not just chopped. Seasonings may be varied according to personal preference. Worcestershire sauce may be added. Tabasco sauce can be used instead of cayenne pepper.

This may be used as a stuffing in a turkey or large hen. It may also be put in a greased casserole dish and baked in a 350° oven for 20 minutes.

The Mississippi Cookbook

Chicken Dressing

1 pan hot corn bread
3 slices loaf bread (soaked in
   evaporated milk)
1 whole onion (1 big or 2 small)
3 boiled eggs

1 raw egg
1 stick oleo
Salt and pepper to taste
Juice off of boiled chicken
1 teaspoon poultry seasoning

Mix all together. Add enough juice of chicken to make kinda soupy.
Bake at 350° until golden brown, about 45 minutes to 1 hour.

Seasoned With Love

Stuffed Cornish Hens

8 Cornish hens
1 cup wild rice
3 tablespoons butter
$^1/_2$ cup toasted almonds
$^1/_2$ cup chopped onion

1 teaspoon salt
1 teaspoon thyme
$^1/_2$ teaspoon marjoram
8 bacon strips

Cook and drain rice. Sauté onion in butter. Mix with rice, almonds,
salt and herbs. Salt and pepper hens and stuff with rice mixture. Put
strip of bacon over hens. Cook, uncovered, for $1^1/_2$ to 2 hours at
325° basting occasionally with drippings.

The Country Gourmet
(Mississippi Animal Rescue League)

Other than catfish, Mississippi's many fresh water lakes and streams
abound with numerous varieties of fish, some of the most common
being bass, bream, crappie and perch. The coastal waters of the Gulf provide
numerous varieties of salt water fish.

Grandmother's Turkey Hash on Waffles

4 tablespoons butter
1/2 cup flour
1 quart turkey or chicken stock
1/2 tablespoon salt
1/4 teaspoon pepper
1/2 teaspoon paprika

8 cups diced cooked turkey
1/4 cup chopped pimiento
1/4 pound mushrooms, fresh or canned
1 1/2 tablespoons chopped parsley

In a double boiler melt butter and slowly add flour to make a thick paste. Add turkey stock, stirring constantly to prevent lumping, and cook until smooth. Season with salt, pepper and paprika. Add remaining ingredients. (If fresh mushrooms are used, prepare by sautéing until brown in additional melted butter.) Heat thoroughly over boiling water and keep hot until ready to serve. Serve hash over waffles or patty shells. May be prepared in advance. Serves 15.

This is a grandmother's recipe which has been used for 65 years at special family gatherings. It is a good use for leftover turkey.

Southern Sideboards

Other Mother's Turkey Croquettes

1 1/2 tablespoons butter
3 tablespoons flour
1/2 cup chicken broth
1/2 cup milk
1 1/2 cups ground or chopped turkey
1/4 teaspoon celery salt
1/2 teaspoon salt

1 teaspoon lemon juice
1 teaspoon chopped parsley
Dash Worcestershire
Hint onion
Egg
Milk
Cracker crumbs (finely chopped)

Melt butter, add flour. Stir in liquids gradually and cook until thick. Add seasonings and meat. Mix well. Let set until cold. Form croquettes. Roll in egg and milk then cracker crumbs. Fry till brown. Chicken or cooked beef may be used instead of turkey.

Into the Second Century

Game

One of Mississippi's typical "ole fishin' holes."

Wings and Tails Etouffée
(Duck and Shrimp Etouffée)

Etouffée is the word for the "smothered" in sauce dishes so popular among Gulf States hunters and gourmets everywhere. This is a very rich, delicious dish that has never failed to bring gestures of gastronomic exhilaration. The following recipe will serve four as an ample entree, or in small part-cup quantities as a light lunch or delicious first course.

2 tablespoons flour	Dash cayenne pepper
1/2 cup butter or margarine	1 cup cooked duck meat
1 1/2 cups chopped onion	1/2 cup hot water
1/2 cup chopped green pepper	1 pound shrimp, peeled and
1/2 cup chopped celery	deveined
3 cloves garlic, minced	Dash Tabasco sauce
1 1/2 cups bloody mary mix	Lemon juice
2 tablespoons celery soup	Salt

Brown flour to a light tan in a small iron skillet and set aside. Melt butter in a 2-quart saucepan and sauté onions until transparent; add green peppers and celery and sauté for two minutes more. Add garlic and flour; mix, and follow with celery soup, bloody mary mix, cayenne, duck, and 1/2 cup hot water with stirring. Allow to simmer just below a boil for a few minutes to blend flavors. Add shrimp and continue to cook until shrimp are red and tender. Correct seasoning with a few drops of Tabasco, a tablespoon or less of lemon juice, and very little salt if still needed. Serve over white rice on warm plates or in gumbo bowls. Etouffées are also served in small bowls as an appetizer with rounds of toasted French bread on the side.

Answering the Call to Duck Cookery

Mississippi is in the path of waterfowl migrations, making ducks and geese plentiful. Hunting these and other abundant game is a much enjoyed sport in the state.

Crock-Pot Duck

The crock-pot is ideally suited for use in the duck camp supplied with electric power. The following recipe is particularly suited for the crock and well worth some experimentation with this labor saving cooker.

When at camp, use duck taken the previous day; brown ducks and cut up vegetables the evening before so you can quickly put this together and turn on the pot before you head out the door in the morning. A mouth watering, ready to serve treat will be ready when you return from the hunt in the evening.

2 ducks, skinned	2 carrots
$^1/_2$ cup cooking oil	$^1/_2$ cup sauterne
Oregano	2 onions, quartered
Garlic salt	2 sticks celery
Lemon pepper	4 potatoes

Trim fat from ducks, rinse and blot dry. Brown in cooking oil over high heat; remove and set aside. Dust birds with oregano, garlic salt and lemon pepper inside and out. Cut 2 carrots to fit the crock and add to the bottom of the pot to act as a rack for the fowl. Add wine and birds to the pot along with onions, celery, and 4 or more peeled potatoes. Cover and cook on low heat for 8 hours. Remove ducks, discarding stuffing and carrot racks. Serve with potatoes.

Answering the Call to Duck Cookery

Connie's Duck

This is an example of great duck cookery. This recipe, and modifications, thereof, are widely used at duck lodges where excellent duck in quantity is needed to feed a host of starving hunters. The quantities below will accommodate the number of ducks which will conveniently fit into a 9x13-inch roasting pan.

4 ducks

Liquid margarine (or melted butter)

Garlic salt

Celery Salt

Lemon pepper

Oregano

Celery stalks, cut in 2-3 inch pieces

1 onion, quartered

1 green (bell) pepper cut in 1-inch strips

$1/4$ pound butter or margarine

1 cup chicken bouillon or stock

1 cup white wine

Rinse duck in cold water and blot dry. Coat inside and out with liquid margarine. Sprinkle garlic salt, celery salt, lemon pepper, and oregano inside and out. Stuff the cavity with celery, onion and green pepper. Heat one cup water and dissolve bouillon cube. Melt butter in bouillon and add wine. Set aside. Select a baking pan with 2-inch sides; line pan with heavy duty aluminum foil allowing one inch over each side. Place ducks in the pan and add sauce (do not pour liquid over ducks). Cover with foil and secure with pan bottom foil to form a tight seal around the edge. Bake 1 to 2 hours at 325°. Remove ducks and discard stuffing. Degrease gravy and strain into a preheated gravy boat. Serve.

Optional: Those who enjoy boiled onions as much as we do will find them excellent when cooked with duck. About a half hour before serving, fold the foil back and add 2 peeled white onions per serving. Reseal foil and return to oven. Serve onions in a warm bowl with a little of the degreased pan juices.

Answering the Call to Duck Cookery

Cumberland Sauce

Cumberland is the classic orange sauce served with roast duck. There are many recipes given for sauces named Cumberland, but this one is a foundation; unsurpassed in simplicity and flavor.

3 oranges
$^1/_2$ cup light Karo syrup
$^1/_2$ cup currant jelly
$^1/_2$ teaspoon dry mustard

1 dash cayenne
$^1/_8$ pound melted butter or margarine

Juice two oranges and strain into a saucepan. Slice the third orange very thin. Add syrup, jelly, mustard, and cayenne and heat with stirring until smooth. Add butter, mix, and simmer for 20 minutes. Serve in a gravy boat or in heavy, prewarmed individual sauce bowls with cooked orange slices to garnish.

Answering the Call to Duck Cookery

Marchand de Vin

3 tablespoons flour
1 cup beef stock or bouillon
1 cup dry red wine
1/4 pound butter or margarine
1/3 cup finely chopped green
  onion tops

1/3 cup finely chopped
  mushrooms
1/2 cup finely chopped ham
6 cloves garlic, chopped
Dash cayenne

Brown flour in a small iron skillet to a light tan; remove from heat and set aside. Dissolve bouillon cube in 1 cup water over low heat; add wine, mix and remove from heat. Melt butter in a saucepan large enough to mix without splattering. Add onion tops and sauté for a few minutes until tips are brown. Add mushrooms, ham, garlic, and cayenne; simmer for one minute. Add flour and mix thoroughly. Add the warm wine-bouillon in quantities less than 1/4 cup with constant stirring; mixing should be complete before the next addition. An electric mixer works well for the weak arm stirrer. Set speed to slow blend and add wine-bouillon in small amounts. Simmer over low heat for one hour; stir as required.

Serving this sauce over grilled, unseasoned steak is a classic, but it is also delicious with other red meats and especially duck paillards.

Answering the Call to Duck Cookery

Pailliards—a piece of beef or veal usually pounded thin and grilled.

Mississippi Delta Duck

4 duck breasts
8 slices bacon
1 onion, sliced and separated
   into rings
1 lemon

Pepper to taste
1 cup soy sauce
$1/2$ cup Worcestershire sauce
Lemon pepper
Salt

Fillet meat from bone, making 8 duck breast halves. Wrap each half with a slice of bacon; secure with a toothpick. Layer the bottom of a covered container with $1/2$ the onion rings; place duck breasts on top. Squeeze lemon over duck; season with pepper. Combine soy sauce and Worcestershire sauce; pour over duck. Sprinkle generously with lemon pepper. Top with remaining onion rings. Marinate for 6 hours; turn duck after 3 hours. Cook in a water smoker with the top on for 20 minutes; turn and cook for 25 additional minutes. Add salt to taste when cooked. Serves 4.

Taste of the South

Doves Wonderful

Doves, 3 per person
Burgundy, enough, when
   mixed with water to cover
   doves
Water

Onions, chopped, 1 onion per
   9-10 doves
Bacon, $1/2$ slice for each dove
Butter
Salt and pepper

Marinate doves for 10 to 12 hours in a mixture of equal parts of burgundy and water and the onions. The marinade must cover the doves! At the end of marinating, remove doves, saving marinade. Wrap each dove with half slices of bacon, securing with a toothpick. Place doves, breast side down, on a cookie sheet that has been lined with foil. Cook over grate on a covered grill, sprinkling frequently with marinade. Cook until done (about 2 hours). About 15 minutes before doves are done, pour 1 cup of burgundy over them. Truly a Mississippi treat!!

Great Flavors of Mississippi

Quail in Red Wine

6 quail or dove
Brandy
Flour
6 tablespoons butter
2 cups sliced mushrooms
1/4 cup butter

1 cup consomme
1 cup dry, red wine
1 stalk celery
Salt and pepper
Juice of 2 oranges, strained

Split birds in half and rub with a cloth soaked in brandy. Dust with flour. Melt 6 tablespoons butter in casserole or black skillet. Add quail and cook till brown. Add consomme, wine, celery, salt and pepper. Cover and simmer 30 minutes or till quail are very tender. Discard celery and add orange juice . Serve with wild rice. This dish can be cooked 1n 300-350° oven instead of over simmering heat. Serves 6.

Gardeners' Gourmet II

Quail and Cream

12 quail
6 tablespoons butter
1 apple, chopped
2 small onions, chopped
3/4 cup celery
1/4 cup brandy
1 beef bouillon cube

3 tablespoons flour
1 can chicken broth
   (Swanson's)
1/2 teaspoon sage
1/2 teaspoon garlic salt
1/4 cup vermouth
1/2-3/4 cup cream

Sauté quail, vegetables, and apple in butter. Heat brandy, and add to quail and vegetables. Ignite; then, boil down. Next, add flour, then bouillon cube, broth, sage, vermouth, and garlic salt; cook until tender. When done (all tender), add the cream to the gravy. DELICIOUS!

Great Flavors of Mississippi

Venison Pepper Steak

2 pounds venison steak
1/2 cup butter
Dash of garlic salt
Dash of powdered ginger
1/2 cup soy sauce
1 cup beef bouillon

3 green peppers, sliced
6 scallions, sliced (including
  tops)
Salt and pepper
4 tablespoons cornstarch
1/2 cup water or white wine

Remove all tendons and slice steak in thin strips (better to cut if slightly frozen). Cook over medium heat in butter with garlic and ginger until well browned. Add soy sauce and bouillon; cover and simmer until tender. Add pepper and scallions; cook a few minutes more. Add cornstarch mixed with wine or water and stir on low heat until sauce is clear and thickened. Serve with rice or Chinese noodles.

Madison County Cookery

Venison Spaghetti Sauce

2 tablespoons oil
5 pounds ground venison
2 tablespoons dehydrated
   parsley flakes
2 cups finely-chopped onion
1 cup finely-chopped bell
   peppers
2 quarts tomatoes
18 ounces tomato paste
1 (8-ounce) jar sliced
   mushrooms and the juice
1 teaspoon sage

2 teaspoons basil
2 teaspoons oregano
2 bay leaves
5 cloves garlic, minced
4 tablespoons sugar
3/4 cup finely-chopped celery
1/2 teaspoon cayenne pepper
2 teaspoons black pepper
Salt to taste
1 (5 1/4-ounce) bottle Heinz 57
   sauce

Heat oil in Dutch oven; add meat a little at a time until all is
browned. Add all other ingredients; simmer 3 to 4 hours, stirring
occasionally to prevent sticking, adding water as necessary.
Remove bay leaves before serving.

Note: This sauce keeps well in freezer.

Accent One

Meats

Brice's Cross Roads Battlefield, west of Baldwin.

My Sunday Roast

5 or 6-pound rump roast	1 teaspoon black pepper
2 teaspoons Lawry's seasoning salt	1/2 stick oleo
1 1/2 teaspoons Accent	3 cups water
	4 cups cooked rice

Season roast generously with salt, pepper and Accent. Place in 2-inch deep baking pan and cut oleo in pats to go under your roast. Preheat oven to 325°. Cook for 2 hours. Remove roast from oven and pour grease out of pan (this is good for Yorkshire pudding). Add water and mix well with "dregs" in pan, scraping bottom of pan. Put roast back in gravy and baste. Cook another hour. Taste your gravy during last hour to see if you need more salt. Accent enhances the flavor. When done, take roast out of gravy to be sliced. Serve with rice, as this gravy is true pan gravy. My family loves it.

Variation: Add a can of mushrooms and juice to gravy and reheat. If you like a thick gravy, take 1 1/2 tablespoons of grease and brown 2 tablespoons flour in it. Add 1 cup water and cook until smooth. Add this to your pan gravy last hour of cooking.

YORKSHIRE PUDDING:

1/3 cup of hot beef grease drippings from a rib roast or rump roast	2 teaspoons baking powder
	1/2 teaspoon salt
1 1/2 cups flour	2 eggs, separated
	1 cup milk

Sift together flour, baking powder, salt. Add beaten egg yolks, then milk and mix well. Fold in stiffly beaten egg whites. Pour into 1-quart baking dish containing hot beef drippings. Swirl grease in dish so it will be all over. Bake in hot oven at 475°. Serve with prime rib; fit for a king!

The Country Gourmet (Miriam G. Cohn)

Peppered Roast of Beef

2 beef bouillon cubes
4 tablespoons boiling water
2 tablespoons black
   peppercorns, coarsely
   cracked

1 (4-5 pound) boneless rib roast

In a small bowl, dissolve the bouillon cubes in hot water. Add the cracked peppercorns and let the mixture stand for 1 hour. Using the palm of the hand, press the pepper mixture into both sides of the roast. Place the roast in a shallow pan, and pour any remaining pepper mixture over the meat. Cover tightly and refrigerate for 12 to 15 hours. Remove meat from marinade and wrap it in foil. Place in a shallow roasting pan and roast at 350° for 2½ hours. Remove foil and cook the meat uncovered at 400° for 20 minutes more. Place meat on a heated platter and spoon sauce over top.

SAUCE:

½ cup butter or margarine,
   melted
½ teaspoon garlic salt
1½ teaspoons onion salt
2 tablespoons Worcestershire
   sauce

1 tablespoon lemon juice
½ teaspoon salt
2 tablespoons minced parsley

In a saucepan, heat the butter and add the garlic salt and onion salt. Stir in the Worcestershire sauce, lemon juice, salt, and parsley. Heat until well blended, and serve over prepared roast.

Note: Sauce recipe may be doubled, in order to have an extra amount to pour over the roast at each person's plate, serving it from a small pitcher or sauceboat at the table.

Come and Dine

Steak Madrid

4 small round steaks (1 large, cut into 4 pieces)	4 tablespoons shortening
1 cup flour	2 cups Cheddar cheese, grated
	1 small jar pimento, diced fine

Remove bone from steak and score around edges. Lightly dredge in flour and brown each one on both sides in shortening. Place ¹/₂ cup grated Cheddar and 1 teaspoon diced pimento on each steak and fold together the edges of steak and secure with toothpicks. Place steaks into greased baking dish and cover with Spanish Sauce. Cover baking dish and place in preheated oven at 350° and bake for 1 hour, or until tender.

SPANISH SAUCE:

Fat from ¹/₂ pound bacon	Dash thyme
1 cup onion, diced fine	1 teaspoon garlic salt
1 bell pepper, diced fine	¹/₈ teaspoon chili powder
¹/₂ cup celery, diced fine	1 cup brown sauce or gravy
1 clove garlic, diced fine	1 cup tomato sauce
Dash of oregano	1 cup peeled tomatoes
1 tablespoon Worcestershire sauce	¹/₂ cup tomato paste
4 drops Tabasco	¹/₄ cup cooking sherry
1 bay leaf	Salt and pepper to taste

Place bacon fat in skillet and sauté onion, bell pepper, celery, garlic and chili pepper until soft. Stir in other ingredients and simmer about 5 minutes. This can be made up in advance.

Madison County Cookery

Whiskey Beef Stew

2 1/2 pounds chuck roast, cut into cubes
3 tablespoons margarine
2 tablespoons brandy
3 tablespoons flour
2 bouillon cubes
2 tablespoons tomato paste
1 1/2 cups burgundy
3/4 cup dry sherry
3/4 cup port

1 can beef bouillon
1/8 teaspoon pepper
4 peppercorns
3 bay leaves
Pinch of thyme
1 clove garlic, minced
1 (16-ounce) can white onions
1 (16-ounce) can button mushrooms, drained

In a large Dutch oven, brown beef cubes in margarine. Remove beef from oven, add brandy, and heat until a vapor rises; ignite brandy, and add beef. Remove beef again; stir in next 3 ingredients, blend, and add next 4 ingredients. Next, add beef, pepper, peppercorns, bay leaves, thyme, and garlic; turn off the heat, add onions and mushrooms. Cover, put in the refrigerator; let stew sit overnight. Heat (the next day) at 325° for 50 to 60 minutes. Serve over rice. Serves 6-8.
SCRUMPTIOUS IN THE WINTER AND MEN LOVE!!!

Great Flavors of Mississippi

Oven Beef Stew

2 tablespoons flour
1 1/2 teaspoons salt
2 tablespoons shortening
1 1/2 pounds beef chuck, cut in 1-inch chunks
2 (10 1/2-ounce) cans condensed tomato soup
1 1/2 cups chopped onion

1/2 teaspoon dried, crushed basil
4 medium potatoes, pared and cubed
4 medium carrots, cut in 1-inch pieces
1/2 cup dry red wine (or water)

Combine flour, salt, and dash of pepper; coat meat cubes and brown in hot shortening in a Dutch oven. Add soup, 2 1/2 cups water, onion, and basil. Cover and bake at 375° for 1 hour. Add potatoes, carrots, and wine. Cover and bake 1 hour longer, or until tender.

The Pick of the Crop

Carbonnade Flamande

In the 1860's and '70's there was a substantial German migration to the Natchez area. Their influence on the cuisine of Natchez is illustrated in this beef stew recipe in which beer and vinegar are used in the sauce instead of the usual French red wine.

1 cup flour	1/2 teaspoon pepper
8 tablespoons bacon grease	5 pounds chuck, sliced into
Olive oil	1/4-inch pieces
1 cup chopped green onions	2 cups thinly-sliced
5 cups thinly-sliced white	mushrooms
onions	1 can beer
Dash of thyme	2 bay leaves
2 cups beef stock	2 tablespoons wine vinegar
2 tablespoons sugar	Grits, rice, or noodles
1/2 teaspoon salt	

Make a roux by browning three-quarters cup flour in a heavy skillet until it is pepper-colored. Add 4 tablespoons bacon grease and enough olive oil to make a paste. Cook until it is chocolate colored, approximately 20 minutes. Stir in green onions, 2 cups white onions, and thyme and cook over low heat until the onions are transparent. Add beef stock and make a smooth gravy. (This mixture can be smoothed in a blender if necessary.)

Dredge meat in 1/4 cup flour, sugar, salt, and pepper mixed together. Brown in 4 tablespoons bacon grease and remove to paper towels to drain.

In an oven-proof casserole dish arrange layers of meat, remaining onions, and mushrooms. Add beer, gravy, and bay leaves. Cover and bake at 350° 2-3 hours or until meat is tender. Sprinkle with vinegar before serving.

Serve over grits, rice, or noodles. Serves 8-10.

Cook with a Natchez Native

Beef Stroganoff

3 tablespoons flour
1 ¹/₂ teaspoons salt
¹/₄ teaspoon pepper
1 pound beef tenderloin,
  ¹/₄-inch thick
1 clove garlic, cut
¹/₄ cup butter or margarine

¹/₂ cup minced onions
¹/₄ cup water
1 (10 ¹/₂-ounce) can condensed
  chicken soup, undiluted
1 pound sliced mushrooms
1 cup commercial sour cream
Snipped parsley, chives or dill

Combine flour, salt and pepper. Trim fat from meat. Rub both sides of meat with garlic. With rim of saucer, pound flour mixture into both sides of meat. Cut meat into 1 ¹/₂ or 1-inch strips. In hot butter in Dutch oven or deep skillet, brown meat strips, turning them often. Add onions; sauté until golden. Add water; stir to dissolve brown bits in bottom of Dutch oven. Add soup and mushrooms; cook, uncovered, over low heat stirring occasionally, until mixture is thick and meat is fork tender, about 20 minutes.

Just before serving, stir in sour cream; heat but do not boil. Sprinkle with parsley. Serve with hot fluffy rice or wild rice, boiled noodles or mashed potatoes. Makes 4-6 servings.

Hospitality Heirlooms

Barbecued Brisket

1 (5-6 pound) beef brisket
3 ounces liquid smoke
Garlic Salt
Onion Salt
Celery Salt
5 tablespoons Worcestershire
   sauce

6 ounces barbecue sauce
2 tablespoons all-purpose flour
$1/2$ cup water
Salt and pepper

Sprinkle liquid smoke and salts over brisket placed in a baking dish sprayed with non-stick cooking spray, and refrigerate overnight. When ready to bake, sprinkle with Worcestershire sauce, salt and pepper—place foil loosely on top. Cook at 250° for 5 hours, uncover and pour barbecue sauce over meat. Cook without foil for another hour—remove platter and let cool before slicing. Remove fat from sauce remaining in dish. Add flour and water to sauce and stir. Cook until sauce thickens. Serve sauce hot with meat. 10 servings.

Note: Great with rice or on sandwiches with slaw.

Temptations

Tommy's Beef Jerky
Perfect for Boy Scout trips as well as divine with a drink.

Round steak or flank steak (7
   pounds will net about 3
   pounds of jerky)
Lemon pepper
Seasoned salt

Garlic salt
Soy sauce
Juice of 2 lemons
Worcestershire sauce

Have butcher slice meat thin with the grain into strips. If you choose to slice it yourself, it is easier to do if meat is slightly frozen. Be sure to trim off all fat.

Season both sides of meat and marinate it in soy sauce, Worcestershire sauce and lemon juice for about 6 hours or overnight in refrigerator. When ready to bake, place strips on a rack with a drip pan underneath. Cook at 200° for about 6 hours. The meat will be dark and very dry in appearance.

This meat will keep safely for a long time, however, it is so good you'll have trouble keeping it at all.

Pineapple Gold

Brocciole

1-2 round steaks, sliced thin,
   cut into 6-8 pieces
Oil
Salt and pepper
Lemon pepper

Garlic powder
Minced onion
Parsley flakes
Parmesan cheese
Raisins

Make paste with oil and the salt, pepper, lemon pepper, garlic powder, minced onion, parsley flakes, and Parmesan cheese. Add enough of each to suit your taste. Spread over each piece of steak. Put 4-6 raisins on each piece of meat and roll up. Secure with 1 – 2 toothpicks. Brown on all sides in oil. Add to the following tomato sauce:

TOMATO SAUCE:
1/2 cup water
1/2 bottle of Worcestershire
   sauce

1/2 bottle Heinz 57 sauce
1/2 bottle A.1. sauce
1/2 bottle catsup

Add to meat. Simmer about 45 minutes. Stir once in a while. Serve over egg noodles.

Family Secrets

Mock Filet

1 pound ground beef
1 cup cracker crumbs
1 egg, beaten
1/3 cup catsup
1/4 cup lemon juice

1 cup grated cheese
1/4 cup chopped green pepper
2 tablespoons chopped onion
Salt and pepper to taste
Bacon slices

Combine all ingredients except bacon. Preheat oven to 400°. Make into patties and wrap 1/2 slice of bacon around each patty. Bake 15 to 20 minutes.

The Mississippi Cookbook

Veal Parmesan

6 veal cutlets
2 eggs, beaten with 1
tablespoon water
1 1/2 cups cracker meal or bread
crumbs
Salt and pepper
3/4 package spaghetti (6 or 7
ounces)
1 1/2 tablespoons oleo

1 large onion, chopped
1 pod garlic, crushed
1 rib of celery, chopped fine
1 (6-ounce) can tomato paste
2 cups water
1/2 teaspoon oregano
1/2 teaspoon garlic salt
2 tablespoons chopped parsley
1 tablespoon Parmesan cheese

Salt and pepper cutlets. Dip in beaten eggs then cracker meal. Fry in deep fat and drain well. Cook spaghetti according to direction.

To make sauce: Sauté onions and garlic in oleo until light brown, add celery, tomato paste and water and all other seasonings, stirring well. Cook over medium heat for 30 minutes. Place drained spaghetti in buttered 2-quart casserole. Spoon a layer of sauce over spaghetti. Place veal cutlets on top. Spoon remainder of sauce over cutlets. Sprinkle with more Parmesan cheese. Bake at 350° for 20 minutes until bubbly.

The Country Gourmet (Miriam G. Cohn)

Thad Cochran's Favorite Meat Loaf

1 1/2 pounds ground beef
1 cup cracker crumbs
2 beaten eggs
1 (8-ounce) can tomato sauce
with tomato bits
1/2 cup finely chopped onions

2 tablespoons chopped green
pepper
1 medium bay leaf, crushed
Dash of thyme
Dash of Marjoram

Combine all ingredients, place in lightly greased loaf pan. Bake at 350° for 1 hour.

*(Thad Cochran, U.S. Senator) **Mississippi Memories***

In contrast to its antebellum past, Mississippi NASA laboratories at Picayune continue to research and test new probes into the space age.

Intentional Hash

1 (2 1/2-3-pound) boneless
  chuck or round roast
1 (14 1/2-ounce) can beef broth
1 bunch green onions
2 teaspoons potato starch or
  flour

2 tablespoons sage
1/2 teaspoon thyme
Salt and pepper

Buy leanest roast possible. In a 10-inch skillet with lid, place the roast and beef broth. Cover, and simmer until very tender about 1 to 1 1/2 hours.

Remove meat to a platter and de-fat; then chop meat into small pieces. Chop green onions, including tops.

Thicken the broth in the skillet with potato starch (available in specialty food stores). If unavailable, measure the broth and thicken with flour, about 1 1/2 teaspoons per cup liquid mixed with a little water for blending. Potato starch also needs to be blended with a little water to prevent lumping when stirred in. This should be a very thin gravy.

Now, add the chopped meat, onions, sage and thyme. Simmer briefly, salt to taste and continue to simmer for 30 to 40 minutes to develop flavor. Sprinkle generously with black pepper and serve on hot split cornbread.

Note: Most hashes are made from leftovers. This recipe is for a deliberate, straight-forward preparation of a hash from scratch. Hence, the designation, Intentional Hash.

Down Here Men Don't Cook

Meatloaf

1 pound ground beef
2 1/2 cups white bread (soaked
  in evaporated milk)
1 medium onion
1 small green pepper, chopped

2 eggs
1/4 cup flour
Salt and pepper to taste

Mix all ingredients. Put into loaf pan. Cover with about 1/2 cup catsup. Cook 1 to 1 1/2 hours at 350°.

Seasoned With Love

Shredded Beef with Pepper
(Chinese Cooking)

8 ounces tender beef
3 green peppers
1 green onion
3 slices ginger

1 cup peanut oil
1 teaspoon salt
$^1/_2$ teaspoon sugar

MARINADE:
2 tablespoons soy sauce
$^1/_2$ tablespoon wine
1 tablespoon cooked peanut
  oil

2 tablespoons cornstarch
$^1/_2$ teaspoon salt

Shred beef about 1 inch in length. Mix with soy sauce, wine, pea-nut oil, cornstarch, salt. Soak for 1 hour.

Clean green peppers; remove seeds and membrane, cut in halves and shred crosswise. Cut green onion and ginger into 1-inch lengths; shred. Heat peanut oil in pan and fry beef. Stir briskly over high heat about 20 seconds; drain out. Heat another 3 tablespoons oil in pan. Stir-fry ginger and green onion, then add shredded green pepper, salt, sugar and stir well. Add beef; blend thoroughly and serve.

Bell's Best 2

Reuben Pie

1 egg, beaten
1/3 cup evaporated milk
3/4 cup rye bread crumbs
1/4 cup chopped onion
1/4 teaspoon salt
Dash pepper
1/2 teaspoon prepared mustard
1/2 pound ground chuck, browned

1 (8-ounce) can sauerkraut, drained and snipped
12 ounces corned beef, chopped (1 1/2 cups thinly sliced)
Pie pastry for 1 deep-dish pie crust
6 ounces Swiss cheese, grated

In mixing bowl combine first 7 ingredients. Add chuck, sauerkraut and corned beef. Mix well. Place 1/2 of meat mixture into pastry shell and sprinkle with 1/2 of cheese. Cover with remaining meat mixture. Top with cheese and bake at 400° for 25-30 minutes. Serves 6.

Southern Sideboards

Reuben Casserole

1 can sauerkraut (do not drain)
1 cup chopped onion
1 carton sour cream

1 can corned beef
Swiss cheese
1/2 loaf party rye bread, buttered

Mix sauerkraut, onions and sour cream. Spread in baking dish. Crumble corned beef and make layer. Cover with cheese, then bread. Bake at 350° until bread is brown.

Into the Second Century

Spaghetti Sauce

SAUCE:

2 big onions, chopped fine
3 pounds ground steak
Wesson oil
6 (6-ounce) cans thick tomato paste
6-8 cans water
6 cloves garlic, chopped fine
6 pieces celery, chopped fine
2 tablespoons salt
2 tablespoons sugar
3 tablespoons chili powder
2 bay leaves
1 teaspoon leaf oregano
Red and black pepper

Brown onions and meat in Wesson oil, add rest of ingredients. Cover and cook slowly 4 hours. If making meat balls, use half the meat in sauce and half in meat balls. Serves 12.

MEAT BALLS FOR SPAGHETTI:

1 1/2 pounds ground round steak
5 slices bread, moistened (no crust)
2 cloves garlic, chopped fine
2 teaspoons salt
1 tablespoon Parmesan cheese
1 small onion, chopped
1 teaspoon chili powder
4 eggs

Put meat in bowl, add crumbled bread and other ingredients. Add eggs and mix thoroughly. Roll into balls and chill. Fry in Wesson oil until brown, cool. Put in sauce and cook slowly for about an hour. Makes 24 meat balls.

Gourmet of the Delta

Pascagoula — Moss Point
Junior Auxiliary Spaghetti Sauce

1 garlic clove, pressed	4 ribs celery
2 medium onions	1 1/2 pounds ground chuck
1/2 bell pepper	Crisco oil

Finely chop vegetables and sauté in Crisco oil. Brown ground chuck (do not substitute hamburger meat) in oil and combine with the sautéed vegetable mixture in a large pot. Add:

1 (12-ounce) can tomato paste	2 tablespoons Worcestershire
1 (12-ounce) can water	sauce
1 (20-ounce) can tomato juice	1/4 teaspoon baking soda
1 scant tablespoon chili	1/4 teaspoon oregano
powder	1/4 teaspoon basil
1 tablespoon sugar	2 drops Tabasco sauce
Salt and pepper to taste	

Cook slowly for three hours, stirring occasionally. Serve over cooked, drained spaghetti. Serves 12.

May be frozen. Also may be doubled. This was used for JA spaghetti dinners several years.

Bouquet Garni

The Pascagoula River is called "The Singing River" because of its occasional weird singing sound. It is said to be the death chant of a Pascagoula tribe who committed suicide in the waters rather than submit to defeat to the Biloxi Indians.

Lasagna

3 pounds ground chuck
1/2 cup chopped onion
2 (1-pound) cans tomatoes
1 (6-ounce) can tomato paste

Garlic, salt and pepper
2 tablespoons parsley flakes
1 tablespoon basil
1 tablespoon oregano

SAUCE:
Brown chuck, add tomatoes and seasonings. Simmer without lid for one hour.

NOODLES:
Boil 1 pound lasagna noodles in salted water until cooked. Rinse and drain in cold water.

CHEESES:
Combine:

1 pound mozzarello cheese,
   sliced or grated
3 small cartons cottage cheese
1 cup grated parmesan cheese

2 tablespoons parsley flakes
1 tablespoon accent
2 eggs

Assemble by layering noodles, meat sauce, cheeses, then repeat. Heat at 375° for 30 minutes. Cool 10 minutes. Serves 12.

The Pilgrimage Garden Club
Antiques Forum Cookbook

Manicotta

1 package Manicotta noodles,
   cooked

SAUCE:

1 1/2 cups chopped onion
1/2-1 teaspoon garlic powder
2 pounds ground beef
1 (35-ounce) can tomatoes,
   undrained
1 (6-ounce) can tomato sauce
2 tablespoons chopped parsley

1 tablespoon salt
2 tablespoons sugar
1 tablespoon Italian seasonings
1/4 teaspoon pepper
1 (4-ounce) can sliced
   mushrooms, optional

Sauté onion and ground beef — may use a little salad oil, if necessary. Add other ingredients and 1 1/2 cups water, mashing tomatoes with fork. Bring to a boil and reduce heat. Simmer, covered, stirring occasionally, for 1 hour.

FILLING:

2 pounds Ricotta cheese
1 (8-ounce) package Mozzarella
   cheese, diced
1/3 cup grated Parmesan cheese
2 eggs

1 teaspoon salt
1/4 teaspoon pepper
1 tablespoon chopped parsley
1/4 cup grated Parmesan

Combine all ingredients except 1/4 cup Parmesan. Blend well. Spread about 1/4 cup filling down each Manicotta noodle (that has been cooked). Spoon a little sauce in casserole dishes, then place noodles on top. Cover with rest of sauce and sprinkle with Parmesan. Bake at 350°, uncovered, 1/2 hour.

Giant Houseparty Cookbook

Noodles Marmaduke

¼ cup sliced onion
2 tablespoons butter
1 pound ground beef
3 tablespoons sherry wine
1 (10½-ounce) can beef
  consomme
1 (6-ounce) can mushrooms,
  stems and pieces, and juice

3 tablespoons lemon juice
1 teapoon salt
¼ teaspoon pepper
Dash garlic salt
¼ pound medium noodles
1 cup sour cream
Chopped parsley

Sauté onion in butter. Add meat and brown. Stir in sherry, consomme, mushrooms and juice, lemon juice, salt, pepper and garlic salt. Simmer uncovered for 15 minutes. Stir in uncooked noodles and cook for 10 minutes or until noodles are tender. Stir in sour cream. Top with parsley to serve. Serves 6.

A favorite dish for Wednesdays at St. Andrew's Episcopal Cathedral luncheons, this recipe is easily doubled, tripled or quadrupled. If prepared in advance, it may be stored in Pyrex casseroles and heated at 325° until hot. It may also be frozen, thawed and reheated.

Southern Sideboards

Inside Out Ravioli

1 pound ground beef
1 medium onion, chopped
1 clove garlic, minced
1 tablespoon salad oil
1 (10-ounce) package frozen
  chopped spinach
1 (1-pound) can spaghetti sauce
  with mushrooms
1 (8-ounce) can tomato sauce

1 (6-ounce) can tomato paste
1/2 teaspoon salt
1/4 teaspoon pepper
1 (7-ounce) package shell or
  elbow macaroni, cooked
1 cup shredded sharp cheese
1/2 cup soft bread crumbs
2 eggs, well beaten
1/4 cup salad oil

Brown first three ingredients in the 1 tablespoon salad oil. Cook spinach according to package directions. Drain, reserving liquid; add water to make 1 cup. Stir spinach liquid and next 5 ingredients into meat mixture. Simmer 10 minutes. Combine spinach with remaining ingredients. Spread in a greased 9x13x2-inch baking dish. Top with meat sauce. Bake at 350° for 30 minutes. Let stand 10 minutes before serving. Serves 8 to 10.

The Mississippi Cookbook

Supreme Beef Casserole

1 pound ground chuck
1 teaspoon shortening
1 (16-ounce) can tomatoes
1 (8-ounce) can tomato sauce
1 teaspoon salt
2 teaspoons sugar
2 garlic buds, crushed, or
  garlic salt

1 (5-ounce) package egg
  noodles
1 (8-ounce) container sour
  cream
1 (3-ounce) package cream
  cheese
6 green onions, chopped
1 cup grated cheese

Brown beef in shortening and drain. Break up tomatoes and add to beef with tomato sauce, salt, sugar and garlic. Simmer 20-25 minutes. Cook noodles and drain. Mix with sour cream, cream cheese and chopped onions. Grease a 3-quart casserole. Put a small amount of meat sauce, layer of noodles and grated cheese. Repeat and top with meat sauce. Bake at 350° for 35 minutes. May be frozen and reheated to serve. Serves 6 to 8.

Madison County Cookery

Seashell Provolone Casserole

3 medium onions, finely
  chopped
1/4 cup butter or oleo, melted
1 1/2-2 pounds ground beef
1 (15 1/2-ounce) jar plain
  spaghetti sauce
1 can (or 2 cups) tomatoes
1 (16-ounce) can mushroom
  stems and pieces

1 teaspoon garlic salt
1 (8-ounce) package seashell
  macaroni
1 (8-ounce) package Provolone
  cheese, sliced
3 cups sour cream
1 cup (4 ounces) shredded
  Mozzarella cheese

Sauté onions in butter in a large skillet just until tender. Add ground beef; cook until browned, stirring to crumble meat; drain. Add spaghetti sauce, tomatoes, mushrooms, and garlic salt to meat mixture. Stir well and simmer 20 minutes.

Cook macaroni according to package directions, except reduce salt to 1 1/2 teaspoons; drain. Place half of macaroni in a deep 4-quart greased casserole; layer with half of meat sauce, half of Provolone, and half of sour cream. Repeat layers and top with Mozzarella. Cover and bake at 350° 30 minutes; uncover and bake another 15 minutes. Serves 12.

The Country Mouse

Moussaka

1 pound ground beef
1 clove garlic, minced
1 (16-ounce) can stewed
   tomatoes
2 (8-ounce) cans tomato sauce
1 envelope onion soup mix
1/2 teaspoon oregano
1 medium eggplant

2 eggs beaten with 1
   tablespoon water
1 cup bread crumbs
Olive oil for frying
1/2 cup Parmesan cheese
1/2 pound Mozzerella cheese,
   cubed

Brown meat. Stir in garlic, stewed tomatoes, tomato sauce, onion soup mix, and oregano. Cover and simmer 15 minutes. Pare eggplant. Cut crosswise in 1/4-inch slices. Dip eggplant into egg-water mixture and then into bread crumbs. Brown in hot olive oil. Alternate layers of eggplant, cheeses, and sauce in a 9x13-inch pan or casserole dish. Bake at 350° for 30 minutes. Serves 8.

The Gulf Gourmet

Red Beans and Rice

2 pounds red kidney beans
2 cups onion, chopped
1/2 cup green pepper, chopped
1 1/2 cloves garlic, mashed
2 tablespoons parsley
1 pound cured ham, cubed
1 pound smoked sausage,
   sliced

1 ham bone, optional
1 tablespoon salt
1/2 teaspoon pepper
1/4 teaspoon cayenne
2 bay leaves
1/2 teaspoon thyme
2 quarts water
2 cups raw rice, cooked

Soak beans overnight in water to cover. Add remaining ingredients, except rice. Cook on low heat 3 hours. Stir the mixture only once every half hour. Serve over fluffy rice.

The Pick of the Crop

Pork Chops in Mushroom Gravy

2 (1-inch thick) loin pork chops
2 tablespoons all-purpose flour
1 teaspoon paprika
Salt and pepper
1 tablespoon vegetable oil

1 small onion, minced
1/2 green pepper, minced
6-8 mushrooms, chopped
1 cup milk
Juice of 1/2 lemon

Remove excess fat from edge of chops. Combine flour, paprika, salt and pepper; dredge chops in mixture. Set aside remaining flour mixture. Brown chops in oil and remove to shallow casserole. Add onion, green pepper and mushrooms to skillet; sauté until soft. Add reserved flour mixture; cook, stirring, 3 minutes. Blend in milk and cook until thickened, stirring constantly. Stir in lemon juice. Pour sauce over chops; cover and bake at 350° for 1 hour. Remove cover and bake 10 more minutes. Yield: 2 servings.

Bell's Best 2

Pork Roast Barbecue

1 (5-6 pound) fresh pork
    shoulder roast
3 parts hickory-flavored
    barbecue sauce

1 part hot barbecue sauce or
    more if desired
1/3-1/4 cup vinegar, optional

Wrap roast tightly in foil; bake in an iron skillet at 225° for 8-9 hours. Drain; remove bone and fat. Shred meat. Combine sauces. Add vinegar if a sharper flavor is desired. Moisten meat with sauce. Serve hot on buns. Serves 10-12.

Taste of the South

Sweet and Sour Pork

1 pound pork, cut into $^1/_2$-inch
   cubes
$^1/_2$ teaspoon Worcestershire
   sauce
2 teaspoons soy sauce
2 teaspoons sherry
$^1/_2$ teaspoon fresh ginger,
   ground or 1 piece candied
   ginger, sliced

$^1/_2$ teaspoon salt
2 beaten eggs
1 cup flour
1 tablespoon cornstarch
$^1/_2$ teaspoon salt
Oil for frying

Marinate the cubed pork in the mixture of Worcestershire and soy sauces, sherry, ginger and $^1/_2$ teaspoon salt. When pork has fully marinated, dip cubes into a batter of the beaten eggs, flour, cornstarch and $^1/_2$ teaspoon salt. Fry in deep hot oil until nicely browned. Drain on paper toweling.

SWEET-SOUR SAUCE:

$^1/_2$ cup water
$^1/_2$ cup sugar
$^1/_4$ cup vinegar
1 teaspoon cornstarch
1 teaspoon soy sauce

1 small tomato, chopped
1 teaspoon sweet pickles
1 teaspoon sweet ginger,
   shredded

Mix first five ingredients and bring to boil on slow fire, stirring constantly. When thick, add tomatoes, pickles and ginger. Place fried pork on platter and pour sauce over.

Giant Houseparty Cookbook

 Antebellum Mississippians served some form of pork and corn at every meal, because both were easily grown, stored and prepared.

Pork Chops-American
(Southern Style)

STUFFING:

$^1/_2$ cup chopped onions
$^1/_4$ cup butter or oleo
1 clove garlic, chopped
$^1/_2$ cup chopped celery
1 cup bread crumbs
2 cups corn bread, crumbled

1 egg, slightly beaten
$^1/_3$ cup chopped parsley
1 tablespoon poultry
   seasoning
Salt and pepper

In skillet, sauté onions in butter. Add garlic and celery and cook until tender. In a bowl, combine bread crumbs, corn bread, egg, parsley, poultry seasoning, salt and pepper. Toss to mix with sautéed onions, garlic and celery.

OTHER INGREDIENTS:

6 (1 $^1/_2$-inch thick) rib chops,
   about 3 $^1/_2$ pounds, slit or
   with pocket
2 tablespoons shortening or
   butter

1 cup apple juice
$^1/_2$ teaspoon dried basil leaves
Salt and pepper
Lemon wedges
Parsley sprigs (to decorate)

Wipe chops and trim off fat. Stuff and hold together with tooth picks. In heavy Dutch oven or skillet, brown chops on both sides in two tablespoons of shortening. Overlap chops in Dutch oven or deep skillet. Sprinkle with basil, salt, pepper and apple juice. Bake in 350° oven 30 minutes. Arrange on serving platter. Garnish with lemon wedges and parsley. Six servings.

My Mother Cooked My Way Through Harvard
With These Creole Recipes

Canadian Bacon Steaks

1 whole bacon, cut in half to
  cook
¹/₄ box brown sugar

Honey
Parsley and fruit sections

Most bacons have been pre-cooked and should be cooked only enough to heat—about 45 minutes to 1 hour at 325° basting often. Put in Dutch oven. Sprinkle about ¹/₄ box brown sugar over the two halves, drizzle honey over this. Turn and repeat in about ¹/₂ hour. Keep covered.

    When ready to serve, cut into ¹/₂-inch circles to resemble tiny ham steaks. Arrange attractively on large tray. Serve with a bowl of orange raisin sauce. Decorate with parsley between each row of slices. You can use most any kind of fruit sections with the parsley for color.

ORANGE RAISIN SAUCE:

2 tablespoons flour
¹/₄ cup brown sugar
1 cup water
¹/₂ cup to 1 cup seedless raisins
  (preferable white)
Dash salt

1 tablespoon butter
¹/₂ cup orange juice
Juice and grated rind of 1
  lemon

Blend sugar and flour. Add water. Cook over low heat until smooth and thickened. Add raisins and other ingredients. Cook slowly for an additional 15 minutes. The sauce can be made ahead of time and reheated.

Special Menus for Very Special Occasions

Straw and Hay

4-ounces white linguine
4-ounces green linguine
Boiling salted water
1/2 cup butter or margarine
8-ounces cooked ham, cut in
    thin strips
3/4 cup cooked green peas

1 (2 1/2-ounce) jar sliced
    mushrooms, drained
2 egg yolks, well beaten
1 cup whipping cream
1 cup Parmesan cheese,
    (4-ounces), freshly grated

Cook white and green linguine in boiling salted water until tender. Drain and return linguine to pot. Add butter, ham, peas and mushrooms. In a small bowl, beat egg yolks and cream with a fork or whisk until foamy. Slowly add cream mixture to linguine, mixing well. Stir in 1/2 cup Parmesan cheese. Stir gently over medium heat, until mixture is thickened. Serve on individual plates. Sprinkle with remaining Parmesan cheese.

Note: Makes 6 appetizer servings, or 4 dinner size portions.

Temptations

Ham-Egg-Mushroom Pie

1 (9-inch) unbaked pie shell
    (use self-rising flour and
    omit salt)
1/2 cup light cream
4 eggs, beaten
4 slices ham, cut up

1 cup fresh mushrooms, sliced,
    or 1/2 cup canned mushroom
    pieces
1/2 cup cheese, grated
Salt and white pepper

Make pie crust. Beat cream into eggs. Mix ham, mushrooms, and cheese and place in pie shell. Pour in eggs. Season. Bake at 425° about 30 minutes. Serves 6-8.

The Twelve Days of Christmas Cookbook

Ham and Turkey Layer

16 slices bread, trimmed
8 slices ham
8 slices turkey
8 slices medium cheese

6 beaten eggs
3 cups milk
$^1/_2$ teaspoon salt
$^1/_2$ teaspoon dry mustard

In a greased 3-quart casserole layer bread, turkey, ham and cheese, (bread on bottom). Mix together eggs, milk, salt and mustard; pour over top of layers. Let set in refrigerator overnight. Next day, mix together:

2 cups corn flake crumbs

1 stick butter

Put over top. Bake for 1 hour at 350°.

Tasting Tea Treasures

Sausage Casserole

1 pound good bulk sausage
$^1/_4$ cup chopped onion
1 cup sliced celery
1 $^1/_2$ cups uncooked rice
2 (14-ounce) cans chicken
   broth

$^1/_2$ cup slivered almonds,
   toasted
1 tablespoon soy sauce

Fry sausage, stirring; do not brown. Sauté celery and onions in small amount of sausage grease. Drain sausage well and add to rice, sautéd celery and onions. Pour in chicken broth. Add almonds and soy sauce. Bake in large covered casserole (3-quart) about one hour at 350°. Stir before serving.

Best of Bayou Cuisine

Smoked Ham

14-pound ham (I prefer
  Southern Belle)
2 (8-ounce) cans crushed
  pineapple
2 cups brown sugar

2 tablespoons mustard
2 teaspoons dry mustard
Juice of 2 lemons
Dash salt

Build fire on charcoal grill and let temperature reach 300°. Place ham on spit inserting spit forks at both ends. Test for balance. Insert meat thermometer into center of thickest part of ham. Attach spit and start motor so that ham will turn slowly. Thermometer should register 140° degrees for pre-cooked ham and 170° for uncooked ham. I cook pre-cooked ham about 3 hours.

To prepare ham glaze, drain pineapple and reserve syrup. Combine pineapple, sugar, mustards, lemon juice, and salt. Stir to mix well and add as much of the reserved syrup as needed to have mixture of spreading consistency, Spread glaze over ham during last ¹/₂ hour of cooking.

The Cook's Book

Raisin Sauce

2 cups seedless raisins
1 cup chicken stock
2 tablespoons flour
Juice of 1 lemon

1 cup sugar
1 teaspoon cinnamon
Dash of ketchup

Soak raisins until tender and plump. Drain. Make brown gravy of chicken stock and flour. Add lemon juice, cinnamon, sugar, raisins and ketchup, and let cook over low fire until desired thickness— about 10 minutes. This is delicious with baked ham.

Inverness Cook Book

Seafood

Catch of the day. Off Mississippi Gulf Coast.

Crunchy Catfish Kabobs

2 pounds catfish fillets, fresh
  or frozen
12 small white onions, peeled
18 large mushroom caps
12 cherry tomatoes
12 large pimento stuffed olives
2 cups herb seasoned croutons
1/2 cup oil
1/2 cup teriyaki sauce or soy
  sauce
1/2 cup chopped onion
1/3 cup fresh lemon juice
1 cup boiling water

2 tablespoons whole coriander
  or caraway seed
1 tablespoon sugar
10 shelled Brazil nuts or 20
  pecan halves
2 cloves garlic, peeled
1/2 teaspoon white pepper
1/4 teaspoon liquid hot pepper
  sauce
3 cups cooked rice
Parsley sprigs, cherry
  tomatoes, and red and green
  pickled cherry peppers for
  garnish

Thaw fish if frozen; cut into 1-inch pieces. Parboil small white onions in water for 5 minutes; drain. In a large shallow dish combine fish, small white onions, mushroom caps, tomatoes and olives. Crush croutons in a blender, processor or with a rolling pin to make fine crumbs. Place in a shallow dish.

In a blender or food processor place oil, teriyaki sauce, chopped onion, lemon juice, coriander seed, sugar, nuts, garlic, pepper and hot pepper sauce. Blend until onion and nuts are finely chopped and marinade is well blended. Pour marinade over fish and vegetables, stirring well to coat all pieces. Cover and refrigerate 1 hour, stirring once or twice while marinating. Drain; reserve marinade.

Roll fish pieces in crumbs. Thread fish and vegetables, alternately, on 6 skewers approximately 16 inches long. Place on a greased broiler pan. Broil about 9 or 10 inches from heat source for 8 to 10 minutes or until fish is opaque and flakes easily when tested with a fork. About 1 minute before cooking time is finished, brush any remaining marinade over kabobs. Serve kabobs over cooked rice. Garnish with parsley sprigs, cherry tomatoes and pickled cherry peppers. Yield: 6 servings.

Mississippi Memories

Catfish Cajun Piquant

1 large green pepper, cut in
   thin strips
$1/2$ cup shallots including tops,
   sliced
1 stalk celery, minced
1 (16-ounce) can tomatoes,
   chopped fine
1 (8-ounce) can tomato sauce

$1/2$ teaspoon thyme
1 bay leaf
1 clove garlic, minced
1 teaspoon sugar
Salt to taste
Pepper to taste
Dash Tabasco
$1 1/2$ pounds catfish fillets

Simmer the onion, green pepper, and celery in a little water until tender. Add all remaining ingredients except fish and simmer 15 minutes. Layer the fillets in the bottom of a shallow baking dish and pour sauce over them. Add more Tabasco if desired.

Bake in a 350° oven for 20 to 25 minutes or until fish flakes with a fork. Remove the bay leaf. Serve with rice. Serves 4. Can partially do ahead.

This is good low calorie fare, proving that catfish does not necessarily have to be fried to be good. Remember, the more Tabasco sauce, the more piquant the dish. Take care. Note also this is a low-salt dish, and it's best with Mississippi Delta farm-raised catfish.

Standing Room Only

"The Catfish Capital of the World" is located in Humphreys County. Mississippi processes over 90% of the farm-raised catfish produced in the United States.

Farm Raised Catfish Pizza

HUSH PUPPY CRUST:

1 1/3 cups pie crust mix   4-5 tablespoons cold water
2/3 cup hush puppy mix

In a medium mixing bowl, combine pie crust mix and hush puppy mix. Add water gradually until mixture clings together and can be rolled into a ball. With fingertips, press dough into a lightly greased 12-inch pizza pan.

TARTAR TOPPING:

1(10 3/4-ounce) can cream of   2 tablespoons chopped
   onion soup   pimento
1/3 cup mayonnaise
1/4 cup finely chopped dill
   pickle

Combine all ingredients; blend well.

PIZZA:

2 cups cooked, flaked farm   1 1/2 teaspoons margarine,
   raised catfish   softened
1 1/2 cups grated Cheddar or   Hush Puppy Crust
   American cheese   Tartar Topping
1/4 cup hush puppy mix

Sprinkle half the cheese over the Hush Puppy Crust. Place the flaked fish on top of the cheese. Pour the Tartar Topping over the fish and sprinkle with remaining cheese. Combine hush puppy mix and margarine; sprinkle over top of cheese. Bake in a hot oven at 400° for 20-25 minutes. Serve hot. Serves 6.

Bell's Best

Blackened Catfish Pecan

6 catfish fillets
1 tablespoon Fines Herbes
1 teaspoon red pepper
1 1/2 teaspoons white pepper
4 teaspoons paprika
1 teaspoon salt

1 stick butter, melted (no
   substitute)
1/2 cup broken pecans
Chopped parsley
Lemon slices (optional)

Dry fish well. Combine seasoning and sprinkle generously on both sides of fillets. Heat a black iron skillet, large enough to accomodate all the fish at one time, over high heat until it is beyond the smoking stage and looks gray on the bottom-at least 5 minutes. Skillet cannot get too hot. Dip seasoned fillets into melted butter and put in skillet, leaving fire on high. Cook 1 1/2 minutes. Turn and cook another 1 1/2 minutes. Test for flakiness. When flaky, reduce heat, remove fish and place around mound of hot buttered rice on large platter. Turn heat down. Add pecans to butter in skillet and sauté, watching closely to keep from burning. Pour browned pecans over rice and fish. Sprinkle with chopped parsley and garnish with lemon slices.

Into the Second Century

Catfish Fillets Meuniere

Soak catfish fillets for 1 hour or more in a mixture of egg and milk, seasoned with salt, pepper, and a dash of hot sauce. Shake fillets in seasoned flour and fry until golden brown. Serve fillets on a warm platter with a generous amount of Sauce Meuniere spooned over them.

SAUCE MEUNIERE:

1/2 cup butter
1 tablespoon chopped green
   onion tops
1 tablespoon chopped fresh
   parsley
2 tablespoons Worcestershire
   sauce

3 tablespoons lemon juice
1/2 teaspoon salt
1/2 teaspoon pepper
Few drops of bottled brown
   bouquet sauce

Simmer all ingredients at least 15 minutes. Serve over fish.

Festival

Farm-Raised Catfish Williamsburg

1 teaspoon salt, divided
8 (4-ounce) catfish fillets or
　　equivalent
1 (2-ounce) bottle Tabasco

1 teaspoon pepper
2 cups cornmeal mix
4 cups oil or more if needed

Lightly salt fish on both sides; liberally sprinkle and rub fish with Tabasco. Refrigerate for 1 hour. Combine pepper, cornmeal mix and remaining salt. Dredge fish in cornmeal mixture; drop into oil heated to 375°. Cook until golden brown or about 5 minutes; drain well. CAUTION: Do not overload oil with fish. Temperature of oil during cooking should not drop below 360°. Four cups of oil will cook about 2 fillets at a time. Serves 4.

Taste of the South

There are three national cemeteries in Mississippi—in Vicksburg, Corinth, and Natchez.

Stuffed Flounder

2 eggs
2 cups cooked shrimp or
   crabmeat
1 cup cream
2 tablespoons butter

$^1/_2$ cup mushrooms
2 teaspoons chopped chives
1 tablespoon flour
4 tablespoons sherry
4 flounders ($^3/_4$-pound each)

Mix the shrimp, egg, and cream together. Melt butter, add mushrooms and chives, and sauté until soft; add flour and cook until bubbly. Add shrimp mixture, sherry and cook until thick. Slit the flounder along the backbone and cut the flesh of the fish away from the bone, but leave intact. Spoon as much stuffing into the slit as possible. Top with butter and bake in 300° oven until done, about 30 minutes.

If you want to use fewer flounders, the stuffing may be made as directed, and the remainder can be stored in the refrigerator for use at a later date.

The Pick of the Crop

Cheesy Catfish

6 pan-dressed catfish or 2
   pounds small fillets
$^3/_4$ cup Parmesan cheese
$^1/_4$ cup flour
$^1/_2$ teaspoon salt

$^1/_2$ teaspoon pepper
1 teaspoon paprika
1 egg, beaten
1 tablespoon milk
$^1/_4$ cup margarine, melted

Combine cheese, flour, salt, pepper, and paprika in bowl. Mix egg and milk. Dip fish in egg mixture and then in cheese mixture to coat well. Place aluminum foil in 13x9x2-inch baking dish and place fish on foil. Pour margarine over fish and bake at 350° until golden brown.

Festival

Tommy's Red Snapper

1 whole large red snapper (5 or 6 pounds)	OR a small to medium whole snapper per person

Score whole fish by cutting deep gashes in both sides crosswise of the fish.

Season fish inside and out with salt and pepper. Place a slice of lemon in each fish or several slices in the large fish. Also place lemon slices on top.

Place fish in broiler pan without rack. Bake at 325° for about 20 minutes. Then pour the lemon juice over the fish. Spoon the mushroom and artichoke sauce over the fish. Continue baking fish until it is tender and flaky (15 minutes or more).

MUSHROOM-ARTICHOKE SAUCE:

1 stick butter (¹/₄ pound)	OR you may use 1 can
2 little green onions, chopped	artichoke hearts, quartered
1¹/₂ cups fresh mushrooms, sliced	¹/₄ cup chopped fresh parsley
	¹/₂-1 cup dry white wine
1 can artichoke bottoms, cut in bite-size pieces, if you are feeling extravagant	3 tablespoons lemon juice, freshly squeezed

Melt butter and sauté onions. Add sliced mushrooms and artichoke bottoms and sauté gently. Add parsley and wine and toss lightly. Set aside until ready to use.

Pineapple Gold

Salmon Mold Supreme

1 tablespoon gelatin	1 tablespoon grated onion
1/4 cup cold water	1/2 cup chopped parsley
1 (1-pound) can salmon	1/2 cup chopped celery
1 cup sour cream	1/2 cup stuffed olives
1/2 cup mayonnaise	3/4 teaspoon salt
1/2 cup salmon liquid or water	2 tablespoons lemon juice

Soak gelatin for 5 minutes. Heat salmon liquid to dissolve; add sour cream and mayonnaise and stir until smooth. Add salmon and remaining ingredients. Pour into well-greased mold. Chill until firm. Cucumber slices may be used to garnish.

DAR Recipe Book

Salmon Loaf
(Low Calorie)

1 cup bread crumbs	1/2 teaspoon onion juice
1 cup scalded, skim milk	2 egg yolks
1 cup canned salmon	1 teaspoon lemon juice
1 teaspoon salt	2 egg whites
1 tablespoon oleo	

Add bread crumbs to scalded milk. Stir in other ingredients except egg whites, and mix well. Beat egg whites until stiff. Fold into salmon mixture and pour into buttered casserole. Bake in a pan of water at 375° for 30 to 45 minutes. Can be served with creole sauce. Serves 6. Approximately 170 calories per serving; 1/3 bread exchange; 2 meat exchanges.

The Cook's Book

Deluxe Fresh Salmon

6 medium carrots, peeled and
  sliced thin
1 large onion, chopped small
4 ribs of celery, chopped small
3/4 stick oleo
2 tablespoons lemon juice
4 fresh salmon steaks, 1-inch
  thick

1/4 teaspoon salt
1/4 teaspoon pepper
1 teaspoon Accent
1 teaspoon Worcestershire
  sauce
Dash of Tabasco

Cook carrots in water until almost tender. Sauté onions in oleo until light brown. Add chopped celery and cook 10 more minutes. Add drained carrots and cook 10 more minutes. Place these vegetables in a greased rectangular casserole dish. Before seasoning salmon, if there is any gray skin that surrounds salmon, remove. Season salmon with salt, pepper and Accent. Place salmon on top of vegetables and add lemon juice, Tabasco and Worcestershire sauce. Bake at 350° for 30 minutes. Will serve 4.

    This dish is very special and unusual.

The Country Gourmet (Miriam G. Cohn)

Pascagoula Shrimp Boil
with Peppy Seafood Sauce

3 ounces prepared shrimp
  boil (commercial spice mix)
1 small onion, sliced
1 lemon, sliced
1 clove garlic, sliced

1 gallon water
$1/2$ cup salt
5 pounds shrimp, fresh or
  frozen

Tie the shrimp boil, onion, lemon and garlic in a piece of cheese-cloth. Place water in large container. Add salt and bag of seasonings. Cover and bring to boiling point over a hot fire. Add shrimp and return to boiling point. Cover and cook 5 minutes or until shrimp are tender. Drain.

Note: If shrimp is to be used for salad or cocktails, cook as above, remove from water, peel, devein, and chill.

PEPPY SEAFOOD SAUCE:

$1/2$ cup chill sauce
$1/2$ cup catsup
3 tablespoons freshly
  squeezed lemon juice
1 tablespoon horseradish
1 tablespoon mayonnaise or
  salad dressing

1 teaspoon Worcestershire
  sauce
$1/2$ teaspoon onion, grated
$1/4$ teaspoon salt
3 drops Tabasco sauce
Dash pepper

Mix ingredients well. Serve with shrimp.

Dixie Dining

 Two of Mississippi's borders are great bodies of water: The Mississippi River and The Gulf of Mexico.

Shrimp Fritters

1 pound medium shrimp	4 eggs
1 cup water	1 teaspoon salt
1/4 cup butter	2 teaspoons paprika
1 cup flour	1/3 teaspoon cayenne pepper

Shell shrimp, leaving tails on. Make a cut deep, but not all the way through, backs of shrimp and spread, butterfly fashion.

Bring 1 cup of water and 1/4 cup of butter to a boil in medium saucepan. Add flour all at once, stirring vigorously until mixture leaves sides of pan. Remove from heat and add the eggs, one at a time, beating after each addition until smooth. Stir in the salt, paprika and cayenne pepper. Dip shrimp in mixture and drop in hot, deep fat. Fry until golden brown, turning once. Drain on paper toweling and serve. (Serves 2.)

My Mother Cooked My Way Through Harvard
With These Creole Recipes

Lemon-Garlic Broiled Shrimp

2 pounds shrimp (medium, peeled)	1/4 teaspoon black pepper
2 cloves garlic, halved	1/2 teaspoon hot sauce
1/4 cup butter	1 tablespoon Worcestershire sauce
3 tablespoons lemon juice	3 tablespoons chopped parsley
1/2 teaspoon salt	

Place shrimp in single layer in a large flat pan; set aside. Sauté garlic in butter until garlic is brown; remove and discard garlic. Add next five ingredients, stirring well; pour mixture over shrimp. Broil shrimp four inches from heat source for eight to ten minutes, basting once. Sprinkle with parsley; serve immediately. Serves 6.

Gardeners' Gourmet II

Shrimp Creole

1/4 cup flour
1/4 cup oil
2 cups chopped onions
1/2 cup chopped green onions,
  and tops
2 buds garlic, minced
1 cup chopped green pepper
1 cup chopped celery, with
  leaves
2 bay leaves
3 teaspoons salt

1/2 teaspoon pepper
1 (6-ounce) can tomato paste
1 (16-ounce) can tomatoes
1 (8-ounce) can tomato sauce
1 cup water
5 pounds raw shrimp, peeled
  and deveined
Dash of Tabasco
1/2 cup chopped parsley
Juice of 1/2 lemon

In a Dutch oven or large heavy pot, make a roux of flour and oil. Add onions, green onion, garlic, green pepper, celery, bay leaves, salt, and pepper. Sauté, uncovered, over medium heat until onions are transparent and soft. Add tomato paste and sauté 3 minutes. Add tomatoes, tomato sauce, and water. Simmer for 45 minutes to 1 hour, stirring occasionally. Add shrimp and cook until shrimp are just done, about 5 minutes. Add Tabasco, parsley, and lemon juice. Stir, cover and remove from heat.

This is best prepared several hours before serving. Let stand so seasonings and flavors can blend. Heat, but do not boil, and serve over rice. Serves 10.

The Gulf Gourmet

Seafood Casserole in Toast Cups

1 (8-ounce) can mushroom
   stems and pieces, or ¹/₂ cup
   fresh sliced mushrooms
1 stick plus 1 tablespoon
   margarine
1 ¹/₂ pounds cooked shrimp
1 can crabmeat

¹/₄ cup sherry
3 cups milk
7 level tablespoons flour
2 egg yolks
Salt and pepper to taste
Buttered bread crumbs

Sauté mushrooms in 1 tablespoon margarine. Soak seafood for one hour in the sherry. Combine with highly seasoned cream sauce made of the milk, 1 stick margarine and flour. Cook over hot water. Add beaten egg yolks and salt. Do not boil. Place in greased casserole; cover with buttered bread crumbs. Bake at 350° until hot and bubbly. Fill toast cups with baked mixture.

TOAST CUPS:
12 slices bread   ¹/₂ stick margarine, melted

Roll 12 slices of fresh and trimmed bread with rolling pin until thin and press each slice into a large muffin tin. Brush lightly with melted margarine. Bake for 1 hour at 250° or until lightly browned.

I Promised A Cookbook

Shrimp Remoulade

2 cups mayonnaise
   (homemade, if possible)
5 tablespoons creole mustard
4 tablespoons grated onion
4 tablespoons grated celery

4 ounces fresh lemon juice
4 tablespoons fresh chopped
   parsley
Salt, cayenne pepper, to taste

Combine all ingredients and chill for two hours to enhance seasonings. Use over boiled shrimp and lettuce.

Down Here Men Don't Cook

Shrimp on Holland Rusk with Ned's Dressing

Cream Cheese
Pinch salt
Mayonnaise to taste

Holland Rusk
Lettuce, shredded
Shrimp, cooked and deveined

Season cream cheese with salt and mayonnaise and spread on Holland Rusk. Cover with shredded lettuce and shrimp. Before serving, cover with Ned's Dressing.

NED'S DRESSING:

1/2 cup Wesson oil
1/2 cup or less, sugar
1/2 cup vinegar
1 teaspoon paprika

1/2 cup chili sauce or catsup
1/4 cup water
1 teaspoon salt
1 small onion, grated

Mix well with beater.

DAR Recipe Book

Barbecued Shrimp

8-10 pounds jumbo shrimp (20 per pound), shells and tails on
1 pound butter
1 pound margarine
6 ounces Worcestershire sauce
8 tablespoons finely ground black pepper

1 teaspoon ground rosemary
4 lemons, sliced
1 teaspoon Tabasco
4 teaspoons salt
2-4 cloves garlic, optional

Preheat oven to 400°. In a large saucepan, melt butter and margarine. Add Worcestershire sauce, pepper, rosemary, lemons, Tabasco sauce, salt, garlic and mix thoroughly. Divide shrimp between two large shallow pans. Pour heated sauce over each pan; stir well. Cook shrimp, turning once during baking, 14 to 20 minutes. Shells should be pink, meat white — not translucent.

Giant Houseparty Cookbook

Itajun Shrimp

4 pounds jumbo fresh shrimp
2 sticks unsalted butter
½ bottle Golden Blend (or
    other) Italian dressing
¼ cup pure virgin olive oil
¼ teaspoon basil

¼ teaspoon thyme
¼ teaspoon oregano
¼ teaspoon rosemary
½ teaspoon Tony Chachere's
    Creole Seasoning
6 "knees" garlic

Wash shrimp and let drain in colander. Melt butter in oblong pan. Add all ingredients except shrimp. Mix well, then place shrimp in the sauce and stir well. Bake uncovered at 350° for 30 minutes, stirring twice during cooking. Serve with hot French bread.
    Serves 6-8.

Natchez Notebook of Cooking

Nevie's Stove-Top Scampi

1½ pounds jumbo shrimp,
    peeled, deveined and
    butterflied
3 tablespoons olive oil
3 tablespoons butter

3 tablespoons lemon juice
3 tablespoons vermouth
1 clove garlic, finely minced
Seasoned salt, to taste
White pepper, to taste

Heat olive oil in large skillet over medium high heat; add butter and turn to medium heat. Add garlic and sauté for 2 minutes, carefully coating pan. Place shrimp into pan; lightly brown on one side and turn. After turning, sprinkle with lemon juice, salt and pepper. Turn heat up to medium high for quick browning. Sprinkle with vermouth evenly. Swirl shrimp and seasonings together. Turn off heat, cover and set off to side. Serve immediately. Yield: 6 appetizer or 2 main course servings.
    Note: This may be used as an appetizer, first course or main dish. Quick and easy!

Mississippi Memories

Bob's Jambalaya

1 ¹/₂-2 pounds large shelled
  shrimp
1 pound sausage
1 large onion, chopped
1 green pepper, chopped
1 bunch green onions, chopped
2 cloves garlic, minced
3 large tomatoes, peeled and
  diced
2 cups long grain rice

2 cups water
Flour
Salt
Pepper
Red pepper
Thyme
Cayenne pepper
Bay leaves
2 tablespoons chopped fresh
  parsley

Brown sausage, remove. Add flour and bacon drippings to make a dark roux. Add onions, green pepper, garlic and sauté until tender. Add tomatoes and cook for 10 minutes. Add shrimp and simmer until they turn pink. Gradually add water, stirring occasionally. Then add rice, seasonings and sausage. Bring to a boil, lower heat and cook for 1 hour, covered tightly, until rice is tender. Garnish with parsley.

    Serves 6 to 8. Double the recipe to serve a large crowd.

Note: Use a big pressure pot to cook this stuff in.

Down Here Men Don't Cook

Shrimp and Artichoke Casserole

2 pounds shrimp	1 (No. 2) can artichoke hearts

Boil, shell, and devein shrimp. Place shrimp in greased baking dish with quartered artichoke hearts. Pour over them the following sauce:

SAUCE:

2 tablespoons butter	1 tablespoon lemon juice
3 tablespoons flour	1 tablespoon Worcestershire
1/2 teaspoon paprika	3 tablespoons sherry
1/4 teaspoon red pepper	1 cup sharp grated cheese
1 pint Half & Half cream	1 teaspoon hot mustard
1 tablespoon catsup	(optional)

Make sauce of butter, flour, cream, paprika, and red pepper. Cook until thick. Then add catsup, lemon juice, Worcestershire, sherry, mustard and cheese. Pour sauce over shrimp and artichokes and add a little grated cheese on top. Heat in moderate oven.

Inverness Cook Book

Eggplant Lynette
(from Jerry Psanos, The Fisherman's Wharf)

2 medium eggplants	3 tablespoons margarine
1 medium onion	3 tablespoons olive oil
1 bell pepper	Salt and pepper to taste
1 stalk celery	1 cup oyster juice (optional)
1/2 pound deveined and	4 tablespoons butter
chopped shrimp	1 cup fresh lump crabmeat

Steam eggplant until tender. Let cool and slice lengthwise. Remove pulp, leaving 1/4 inch around skin of the eggplant. Reserve pulp. Sauté chopped onion, bell pepper and celery in margarine and olive oil. Add salt, pepper, oyster juice and pulp. Stuff all ingredients in eggplant shell and bake at 450° until brown crust appears. In separate skillet, melt butter and add crabmeat. Top on eggplant just before serving.

Hospitality Heirlooms

Shrimp in Sour Cream

1 pound cooked, cleaned
   shrimp, fresh or frozen or 4
   (4¼- to 5-ounce) cans shrimp
1 (4-ounce) can sliced
   mushrooms, drained
2 tablespoons chopped green
   onion
2 tablespoons butter or
   margarine, melted

1 tablespoon flour
1 (10¾-ounce) can condensed
   cream of shrimp soup
1 cup sour cream
Dash pepper
Toast points or patty shells

Thaw frozen shrimp or drain canned shrimp. Rinse canned shrimp with cold water. Cut large shrimp in half. Cook mushrooms and onions in butter until tender. Blend in flour. Add soup and cook until thickened, stirring constantly. Add sour cream, pepper, and shrimp. Heat, stirring occasionally. Serve on toast points or in patty shells. Serves 6.

Bouquet Garni

Seafood Mousse

1 tablespoon unflavored
   gelatin, softened in ¼ cup
   cold water
1 cup hot sour cream (do not
   boil)
1 pound or 2 cups seafood
   mixture (crab and shrimp)
¼ cup mayonnaise

¼ cup green onions, chopped
1 tablespoon onion, grated
¼ cup celery, finely chopped
1 cup whipping cream,
   whipped
Salt and pepper to taste
Few drops Tabasco & lemon
   juice

Add softened gelatin to hot sour cream. Cool. Add seafood, mayonnaise, onion, and celery. When mixture begins to congeal, fold in whipped cream. Correct seasonings and pour into a wet mold. Chill.

Natchez Notebook of Cooking

Scallops and Crabmeat

4 tablespoons butter
1 pound fresh bay scallops
Fresh lemon juice
Salt to taste
3 tablespoons chopped bell
　pepper
3 tablespoons finely chopped
　onion
1/4 pound fresh mushrooms,
　sliced
1 stick butter
3/4 cup flour

1 cup half-and-half
1 cup milk
1/4 teaspoon salt
1/4 cup dry white wine
Generous dash nutmeg
Dash cayenne pepper
3 tablespoons chopped
　pimiento
1 1/2 cups whipping cream
3 tablespoons butter
1 pound fresh lump crabmeat
Salt and pepper to taste

Melt 4 tablespoons butter in heavy skillet over medium heat and
sauté scallops, one-half at a time, until slightly brown; remove with
slotted spoon, sprinkling with lemon juice and a touch of salt. Add
bell pepper and onion; simmer until tender; add mushrooms; simmer 3 minutes, adding butter as needed; remove from heat.

Melt 1 stick butter in double boiler over low heat; add flour, stirring until smooth. Pour in half-and-half and milk, stirring occasionally until sauce thickens. Add salt, wine, nutmeg, cayenne,
pimiento, whipping cream, and 3 tablespoons butter. Pour vegeta-
ble-mushroom mixture into sauce; add scallops and gently fold in
crabmeat. Heat and serve in patty shells or on toasted bread. Serves
6 to 8 as an entrée.

Note: If bay scallops are not available, substitute sea scallops, cut
in half. May be served from a chafing dish as an appetizer.

Accent One

King Crab au Gratin

1 (6-ounce) container crabmeat
3 tablespoons butter
3 tablespoons flour
1 cup milk
1/2 cup light cream
1/2 cup chicken broth
3/4 cup shredded sharp
    Cheddar cheese

1 (4-ounce) can sliced
    mushrooms, drained
2 tablespoons grated onion
1 teaspoon salt
1/4 teaspoon paprika
2 tablespoons white wine
1/4 cup fine bread crumbs

Defrost crabmeat. Melt butter in saucepan. Stir in flour until smooth. Gradually stir in milk, cream and broth. Cook, stirring constantly, over low heat until sauce is smooth and thick. Add cheese, mushrooms, onion, salt, paprika and wine. Stir until cheese is melted. Stir in chunks of crab. Pour mixture into well-greased 1 1/2-quart casserole. Sprinkle bread crumbs over top. Bake at 400° for 10-15 minutes or until top is golden brown.

Bell's Best

Luncheon Muffin Round

Butter
4 English muffins
2 packages frozen broccoli
    spears, cooked and drained
1 pound lump white crabmeat
Slivered toasted almonds,
    chopped

2/3 cups finely chopped celery
1 cup mayonnaise
Salt and pepper to taste
8 slices American cheese
Paprika

Split and butter muffins and top each with three broccoli spears. Mix remaining ingredients except cheese and paprika and mound the mixture on top of broccoli. Top with cheese slices and sprinkle with paprika. Bake at 400° for 20 minutes. Serves 8.

Serve with potato chips, tomato wedges, pickles, radish roses, and parsley for a pretty luncheon plate.

Bouquet Garni

Crab Mousse

1 tablespoon gelatin
1/4 cup mayonnaise
2 tablespoons lime juice
2 tablespoons lemon juice
1 tablespoon parsley, chopped

1 tablespoon chives, chopped
1 tablespoon prepared mustard
Salt and pepper to taste
2 cups flaked crabmeat
3/4 cup heavy cream, whipped

Soften 1 tablespoon gelatin in 3 tablespoons cold water and dissolve it over hot water. Mix gelatin with 1/4 cup mayonnaise, 2 tablespoons each of lime and lemon juice, 1 tablespoon each of parsley and chives, 1 tablespoon prepared mustard, and salt and pepper to taste. Fold in 2 cups flaked, fresh crabmeat. (The lump crabmeat is not as delicate as the other). Fold in the 3/4 cup heavy cream, whipped.

Pour the mixture into a buttered ring mold and chill until set. Unmold the mousse on a chilled platter and garnish with thin slices of lime.

Fill the center with avocado mashed with lemon juice, a little mayonnaise, and a dash of Worcestershire. Sprinkle top with chopped chives.

This can also be made into individual salads and is delicious for a luncheon. It is pretty in a fish mold without the avocado.

Pineapple Gold

Baked Crab and Mushrooms

3/4 cup chopped fresh
  mushrooms
2 tablespoons margarine, more
  if needed
1/2 cup heavy cream

3 tablespoons sherry
1/2 teaspoon tarragon
1 cup crab meat
1 teaspoon cornstarch
1/2 cup diced mild white cheese

Wash mushrooms; chop and sauté in margarine. Add cream, sherry and tarragon. Boil, stirring frequently, until liquid is reduced by half. Blend crab meat and cornstarch. Add to cream mixture in skillet. Simmer 5 to 10 minutes. Put in baked pastry shells or ramekins; top with cheese. Heat until cheese is bubbly. *Can be made ahead.*

Just a Spoonful

Almond Topped Crab Quiche

Pastry for 9-inch pie shell
1 cup shredded Swiss cheese
1/2 pound fresh crabmeat
2 green onions, sliced
3 eggs
1 cup half & half

1/2 teaspoon salt
1/2 teaspoon grated lemon rind
Dash of dry mustard
Dash of pepper
1/4 cup sliced almonds

Line a 9-inch quiche dish with pastry. Trim excess from edges. Bake at 400° for 3 minutes; remove from oven, gently prick with fork. Bake 5 minutes longer. Cool on rack. Sprinkle cheese in pastry shell. Remove cartilage from crabmeat and place crabmeat on top of cheese. Sprinkle with green onion. Beat eggs until foamy; stir in half & half, salt, lemon rind, dry mustard and pepper. Pour into pastry shell. Sprinkle with almonds. Bake at 325° for 1 hour. Let stand 10 minutes before serving.

Hospitality Heirlooms

Deviled Crabs

4 teaspoons butter
3 teaspoons flour
1 cup milk
2 cups cooked crab meat
Juice of 1 lemon
2 hard boiled eggs, chopped
1 teaspoon pepper, red or
   black

1 teaspoon dry mustard
3 tablespoons chopped onion
1 teaspoon salt
1/2 cup toasted bread crumbs
4 teaspoons melted butter

Melt butter, stir in flour and gradually add milk. Cook until thick. Remove from heat, add crab meat, all seasonings, and eggs. Place mixture in crab shells, if available, or in greased baking dish. Sprinkle with bread crumbs and butter. Bake at 400° for 15 minutes.

Inverness Cook Book

Bravo Oyster Spaghetti

1 stick salted butter
1/2 cup plus 3 teaspoons olive oil, divided
8 large cloves garlic, peeled and cut in pieces 1/3-inch thick
3 teaspoons dried basil or 1/2 cup fresh
3 tablespoons finely minced fresh parsley

1 teapoon freshly ground pepper
6 1/2 teaspoons salt, divided
2 pints fresh shucked oysters (about four dozen medium-sized oysters, drained. Do not use large oysters.)
6 quarts cold water
24 ounces linguine

In a heavy 2-quart saucepan or iron skillet, melt the salted butter over low heat; add 1/2 cup olive oil, mixing thoroughly, and heat 4 minutes. Add cut garlic cloves and cook over medium heat just until they begin to brown, about 5 minutes; remove immediately with a slotted spoon. Be very careful to cook the garlic just until it begins to brown, because it gets milder the longer you cook it. The garlic, removed from the oil and and drained, makes a tasty (and healthful) hors d'oeuvre for the cook. Add the parsley, basil, pepper and 1/2 teaspoon salt to the butter and oil mixture and simmer for about 4 minutes. Add the drained oysters. It is proper to warm the oysters at this point of preparation, not cook them, about 5 minutes over low heat. Remove the saucepan or skillet from the heat and cover, setting aside.

Cook the spaghetti in a 6 to 8-quart pot or saucepan. Combine 6 quarts cold water, 6 teaspoons salt, 3 teaspoons olive oil, and bring to rolling boil, fast. Add the spaghetti and cook about 7 minutes after water comes to a boil again. Drain in colander thoroughly and then put spaghetti back in pot. Add oyster mixture and mix very gently with a long fork. Cover pot and let it stand on a warming tray or in an oven preheated to 200° about 10 minutes before you serve. Toss the oyster mixture and the spaghetti very well with a large wooden spoon, redistributing the sauce which has settled to the bottom. Serve lots of sauce and oysters on top of the spaghetti. It is acceptable to provide freshly grated Parmesan cheese for garnish, but not necessary. Serves 6. Can partially do ahead.

Serve Bravo Oyster Spaghetti with hot buttered French bread and salad. I prefer this feast served with a good California Cabernet, or, if you prefer a white wine, a good California Pinot Chardonnay.

Standing Room Only

Oysters a la Finella

12 large oysters in the shell
1/4 pound butter
1 cup flour
1 1/2 cups milk
1/2 cup oyster liquor (optional)
1 teaspoon Worcestershire
  sauce

1 teaspoon sherry
Salt, pepper, and paprika to
  taste
1 cup cooked lobster, cubed
12 slices sharp Cheddar cheese

Bake oysters in the deep half of the shell in medium oven until edges curl. Melt butter; blend in flour to form a smooth paste. Slowly add milk, keeping mixture smooth. Add seasonings. Sauce must be thick. Add lobster meat. Divide sauce equally over top of each oyster; then top each with a thin slice of cheese, covering oyster well. Bake in medium oven until hot and cheese is melted. Sprinkle paprika on top. Serves 3.

The Cook's Book

Creamed Oysters

1/2 cup onion, chopped
1/2 cup celery, chopped
1/4 cup butter
1 pint fresh oysters
2 tablespoons all purpose flour
1 teaspoon prepared mustard

1 teaspoon anchovy paste
1/2 teaspoon salt
Cayenne pepper to taste
1 cup light cream
2 tablespoons dry sherry
4 English muffins, split

In skillet or heavy saucepan, sauté onions and celery in butter until tender. Add oysters, undrained. Cook until edges curl. Mix flour, prepared mustard, anchovy paste, salt, pepper into cream. Add to oyster mixture. Cook and stir a few minutes. Add sherry. Serve on heated muffins. Serves 4 to 8.

Dixie Dining

Oyster Mousse
Dr. Dub's Town House Recipe, Served at Stanton Hall Antiques Forum Reception

2 envelopes unflavored gelatin   **¹/₂ cup water**

Soften gelatin in water and set aside.
1 (8-ounce) package cream cheese   **1 cup mayonnaise**

Combine in saucepan, cook over low heat, stirring constantly until cream cheese melts and mixture is smooth. Remove from stove. Stir in:
2 (3³/₄-ounce) cans of smoked oysters, drained and minced.

Add following seasonings:
1 tablespoon Worcestershire sauce   **1-2 minced or grated garlic buds**
Dash of hot pepper sauce or cayenne pepper   **¹/₂-1 teaspoon prepared horseradish**

Add softened gelatin. Spoon into well-greased 3¹/₂-cup fish-shaped mold. (I use vegetable spray on mold.) Cover and chill overnight or until mousse is firm. Unmold and garnish with lemon twists, parsley, ripe and green olives. Serve with Brenner Wafers or other unsalted type of cracker.

The Pilgrimage Garden Club
Antiques Forum Cookbook

Vegetables

Picking cotton in the Mississippi Delta.

Broccoli Casserole with Chopped Peanuts

2 (10-ounce) packages frozen chopped broccoli, cooked and drained
1 (10¾-ounce) can cream of chicken soup
2 tablespoons lemon juice

1 cup chopped salted peanuts
¼ cup mayonnaise
¼ cup chopped onion
2 eggs, beaten
1 cup shredded Cheddar cheese

Mix all ingredients except cheese. Pour into greased casserole. Sprinkle with cheese. Bake at 350° for 30 minutes.

Just a Spoonful

Asparagus Supreme

1 (10½-ounce) can asparagus and juice
Cracker crumbs
4 hard boiled eggs
1 can cream of mushroom soup
3 tablespoons Sauterne wine
Garlic salt (optional)
2 tablespoons butter

3 or 4 dashes Tabasco
1 teaspoon Worcestershire
Salt
Pepper
Sugar
New York State cheese, grated
1 slice bread, trim crust
Blanched almonds, slivered

Into buttered casserole alternate layers of asparagus, eggs, cracker crumbs and mushroom soup which has been mixed with asparagus juice, butter, wine and seasonings. Top with cheese, small pieces of bread and almonds. Bake at 350° for about 20 minutes. Serves 6-8.

Gourmet of the Delta

Artichoke Pie

4 tablespoons butter, melted
1/4 cup chopped onion
1 tablespoon flour
1/2 cup half and half
1/2 cup sour cream
4 eggs
Salt and pepper to taste
1/4 teaspoon ground nutmeg
2 teaspoons fresh parsley,
   chopped

1 1/2 cans artichoke hearts, cut
   in fourths
1 (9-inch) pie crust
1/2 cup shredded Cheddar
   cheese
1/2 cup shredded Swiss cheese
1/4 cup freshly grated
   Parmesan or Romano cheese

Melt butter. Add onion. Cook until tender, stir in flour and add half and half. Cook until thickened. In a small bowl combine sour cream, eggs, salt, pepper, nutmeg and parsley. Add to onion mixture. Place layer of artichoke hearts in pie crust. Cover with Cheddar cheese. Put a layer of artichokes then the Swiss cheese. Pour egg mixture over this. Top with Parmesan cheese. Bake at 350° for 45 minutes. Serve at once.

Into the Second Century

Olive Broccoli

2 (10-ounce) packages frozen
   broccoli spears, cooked and
   drained
2 tablespoons butter or
   margarine

1/4 cup cider vinegar
1/2 cup French dressing
16 stuffed olives, sliced

To the cooked broccoli, add the butter, vinegar, and French dressing. Fold in olives, pour into serving dish, and serve while warm. Yield: 6 to 8 servings.

Come and Dine

Broccoli with Horseradish Sauce

4 tablespoons butter, melted
3/4 cup mayonnaise
1 tablespoon horseradish
1 tablespoon onion, grated
1/4 teaspoon salt

1/4 teaspoon dry mustard
Dash red pepper
2 (10-ounce) packages frozen
   broccoli or 1 head fresh
   broccoli

Combine first seven ingredients and refrigerate until ready to use. Cook broccoli by package directions. If using fresh broccoli, cut into spears and scrape the spear ends with a potato peeler. Cook in boiling salted water for 8 minutes. Broccoli should be crisp. Serve with a spoonful of sauce on top. Sauce will keep for several months in the refrigerator and may be used on roast beef or other vegetables. Serves 6.

Natchez Notebook of Cooking

Brussels Sprouts and Pecans

2 (10-ounce) boxes frozen
   Brussels sprouts
1 cup chicken broth
2 tablespoons chopped onion

1/2 teaspoon salt
1/2 cup chopped pecans
1/2 cup margarine

Mix sprouts with broth, onion and salt. Bring to a boil, reduce heat, cover and cook 10 minutes. Drain and place in warm serving dish. Sauté pecans in margarine 2 to 3 minutes. Pour over sprouts and toss lightly.

Just a Spoonful

Glazed Broccoli with Almonds

2 pounds fresh broccoli
1/2 teaspoon salt
1 beef bouillon cube
3/4 cup hot water
1 cup half & half
1/4 cup butter or margarine
1/4 cup all-purpose flour
2 tablespoons sherry

2 tablespoons lemon juice
1/8 teaspoon pepper
2 teaspoons monosodium
   glutamate
1/2 cup (2-ounces) shredded
   Cheddar cheese
1/4 cup slivered almonds

Trim off large leaves of broccoli. Remove tough ends of lower stalks and wash broccoli thoroughly; separate into spears. Cook broccoli, covered, in a small amount of boiling salted water for 10 minutes or until crisp-tender. Drain well and place in a 12x8x2-inch baking dish. Dissolve bouillon cube in 3/4 cup water; stir in half & half and set aside.

Melt butter in a heavy saucepan over low heat; blend in flour, stirring until smooth. Cook 1 minute, stirring constantly. Gradually stir in bouillon mixture; cook over medium heat, stirring constantly until thickened and bubbly. Stir in sherry, lemon juice, pepper and monosodium glutamate.

Pour sauce over broccoli. Sprinkle with cheese and almonds. Bake at 375° for 25-30 minutes.

Hospitality Heirlooms

John Birch Society Beans
(Willie Morris)

Willie Morris has been editor-in-chief of the *The Texas Observer* and *Harper's*. Among his books are *North Toward Home, Yazoo, The Last of the Southern Girls, James Jones: A Friendship,* and *Terrains of the Heart*. He lives in Oxford, Mississippi.

These beans are so named because of the intense internal reaction they produce. I learned how to prepare them from a border-rat Texan I once knew years ago, and I have been refining them ever since. If you truly care for the diligent creativity which goes into them, they will become more superlative with each effort. One virtue of my beans is that they are open to the infinite possibility. Once you master their basics, you can enhance them with all sorts of things. The imagination must be given sovereign reign. As they say about winning football teams, these beans have momentum.

John Birch Society Beans are perfect for sizeable parties. For ten years I made them every New Year's Day for my Yankee chums at Bobby Van's Saloon in Bridgehampton, Long Island. They never failed to elicit praise from that strange, eclectic assemblage. Bobby Van claimed his beer sales quadrupled on these heady days. "These beans are a portable, built-in barbeque," Lauren Bacall once whispered to me. Some endow them with aphrodisiacal nuances, while others deem them unimpeachable for hangovers. Now that I live again in my native Mississippi, I serve them on New Year's Eve, as I did in the North, for my beans evoke the nostalgias of sorrow, memory, and belonging.

I have only had unsatisfactory moment with the beans. I was cooking them one day in a well-appointed kitchen on Long Island, owned by the painter Warren Brandt, as a condiment for roast suckling pig for a large gathering that evening. Craig Claiborne had arranged to drop by with a photographer to do a piece for *The New York Times* on the beans, which were already famous. He and the photographer arrived and Craig brought out

CONTINUED

CONTINUED

his notebook. After watching me make my beans for several minutes, with a peremptory gesture he put his notebook back in his pocket. "If I wrote about these beans, Punch Sulzberger would fire me," he said. That is the only time I have ever known my friend and fellow Mississippian, Mr. Claiborne, to be wrong. Serve these wonderful beans once and the compliments of your guests will echo in your heart. You will do them again and again.

3 sticks butter or margarine
As many fresh country
    sausages as you can afford
    (Polish sausage will suffice
    if absolutely necessary;
    weiners will do, too. As a
    matter of fact, add a dozen
    weiners to this recipe
    anyway.)
4 large onions
3 large green peppers
3 or 4 jalapeño peppers (fresh
    or canned)
2 dozen mushrooms (fresh if
    possible; if not 3 cans)
6 hard-boiled eggs or more

3 cans water chestnuts
3 big cans peeled tomatoes
A dozen strips of bacon
12 cans, regular-sized,
    barbeque beans (preferably
    Campbell's)
Tabasco
Worcestershire sauce
A lot of chili powder
Salt and pepper
One jar molasses
15 slices of cheese (preferably
    Cheddar, but any kind will
    work, except Gruyere and
    Camembert)

Put all three sticks of butter at the bottom of an extremely large cooking pot. As the butter melts, throw in the sausages and weiners, both well-sliced. Sauté until brown. Throw in the onions, green peppers, jalapeño peppers, and mushrooms (all finely sliced). Allow these to sauté so they will soak into the sausages and weiners.

Put in the hardboiled eggs, sliced. Start mixture about now. Add the water chestnuts, well-diced. Then toss in the canned, peeled tomatoes. Add the strips of bacon, which also need to be sliced. Let them sauté with the other things.

Put in all the barbeque beans, juice included. Stir again vigorously for a long time. Make sure the beans get well-integrated

CONTINUED

John Birch Society Beans CONTINUED

with the previous ingredients. Add large quantities of Tabasco, Worcestershire, and chili powder. In fact, use more chili powder than you think you should. Courage is needed at this point. Salt and pepper a great deal. Continue to stir every minute or so. Add the molasses, all of it at one time. Keep on stirring. Mix in even more chili powder. Allow all this to simmer over a low-to-medium fire on top of the stove for about thirty or forty minutes.

Spread the cheese slices all over the top of the beans. Place the whole pot in an oven heated to about 325°. Keep the beans there for about two hours. But if you do not take them out every now and then to stir, they will stick to the bottom of the pot. Serves 30 to 35 people.

As I suggested earlier, once you have mastered this recipe, you may dramatize the beans with other ingredients, depending on what you have. I once added some chicken livers, for instance, and on other occasions sliced ham, meatballs, fresh sliced tomatoes, garlic, and even some roast pork egg foo yong from the night before. Almost any kind of meat except catfish is a worthy addition to the other items.

My son and I went rather berserk one afternoon making the beans in the kitchen of an Italian restaurant in Bridgehampton for a party that night for a hometown boy, Carl Yaztremski. When the chef was out of the kitchen, David and I surreptitiously tossed in some of the chef's lasagna, which was just sitting there, asking to be used, and some cannelone, and a bit of the antipasta. This combination, even as an afterthought, was remarkable.

Just before serving, open the windows of your home.

The Great American Writer's Cookbook

Annandale Baked Beans

7 (16-ounce) cans pork and
  beans, drained
6 slices bacon, cooked and
  drained
2 bell peppers, chopped and
  cooked in bacon grease
2 onions, chopped and cooked
  in bacon grease

2 tablespoons Worcestershire
  sauce
3 tablespoons liquid smoke
1 tablespoon prepared mustard
1 cup brown sugar
1 can cranberry sauce
Salt and pepper to taste

Put all into crock pot and cook on low for at least 4 hours. If they
look too runny, take off top and cook on high for the last hour.
Serves approximately 16-18.

Madison County Cookery

Barbecued Baked Beans

1 (31-ounce) can baked beans
1 tablespoon Worcestershire
  sauce
1 teaspoon prepared mustard
$^{1}/_{2}$ cup white sugar

$^{1}/_{2}$ cup barbecue sauce with
  onions
$^{1}/_{4}$ cup chopped onions
3 slices bacon

Mix all ingredients except bacon; place in 1$^{3}/_{4}$-quart casserole dish.
Top with bacon. Bake at 350° for 1 hour. Serves 6.

The Mississippi Cookbook

Ro-Tel French Style Green Beans

2 (16-ounce) cans French style
green beans
1 (10-ounce) can Ro-Tel
tomatoes

$^1/_2$ pound mild Cheddar cheese

Drain green beans and add water to cover. Cook on medium heat about 25 minutes. Add Ro-Tel tomatoes and cook 10 minutes. Slice cheese and add to green beans. Cook until cheese melts, stirring often. Serve hot. Yield: 8 servings.

Festival

Harvard Beets

2 tablespoons butter
1 tablespoon cornstarch
1 tablespoon sugar
$^1/_4$ teaspoon salt

$^1/_2$ cup mild vinegar
2 cups cubed, canned, or
freshly cooked beets

Melt butter; add cornstarch, sugar, and salt. Blend well. Add vinegar and cook until thick. Add beets and mix thoroughly. Serves 4-6.

DAR Recipe Book

Over 8,000 years old, The Natchez Trace was originally a Chickasaw Indian trail through Central Mississippi. It was extended, improved, and made a U.S. mail route by 1801. Its 50 inns and trading posts became deserted after steamboats came into use and it fell into disrepair. Today it is a national parkway, lush with unobstructed, natural scenic beauty, and extends from Natchez to Nashville.

Basil Carrots

1 1/2 pounds carrots
1/2 cup firmly packed fresh
  basil leaves, minced

1/4 cup olive oil
1/2 teaspoon salt

Pare carrots; quarter lengthwise and cut into 1 1/2-inch strips. Boil carrots 10 minutes in salted water until barely tender. Drain them and rinse under cold water to refresh them. Pat them dry. Sauté carrots in oil, basil and salt, stirring well until well coated with the mixture and well heated. Serves 6-8. Can partially do ahead.

Standing Room Only

Smothered Cabbage

1 medium cabbage
1/2 cup green pepper, finely
    chopped
1/4 cup onion, finely chopped
1/4 cup butter, melted
1/4 cup all purpose flour
2 cups milk

1/2 teaspoon salt
1/8 teaspoon pepper
1/2 cup mayonnaise
3/4 cup medium Cheddar
    cheese, shredded
3 tablespoons chili sauce

Cut cabbage into wedges, removing core. Cover, and cook for 10 minutes in a small amount of slightly salted boiling water; drain well. Place wedges in a 13x9x2-inch dish; set aside. Sauté green pepper and onion in butter until vegetables are tender. Add flour, and cook 1 minute, stirring constantly. Gradually add milk, cook over medium heat, stirring constantly until thickened and bubbly. Then, stir in salt and pepper, and pour mixture over cabbage. Bake at 375° for 20 minutes. While cabbage is baking, combine mayonnaise, cheese, and chili sauce; mix well. When casserole comes out of the oven, spoon cheese mixture over cabbage wedges, and bake for 5 minutes or more. Serves 8.

Great Flavors of Mississippi

St. Patrick's Casserole

1 medium can chopped turnip
    greens, drained
1 can cream of celery soup
1/2 cup Kraft mayonnaise
Salt and pepper to taste

2 eggs, beaten
2 tablespoons wine vinegar
1 teaspoon horseradish
1 teaspoon sugar
Bread crumbs

Mix in order given. Top with bread crumbs. Bake for 30-40 minutes at 350°.

Tasting Tea Treasures

Sue's Cabbage Pie

1 head cabbage, shredded
1 large onion, sliced

20-30 saltine crackers,
crumbled

CREAM SAUCE:
1 teaspoon salt
1/2 teaspoon pepper
1/8 teaspoon celery seed

1 stick butter
4 tablespoons flour
2 cups milk

Mix butter and flour in top of double boiler; slowly add milk. Stir until mixture starts to thicken. Add seasonings. Layer cabbage, onions, crackers and 1/3 sauce. Repeat and pour remaining sauce over top. Bake 350° for 1 hour.
   Note: This is great with roast.

Tasting Tea Treasures

Steamed Cabbage with Vinegar and Cream

4 slices bacon
1 pound shredded cabbage
Salted water
1 teaspoon sugar

1/8 teaspoon white pepper
1 tablespoon vinegar
Salt to taste
4 tablespoons whipping cream

Cook bacon in large skillet until crisp; remove bacon; drain and crumble. Wash cabbage, discarding wilted and yellow leaves; remove core and discard. Soak cabbage in salted water 30 minutes; drain; do not rinse. Place cabbage in skillet with hot bacon drippings, reducing heat and stirring in sugar, white pepper, vinegar, and salt. Cover with tight-fitting lid, simmering until barely tender. To serve, stir in cream; heat; do not boil; garnish with crumbled bacon. Serves 4.

Accent One

Cauliflower Hollandaise

Trim head of cauliflower and soak, head down, in salted water for 20 minutes. Rinse and cook, covered, base down in plain water to keep vegetable white until just tender. Do not overcook. Drain and serve with Hollandaise Sauce.

PERFECT HOLLANDAISE SAUCE:

2 egg yolks	2 tablespoons lemon juice
1/3 cup vegetable oil	1/4 tablespoon salt

Combine egg yolks and one tablespoon oil in top of double boiler. Cook over hot water. Add rest of oil very slowly, stirring constantly. Cook until thick, add salt and lemon juice, one tablespoon at a time. Stir until thick again. Stir vigorously. Do not re-heat. If sauce separates, beat in one unbeaten egg white with rotary beater. Serve with broccoli, asparagus, green beans, meat and fish.

My Mother Cooked My Way Through Harvard
With These Creole Recipes

Creole Cucumbers

4 large cucumbers, washed and split lengthwise	4 tablespoons butter
2 tablespoons onion, chopped	1 cup bread crumbs
2 tablespoons parsley, chopped	1 cup tomato pulp
	Salt and pepper

Scoop out seed portion of cucumbers and save. Boil the cucumbers in lightly salted water for about 10 minutes. Drain. Sauté onion and parsley in butter. Add other ingredients and the reserved cucumber pulp and cook, stirring, for 5 minutes. Fill cucumber shells with the stuffing and place in a shallow baking dish. Add a small amount of water and bake at 350° for 15 minutes, or until brown on top. Serves 8.

The Twelve Days of Christmas Cookbook

Crispy Fried Okra

1 pound fresh okra, stemmed
   and cut into 1/2-inch slices, or
   1 (10-ounce) package frozen
   cut okra, thawed and dried
1 or 2 egg whites, slightly
   beaten

1/2 heaping cup white cornmeal
1/2-3/4 teaspoon onion powder
1/2 teaspoon salt or to taste
1/4 teaspoon freshly ground
   pepper or to taste
Corn oil

Add okra slices to egg whites and toss until well coated. Combine cornmeal, onion powder, salt and pepper in a plastic bag. Add okra slices a handful at a time to the cornmeal mixture, shaking until thoroughly coated. Remove from the bag and place on a baking sheet. Okra can be refrigerated at this point. Heat oil and fry a small batch of okra at a time. If too much is added at one time, okra will smother rather than fry. Remove from oil, drain on a paper towel and place in a warm oven until all okra is prepared. Serve immediately. Serves 3-4.

Taste of the South

Crusty Corn Casserole

$1/2$ cup margarine
$1 1/4$ cups fine cracker crumbs
$1/4$ cup green pepper, chopped
$1/4$ cup onion, finely chopped
1 tablespoon butter or
   margarine

2 tablespoons flour
1 cup milk
1 large can cream style corn
$1/2$ teaspoon salt
$1/2$ teaspoon sugar
2 eggs or 4 yolks, beaten

Mix margarine and crumbs and press in deep dish pie plate. Cook green pepper and onion in butter, add flour and cook until bubbly; blend in milk and cook until thickened. Stir some of hot mixture into eggs, add to remaining hot mixture, stirring constantly. Add corn, salt, and sugar and mix thoroughly. Pour in pie shell and bake at 400° for 30 or 35 minutes or until set.
   Note: If you want to do two pies, just double everything.

Into the Second Century

Hash Brown Potato Casserole

1 (2-pound) package of frozen
   hash brown potatoes
1 stick of butter or oleo
$1/2$ cup finely chopped onions
1 can cream of chicken soup
   (undiluted)

2 cups sour cream
1 teaspoon salt
1 teaspoon pepper
1 (8-ounce) package of grated
   sharp cheese
2 cups crushed corn flakes

Pour frozen hash brown potatoes in a large shallow casserole dish to defrost. In a saucepan, melt butter or oleo. Add chopped onions, cream of chicken soup, and sour cream. Remove from heat. Add salt and pepper. Mix this mixture well with the potatoes. Top with grated cheese, and top with crushed corn flakes. Bake at 350° for about 1 hour—until hot and bubbly. Do not overbake. May divide in half and freeze part.

The Pick of the Crop

Skillet Potato Pie

1 pound potatoes, cooked and
   cooled
3 tablespoons snipped chives
1/2 teaspoon salt
3 eggs, beaten
1/4 cup light cream

1/4 cup grated Parmesan cheese
1/2 teaspoon salt
Dash pepper
4 tablespoons butter or
   margarine

Peel and shred potatoes. Add chives and 1/2 teaspoon salt. Mix eggs, cream, cheese, salt and pepper. Reserve. Heat 2 tablespoons butter in a 10-inch non-stick skillet over medium heat. Add potatoes, shaping into a pattie. Pour egg mixture over the potato pattie, and reduce heat to low. Cook about 10 minutes, or until potatoes are brown. Invert potato pattie onto a platter. Heat remaining butter in skillet until hot. Slide potato pattie back into skillet, and cook 8 more minutes, or until brown. Cut into wedges and garnish, Yield: 4 to 6 servings.

Come and Dine

Hot Potato Casserole

5 large red potatoes, scrubbed
   in the peeling and each cut
   into 8 pieces
2 large onions, chopped
4 ribs of celery, chopped
1 teaspoon salt

1/2 teaspoon black pepper
1/2 teaspoon Accent
1 1/2 sticks oleo
2 tablespoons parsley flakes
1 teaspoon paprika

Place potatoes into a greased, 2-quart rectangular-shaped baking dish. Put all of the above ingredients over the potatoes, cutting the oleo in pats to put all over and sprinkle paprika last. Cover and bake at 350° for 30 minutes, basting several times. Remove cover and test potatoes, as you just want them fork tender

The Country Gourmet (Miriam G. Cohn)

Easy Sweet Potato Pone

Sweet potato pone was a favorite dish for my grandfather. I can still hear Grandy bidding me to follow him to the big sweet potato patch that grew near the garden "and let's see if we can find a few big enough to dig." When we did, they went into the grated potato dish that's called pone.

1 large sweet potato, or 2 medium	³/₄ cup brown sugar
	¹/₂ cup margarine
1 egg	Vanilla to taste

Peel and grate sweet potatoes. Stir in whole egg, sugar, margarine and flavoring. Place in well-buttered baking dish and bake in slow oven for 45 minutes.

Just a Spoonful

 Vardaman, Mississippi is called The Sweet Potato Capital of the World.

Sweet Potato Casserole

4 large sweet potatoes	3 eggs
1¹/₂ cup sugar	1 teaspoon vanilla
2 small cans crushed pineapple	¹/₂ stick oleo
Marshmallows	¹/₂ teaspoon baking powder

Boil potatoes in salted water. Mash with oleo. Add eggs; stir in sugar and pineapple. Add vanilla and baking powder; stir well. Put in buttered dish and bake for 30 minutes at 400°. During the last minutes of baking time, top with marshmallows.

Top Rankin Recipes

Shoe Peg Corn and Beans

1 cup chopped celery
1 cup chopped onion
1/2 cup chopped green pepper
2 tablespoons butter
1 can cream of celery soup
1 small carton sour cream

1 (12-ounce) can shoe peg corn,
    drained
1 (16-ounce) can French style
    green beans, drained
1/2 cup Ritz cracker crumbs

Preheat oven to 350°. Sauté the celery, onion, pepper in the butter. Combine the soup and sour cream, mixing well. Add sautéed mixture, corn and beans. Pour into a 2-quart casserole dish; sprinkle with crumbs and dot with butter. Bake for 35 to 40 minutes.

Dixie Dining

Mixed Vegetables in Foil

1 (1³/4-pound) can cut green
    beans (boiled with salt,
    pepper, bacon drippings,
    dash of sugar, celery and
    salt)
2 large sliced tomatoes
4 tablespoons melted
    margarine

1/4 cup chopped onion
2 teaspoons prepared mustard
1 teaspoon prepared
    horseradish
1 tablespoon brown sugar
1 teaspoon salt
Dash of pepper

Beat the last seven ingredients, mixing thoroughly. Drain boiled beans and place either in a baking dish for the oven or thick foil for the grill. Place tomatoes on top of beans and dot with the mustard mixture. Cook 40 minutes on rack on grill or at 375° in oven. Serves 4.

The Gulf Gourmet

Spinach Marguerite
(In Honor of Marguerite Watkins Goodman)

$^1/_2$ cup water
20 ounces frozen chopped
   spinach
4 tablespoons butter
2 tablespoons finely-chopped
   onion
2 cloves garlic, pressed
1 tablespoon finely chopped
   celery
1 teaspoon Worcestershire
   sauce

$^1/_2$ teaspoon black pepper
Cayenne pepper to taste
2 tablespoons flour
$^1/_2$ cup evaporated milk
$^1/_2$ cup spinach liquid
6 ounces Jalapeno cheese
Buttered rich cracker crumbs
Paprika
Sliced buttered toasted
   almonds

Pour $^1/_2$ cup water into medium saucepan; bring to a boil; reduce heat and add spinach; cook until tender; drain, reserving $^1/_2$ cup liquid. Melt butter in saucepan over low heat; add onion, garlic, celery, Worcestershire, black pepper, and cayenne pepper; simmer until vegetables are tender. Blend flour into mixture; when sauce is smooth, pour in milk and spinach liquid. Stir until smooth and thick; add cheese and stir until melted. Mix spinach with sauce; pour into greased 1$^1/_2$-quart casserole. Top with buttered crumbs, paprika and almonds. Bake at 350° on center rack until hot and bubbling. Serves 6.

Accent One

English Peas in Pepper Ring

2 large cans English peas
1 tablespoon flour added to 1
   cup milk
1 small jar cocktail onions
3 hard-boiled eggs, cut into
   quarters

2 large or 3 medium bell
   peppers, sliced in $^1/_2$-inch
   rings

Bring peas to a boil. Add flour, milk and onions. Stir until thickened. Add eggs. Serve in pepper rings.

I Promised A Cookbook

"Lou Emma's" Spinach Casserole

3 (10-ounce) package frozen
   chopped spinach
1 small can mushroom pieces
1/2 cup margarine
2 tablespoons flour
1 cup milk

Salt and pepper to taste
Dash Worcestershire sauce
1 can artichoke hearts
1/2 cup sour cream
1/2 cup mayonnaise
1 teaspoon lemon juice

Cook chopped spinach until done, drain well. Sauté mushrooms in margarine then remove mushrooms from skillet and add flour. Gradually stir in milk until smooth. Add spinach, mushrooms and seasonings to taste.

Cut artichoke hearts in half and cover bottom of the casserole. Pour spinach mixture over the artichokes. Heat sour cream, mayonnaise and lemon juice together. Spread over top of casserole. Heat in 350° oven until bubbly. Serves 8-10.

The Pilgrimage Garden Club
Antiques Forum Cookbook

Onion Pie

CRUST:

1 cup saltine cracker crumbs $^1/_4$ cup butter, melted

Mix together and press into a 9-inch pie pan. You may use regular pie crust if you prefer.

FILLING:

3 cups diced onion
$^1/_4$ cup butter
$^1/_2$ pound Swiss cheese, finely grated
1 tablespoon flour

1 teaspoon salt
$^1/_4$ teaspoon cayenne pepper
3 eggs, beaten well
1 cup scalded milk

Sauté onions in butter slowly, stirring constantly until golden. Remove from fire, drain and put into pie shell. Combine cheese, flour, salt, and cayenne; stir in eggs and milk. Pour over onions and bake in a 350° oven for 40 minutes. Cut into small wedges and serve. Yields 8 or more servings. May be used as a main dish if hungry men are not to be fed.

The Gulf Gourmet

Marinated Mushrooms

$^1/_3$ cup red wine vinegar
$^1/_3$ cup salad oil
1 red onion, thinly sliced
1 teaspoon salt
2 teaspoons dried parsley flakes

1 tablespoon brown sugar
1 teaspoon prepared mustard
3 cans mushroom caps or 3 cups fresh mushrooms, steamed 1 minute

Simmer all except mushrooms for 5 minutes. Drain mushrooms, add to marinade. Store in refrigerator for at least 24 hours, or as long as 2 weeks. Remove from refrigerator an hour before serving.

Just a Spoonful

Muenstrously Delicious Onion Casserole

2 tablespoons butter
2 large sweet Spanish onions,
  sliced, separated into rings
2 cups (8 ounces) grated
  Muenster cheese
1/4 teaspoon pepper

1 (10³/4-ounce) can cream of
  chicken soup
1 cup milk
Sliced, buttered, slightly dry
  French bread

Melt butter in large frying pan. Add onion rings. Cover and cook slowly over low heat, stirring often, for 20 – 30 minutes or until soft. Spoon into a 6-cup, fairly shallow baking dish. Spread cheese over top and sprinkle with pepper. Heat soup and milk in same frying pan in which onions were cooked, stirring until smooth. Pour over onion-cheese layer. Stir lightly with tip of knife to let sauce flow to bottom. Overlap enough bread slices, buttered side up, to make a ring around top. Bake in 350° oven 30 minutes or until bread is toasted and sauce is hot. Serves 6-8.

The Country Mouse

Stuffed Mushrooms

2 pints mushrooms
2 tablespoons onion, finely
  chopped
2 tablespoons butter
1/4 cup soft bread crumbs
1/4 cup toasted unblanched
  almonds, finely chopped

2 teaspoons lemon juice
1/2 teaspoon salt
1/4 teaspoon Worcestershire
  sauce
1/2 cup light cream
1/2 cup shredded American
  cheese

Wash mushrooms and remove stems. Reserve caps. Chop stems; sauté with onion in butter in small skillet for 5 minutes until tender. Add crumbs and almonds and cook 2 minutes longer. Stir in lemon juice and seasonings. Fill mushroom caps with stuffing. Place in baking dish. Pour cream around mushrooms. Bake at 400° for 15 minutes. Top with cheese. Bake 10 minutes longer, until cheese melts.

The Gulf Gourmet

Eggplant Creole

1 medium eggplant, peeled and
diced
Salt
4 tablespoons margarine,
divided
3 tablespoons flour
3 large tomatoes, peeled and
chopped
1 small green pepper, seeded
and chopped

1 small onion, peeled and
chopped
1 tablespoon brown sugar
1 teaspoon salt
2 cloves garlic, minced
1/2 bay leaf
1/4 cup dry bread crumbs

Cook eggplant. uncovered, 10 minutes in boiling salted water.
Drain well; place in a greased 1 1/2-quart casserole. In large skillet,
melt three tablespoons margarine. Add flour and stir until blended.
Add to skillet tomatoes, pepper, onion, sugar, salt, garlic and bay
leaf. Cook, uncovered, five minutes, stirring occasionally. Pour
contents of skillet over eggplant. Sprinkle with bread crumbs; dot
with remaining one tablespoon margarine. Bake in 350°oven a half
hour.

Just a Spoonful

Ratatouille

2 small eggplants
3 medium-size tomatoes
2 bell peppers
3 small zucchini squash
2 onions

2 yellow squash
3 tablespoons olive oil
Salt and pepper
1 teaspoon garlic powder
1/4 cup water

Slice eggplants, tomatoes, peppers, zucchini; onions, and squash about 1/4 to 1/2-inch thick. Layer vegetables in casserole which has been oiled with 1 tablespoon olive oil, starting with onions, bell pepper, and vegetables as desired. Repeat until all vegetables are used. Sprinkle salt and pepper, remaining olive oil, and garlic powder over vegetables. Pour 1/4 cup water over casserole. Cover and bake in 275° oven for 1 1/2 hours. Test vegetables for tenderness. Good cold or hot. Serves 8 to 10.

Waddad's Kitchen

Southern Tomato Pie

1 (9-inch) pie crust, cooked
   until it is light brown
2-3 good sized tomatoes
1 tablespoon Italian seasoning
   or to taste
1 tablespoon oregano or to
   taste

1 1/2 teaspoon chives or to taste
Salt and pepper to taste
1 cup sharp cheese, grated
1 cup mayonnaise

Sprinkle tomato slices with seasoning, oregano, chives, salt and pepper; place slices in pie crust. Combine cheese and mayonnaise to make a thick paste; then, cover tomatoes with paste. Bake at 350° until tomato paste is bubbly and the crust is a deep, golden brown.

Great Flavors of Mississippi

Baked Tomatoes Rockefeller

2 (10-ounce) packages chopped
   spinach
2 cups seasoned bread crumbs
6 green onions, chopped
6 eggs, slightly beaten
3/4 cup butter, melted
1/2 cup Parmesan cheese
1/4 teaspoon Worcestershire
   sauce

1/2 teaspoon minced garlic
1 teaspoon salt
1/2 teaspoon black pepper
1 teaspoon thyme
1 teaspoon monosodium
   glutamate
1/4 teaspoon Tabasco brand
   pepper sauce
12 thick tomato slices

Cook spinach according to directions. Add remaining ingredients
except tomato. Arrange tomato slices in a single layer in buttered
9x13-inch baking dish. Mound spinach mixture on tomato slices.
Sprinkle lightly with more Parmesan cheese. Bake at 350° for 15
minutes. The spinach mixture may be made well in advance and it
freezes well. Yield: 12 servings.

Vintage Vicksburg

Baked Cushaw

1 cushaw
2 eggs, beaten
1 3/4 cups sugar
1 1/2 tablespoons flour
1/2 teaspoon baking powder

1 teaspoon nutmeg
1 teaspoon vanilla
1 stick butter (or 1/2 stick oleo
   and 1/2 stick butter)
1/2 teaspoon cinnamon

Cut cushaw into small pieces, removing seeds. Boil in small amount
of water until tender. Peel, mash and mix with all ingredients. Place
in buttered baking pan. Bake at 350° until brown.

Variation: Cut cushaw into serving pieces, remove seeds, and
boil until tender. Do not peel. Sprinkle pieces with a mixture of
brown sugar, nutmeg, and cinnamon. Dot with butter, broil under
flame or bake in 400° oven until sugar and butter bubble. Serve hot.

My Mother Cooked My Way Through Harvard
With These Creole Recipes

Souffled Squash

2 eggs, separated
2 cups cooked squash
1/4 cup finely chopped celery
1/8 cup green pepper, cut fine
1/4 cup finely chopped onion
1 teaspoon sugar

1 teaspoon baking powder
1 tablespoon flour
2/3 cup milk
Salt and pepper to taste
3 tablespoons margarine
1/3 cup cracker crumbs

Beat eggs separately, adding 1 tablespoon of water to both egg whites and yolks. Slice squash and cook until tender. Mash squash, drain. Add celery, green pepper, onion, sugar, baking powder, flour, milk, salt and pepper. Add egg yolks and whites separately. Pour into greased glass or aluminum cups. Top with cracker crumbs and dot with margarine. Cook until lightly brown in 350° oven about 20 minutes. Top with grated cheese, if desired. Serves 8 generously.

This recipe was a specialty of Allison's Wells in its day.

Madison County Cookery

Squash Casserole Henrietta Grayer

5 medium sized yellow squash
1 small onion, chopped
Salt and pepper to taste
3 eggs

Pinch of baking powder
1 tablespoon cornstarch
$1/4$ cup melted butter
1 cup grated cheese

Cut squash in 1-inch pieces and boil with onion, salt and pepper. Drain. Beat eggs, baking powder and cornstarch, add butter, cheese, squash and onions. Put into large mixing bowl and beat until light. Season to taste. Pour into 2-quart casserole and bake at 350° for 30 minutes.

P.S. This is Henrietta's original recipe for yellow squash and it is very good.

Southern Legacies

Zucchini with Black Olives

Whole zucchini
Black olives, pitted and
    chopped
Tony Chachere's Creole
    Seasoning

Parmesan cheese
Butter
Paprika

Parboil whole zucchini in a little water for 5 minutes. Remove from water and cut in half lengthwise. Remove pulp, chop, and add $1/4$ part chopped black pitted olives. Season with Tony Chachere's Creole Seasoning until salt taste is correct. Restuff zucchini shells and sprinkle surface liberally with parmesan cheese. Dot tops with 2-3 pats butter, dust with paprika and bake at 350° until slightly browned. Serve.

Answering the Call to Duck Cookery

Mississippi Caviar

4 (16.5-ounce) cans black-eyed
  peas, seasoned with salt,
  pepper, and ham hocks
1 cup oil
½ cup vinegar
3 bunches green onions,
  chopped

3 cloves garlic, slivered
Salt and pepper to taste
1 jar Trappey's Salad Peppers,
  with juice, chopped in
  blender

Cook peas and seasoning until tender. Then, remove hamhocks and drain well. Add remaining ingredients to the peas, and gently combine. Put peas mixture in a bowl that can be turned to shake and mix. Then, refrigerate for at least 24 hours. The "caviar" can be kept for 2 weeks and gets better all along!

Mississippi Caviar is a must for New Year's Day!

Great Flavors of Mississippi

Mississippi has a renowned musical heritage. Black sharecroppers sang about their troubles and hard times in the Mississippi Delta and "gave birth to the blues"—B.B. King is from Indianola, W.C. Handy, Clarksdale; Elvis Presley (Tupelo) became "The King of Rock and Roll," Jimmy Rodgers (Meridian) was "The Father of Country Music," Leontyne Price, (Laurel) is acclaimed as an opera star of the first magnitude; Charlie Pride (Sledge) is the first black country and western artist inducted into the Grand Ole Opry, and nine-time Grammy Award winner, gospel legend, James Blackwood, is from Choctaw County.

Wild Rice Casserole

1 box Uncle Ben's brown and
   wild rice
1 cup cooked rice
4 tablespoons oleo
1 large onion, chopped fine
1/2 bell pepper, chopped
2 ribs celery, chopped fine
1 (6-ounce) can mushroom
   pieces and juice

1 can onion soup or 1 1/2 cups
   roast gravy
1 teaspoon Accent
2 tablespoons chopped parsly
1/2 teaspoon each salt and
   pepper

Cook wild rice according to box instructions. Add cooked rice.
Sauté onion in oleo with bell pepper and celery for 10 minutes. Add
all other seasonings. Mix well. Put in greased 2 1/2-3 quart casserole.
Bake at 325°, for 30 minutes. Will serve 6.

For 15 guests, I used 2 boxes of wild rice, 1 1/2 cups cooked rice, 2
cans mushrooms, 2 onions, 3 pieces of celery, 1 bell pepper, 2 cups
gravy, 1 teaspoon salt, 1 teaspoon pepper, 2 teaspoons Accent and
2 tablespoons parsley flakes.

The Country Gourmet (Miriam G. Cohn)

Armenian Rice

1 cup rice
2 cups chicken broth
1 stick butter
4 buttons garlic, chopped
1 cup broken nested vermicelli

1 large bell pepper, cut in large
   pieces
1 can mushrooms
1 small can ripe olives, halved
1 can water chestnuts

Wash 1 cup of rice until water is clear. Place washed rice in casserole and cover with chicken broth. Melt 1 stick butter in skillet and
cook garlic until golden brown. Remove garlic and add vermicelli
to butter. Cook the vermicelli until a dark brown. Add remaining
ingredients to casserole and mix well. Place lid on casserole and
cook in 350° oven for about 40 minutes. The rice will be done
when all the broth has cooked away. Serves 8.

Best of Bayou Cuisine

Gourmet Noodles

¹/₄ pound butter	1 clove garlic, minced
¹/₂ pound sliced mushrooms	1 tablespoon lemon juice
¹/₄ cup chopped onion	1 can consomme
¹/₄ cup sliced almonds	4 ounces medium noodles

Melt butter. Add mushrooms, onion, almonds, garlic and cook about 10 minutes on low heat. Add remaining ingredients and cook till noodles are tender, about 10 minutes. Serves 4. Great with steak or roast.

Best of Bayou Cuisine

Apricot Casserole (Lois')

1 (29-ounce can) peeled apricots	¹/₂ box Cheese Ritz crackers
¹/₂ box light brown sugar	¹/₂ stick butter or margarine
3 tablespoons lemon juice	

Remove seed from apricots and drain in colander for 1 to 1¹/₂ hours. Turn apricot cavity up in pyrex pan and sprinkle with sugar and lemon juice to marinate overnight in refrigerator. Just before cooking, crumble crackers coarsely over apricots; drizzle with butter, and bake at 350° for 40 to 50 minutes. Delightful with any meat. Serves 8.

The Cook's Book

Besides "King Cotton," Mississippi's major row crops are soybeans, rice, corn and wheat.

Hot Brandied Fruit

Buffet suppers have become a way of life in Natchez where it is commonplace to have 50 or 60 people to dinner several times a month. Hostesses have learned to perform a bit of magic with this dish, which can be a vegetable at a dinner party, a dessert at a brunch, or both at a buffet supper.

1 (20-ounce) can pineapple chunks	1 cup brandy
1 (28-ounce) can peach halves	Brown sugar
1 (16-ounce) can pitted bing cherries	24 crushed dry almond macaroons
1 (16-ounce) can mandarin oranges	Butter
3 sliced bananas	1 cup sliced toasted almonds
	Sour cream

Drain the canned fruit, reserving its juices. Marinate all the fruit in brandy for 12 hours. Boil the fruit juice until it equals 1 cup fluid. Drain the fruit again and mix the brandy with the fruit juice. Arrange the fruit in layers in a shallow rectangular casserole dish. Sprinkle each layer with brown sugar, macaroon crumbs, slices of butter, toasted almonds, and brandy mixture. The dish should be moist but not mushy. Bake 10-15 minutes at 350°. This can be prepared ahead and baked just before serving. Top with a dab of sour cream. Serves 8.

Cook with a Natchez Native

Bread
and
Breakfast

Rowan Oak, antebellum home of author, William Faulkner. Oxford.

Delicious Buffet Bread

2 packages yeast
$1/2$ cup warm water
1 cup Crisco
$1/2$ teaspoon salt
$1/2$ cup sugar

1 cup boiling water
2 eggs
$5 1/2$ cups flour
1 stick butter or oleo, melted

Dissolve yeast in warm water. Set aside. Combine Crisco, salt, sugar, and boiling water. Cool to lukewarm. Add eggs. Then add yeast mixture. Now add two cups flour and beat until smooth. Gradually add $3 1/2$ more cups of flour, one cup at a time. Let rise until doubled. Knead on floured surface. Roll out $1/2$-inch thick. Cut in small pieces. Dip each piece into melted butter. Place pieces overlapping in a greased tube pan. Let rise until doubled. Bake in 350°, oven for 30 to 40 minutes. Pour remaining melted butter over bread while it is still in the pan. Let set 5 minutes; then turn out on rack to cool. Delicious! Each person pulls off pieces.

The Pick of the Crop

Easy Rolls

2 packages dry yeast
$1 1/4$ cups lukewarm water
$1/2$ cup butter, melted

1 package egg custard mix
$3 1/2$ cups all-purpose flour

Mix in order given. Knead and place in greased bowl in refrigerator or make into rolls and let rise 2 hours. Bake at 400° for 12 to 15 minutes. 24 rolls.

Temptations

Monkey Bread

1 ³/₄ cups sugar, divided
3 teaspoons cinnamon
³/₄ cup pecans, chopped

2 small boxes raisins
1 ¹/₄ sticks oleo
3 cans biscuits

Quarter the biscuits and shake in mixture of ³/₄ cup sugar and the cinnamon. Shake a few pieces at a time. Place 1 can (quarter biscuits) on bottom of ungreased Bundt pan. Add a layer of pecans and raisins. Repeat. Melt oleo and 1 cup sugar together. Bring to a boil. Pour over biscuits, nuts and raisins. Bake at 325° for about 45 minutes. Remove immediately. Cool slightly. Pinch off the pieces with fingers. Don't cut.

Hospitality Heirlooms

 The thick vines seen on many Mississippi roadways are a plant imported from China in the '30's called kudzu, planted by CCC (Civilian Conservation Corps) workers in an effort to stop erosion. It is extremely prolific.

Spoon Rolls

1 package dry yeast
2 cups very warm water
1 ¹/₂ sticks of butter

¹/₃ cup sugar
1 egg, beaten
4 cups self-rising flour

Combine water and yeast. Melt butter and mix with sugar in a large bowl. Add and blend in beaten egg. Add dissolved yeast. Stir in flour until well mixed. Place in airtight bowl and refrigerate. When ready for rolls, drop by spoonfuls into well greased muffin tins. Let rise 20-30 minutes. Bake at 350° until brown, 10-15 minutes.

Natchez Notebook of Cooking

Herb Bread Sticks

2 packages hot dog buns
2 sticks margarine
1 tablespoon garlic juice

2 teaspoons thyme
2 teaspoons basil
2 teaspoons rosemary

Cut buns in eighths. Melt oleo, add garlic juice and other spices. Spread on buns with a pastry brush. Bake at 200° for 4 hours.

Gardeners' Gourmet II

Quick (and I Mean Quick) Herb Rolls

$^1/_2$ cup butter
1 $^1/_2$ teaspoons parsley flakes
$^1/_2$ teaspoon dill weed
1 tablespoon onion flakes

2 tablespoons Parmesan cheese
1 (10-ounce) can Hungry Jack
  biscuits

Melt butter in 9-inch pan. Mix herbs and cheese together and stir into butter. Let stand 15-30 minutes. Cut biscuits into halves and swish around in herb butter to coat all sides. Bake at 425° for 12-15 minutes. This may be prepared ahead of time.

Family Secrets

Sally Lunn

6 tablespoons butter
$^1/_4$ cup sugar
1 large egg
1 $^3/_4$ cups flour

$^1/_2$ teaspoon salt
3 teaspoons baking powder
1 cup milk

Cream butter and sugar. Add well-beaten egg. Sift together flour, salt and baking powder. Add alternately with milk to creamed mixture. Bake in tiny greased muffin tins at 375° about 20 minutes.

The Twelve Days of Christmas Cookbook

Southern Spoon Bread

3 cups milk
1 cup white corn meal
1 teaspoon butter

1 teaspoon salt
1 teaspoon sugar
3 eggs, separated

Scald milk in double boiler and gradually add corn meal. Cook 5 minutes stirring to make smooth. Cool slightly and add butter, salt and sugar. Beat egg yolks and add to mixture. Then fold in stiffly beaten egg whites. Bake in greased 1½-quart-size baking dish in a moderate oven (350°) about 45 minutes. Serve hot from dish in which it was baked with plenty of butter. Yields 6 servings.

The Mississippi Cookbook

 More than half the millionaires in the U.S. lived in the plantations of Natchez during the first half of the last century.

Spinach Corn Bread

1 package "Jiffy" or Mexican
   corn bread mix (Mexican is
   best)
1 stick oleo
1 (6-ounce) carton cottage
   cheese

1 large onion, chopped fine
1 package frozen chopped
   spinach, drained and
   squeezed
4 eggs, well beaten
1/2 teaspoon salt

Melt oleo; add onion, cheese, corn bread mix, spinach, and salt. Mix. Add eggs last and mix well. Bake at 400° for 30 minutes in greased dish or corn bread pan.

Does not brown on top, so run under broiler a few minutes to brown.

Top Rankin Recipes

Gloria's Corn Bread Muffins

1 cup self-rising cornmeal
1 (8-ounce) carton sour cream
1 (8 1/2-ounce) can cream style
   corn

1/2 cup vegetable oil
2 eggs, beaten

Mix all ingredients together and bake at 400° for 20 minutes.

Tasting Tea Treasures

Educated Hush Puppies

1 cup corn meal
1 teaspoon baking powder
1/2 teaspoon sugar
Red and black pepper, to taste
1 egg
1/2 cup all-purpose flour

1 cup water
1/2 teaspoon salt
1/2 cup green onions, finely
   chopped
Dash Tabasco

Mix all ingredients well. Drop by teaspoonfuls into hot grease. Educated Hush Puppies will turn over by themselves.

Madison County Cookery

Applesauce Muffins

2 cups biscuit mix
1 teaspoon cinnamon
¹/₄ cup sugar
¹/₂ cup applesauce
¹/₄ cup milk
1 egg, slightly beaten

2 tablespoons oil
2 tablespoons margarine,
   melted
¹/₄ cup sugar
¹/₄ teaspoon cinnamon

Combine biscuit mix, ¹/₄ cup sugar and 1 teaspoon cinnamon. Stir in applesauce, milk, egg and oil. Beat vigorously for 30 seconds. Spoon into greased muffin tins. Bake at 400° for about 12 minutes. Remove from tins and dip tops in melted margarine, then in cinnamon-sugar mixture. Makes 2 dozen.

I Promised A Cookbook

Ruth's Cranberry Bread

1 cup fresh cranberries
1¼ cups sugar
3 cups flour
4½ teaspoons baking powder
1 teaspoon salt
1 cup milk

3 tablespoons melted butter
2 eggs, slightly beaten
3 tablespoons grated orange
  rind
½ cup chopped nuts

Grind the cranberries coarsely. Add to this ¼ cup sugar and set aside. Sift together 1 cup sugar, flour, baking powder and salt. Blend in milk, melted butter, eggs, orange rind and nuts. Fold in cranberry mixture and pour into greased loaf pan. Cook at 350° for one hour.

P.S. This will make 2 small loaves. Makes delicious sandwiches.

P.P.S. Cranberry bread always is a special holiday treat for my family.

Southern Legacies

Real Biscuits

2 cups self-rising flour
½ teaspoon soda
5 tablespoons butter

1 cup buttermilk
1 package yeast

Sift dry ingredients together. Cut in butter. Dissolve yeast in warm buttermilk. Add to dry ingredients. Work dough as little as possible. Knead one time. Roll out to ½-inch thick and cut with biscuit cutter. Let stand 20 minutes. Cook at 450° for 12 mimutes in preheated oven. Yield: 12 to 14 biscuits.

Festival

Angel Biscuits

5 cups plain flour
1 teaspoon salt
1/2 teaspoon soda
3 teaspoons sugar

3 teaspoons baking powder
1 cup Crisco
2 cups buttermilk
2 packages yeast

Sift dry ingredients 3 times in large bowl. Make a well in flour mixture and add milk and Crisco. Work well. Dissolve yeast in 1/2 cup warm water. Add to flour mixture. Knead well. Roll out on floured surface. Cut biscuits and place in greased pan. Bake at 400° for 15 to 20 minutes. Dough may be kept refrigerated for several days. Makes 40 to 50 biscuits, depending on size of biscuit cutter.

The Cook's Book

Baklava Rolls

1 pound filo dough
1 pound butter

5 cups ground pecans
1/4 cup granulated sugar

If filo dough is frozen, let it thaw overnight in refrigerator. Bring butter to boil, removing foam as it comes to top. Grind pecans and mix with sugar. Cut filo dough into thirds, making about 50 strips. Brush each strip with butter. Add 1 tablespoon pecan mix at top of each strip. Roll each strip and place rolls close together on greased cookie sheet.Bake at 300° until golden brown, about 20 to 25 minutes. Pour cold syrup over rolls. Cool. Store in cookie tin for several weeks.

SYRUP:
2 cups sugar
1 cup water
1 teaspoon lemon juice

1 teaspoon rose water
  (optional)
1 tablespoon honey

Bring ingredients to boil. Cool. Pour over Baklava Rolls.

Waddad's Kitchen

Blintz Soufflé

½ cup butter, softened
⅓ cup sugar
6 eggs
1½ cups sour cream
½ cup orange juice
1 cup flour

2 teaspoons baking powder
Blintz filling
Sour cream (for topping)
Blueberry syrup or assorted
    jams (for topping)

Preheat oven to 350°. Butter a 9x13-inch dish and set aside. In a large bowl mix butter, sugar, eggs, sour cream, orange juice, flour, and baking powder until well blended. Pour ½ batter into 9x13-inch dish. Place remaining ½ aside. Prepare Blintz Filling. Yield: 8 servings.

BLINTZ FILLING:

1 (8-ounce) package cream
    cheese, softened
1 pint small curd cottage
    cheese

2 egg yolks
1 tablespoon sugar
1 teaspoon vanilla extract

In medium bowl or food processor fitted with metal blade, combine all ingredients. Mix until well blended. Drop filling by heaping spoonfuls over batter in dish. With a spatula or knife, spread filling evenly over batter; it will mix slightly with batter. Pour remaining batter over filling. Bake uncovered at 350° for 50 to 60 minutes or until puffed and golden. Serve immediately with sour cream and blueberry syrup or assorted jams. May be made a day ahead. Cover and refrigerate until ready to use. Before baking, bring to room temperature.

Note: This is a wonderful brunch or morning bridge dish.

Vintage Vicksburg

Maw Maw's Apricot Strudel

3/4 teaspoon cinnamon
1/4 cup sugar
3/4 cup ground nuts
2 sticks oleo
1 (8-ounce) package
   Philadelphia cream cheese

2 cups unsifted flour
1 (18-ounce) jar apricot
   preserves
3/4 cup powdered sugar

Mix 1/4 cup sugar, nuts and cinnamon together and set aside. Soften oleo and cream cheese. Mix together add flour. Mix well. Divide dough in 3 portions. Wrap each in foil and refrigerate overnight. It can be frozen. Next day, roll out one portion at a time on a very lightly floured board. Be sure and flour your rolling pin. Spread a thin layer of apricot preserves very gently and lightly over dough. Sprinkle some of nuts and sugar mixture over this. Roll up like a jelly roll, being very careful not to tear dough. Bake on ungreased cookie sheet in a 325° oven for 45 minutes. The top of strudel should be lightly brown when done. Cut on diagonal while hot, 1-inch pieces. Sprinkle with powdered sugar. When cold, sprinkle again. This can be stored in foil and frozen for 3 months. When thawed, sprinkle more sugar.

The Country Gourmet (Miriam G. Cohn)

Zucchini Bread

1 cup cooking oil
3 eggs, slightly beaten
2 cups sugar (1 cup granulated,
   1 cup brown)
2 cups finely shredded
   zucchini
3 cups all-purpose flour

2 teaspoons cinnamon
1 teaspoon salt
1 teaspoon baking soda
1/4 teaspoon baking powder
2 teaspoon vanilla
1 cup chopped pecans

Mix just first 4 ingredients. Add dry ingredients to flour and fold into first mixture. (Do not beat.) Add vanilla and pecans. Pour into greased loaf pans. Bake at 350° for about 45 minutes or until done.

Top Rankin Recipes

Jim Buck Ross' Blueberry Buttermilk Muffins

Editor's Note: Jim Buck supplied this recipe and did attempt to bake them — once.

2 cups all-purpose flour	1 egg slightly beaten
$^1/_2$ cup sugar	1 cup buttermilk
2 $^1/_4$ teaspoons baking powder	$^1/_4$ cup melted butter or
1 teaspoon salt	margarine
1 teaspoon baking soda	1 cup blueberries

Combine dry ingredients in a mixing bowl; set aside. Combine egg, buttermilk and butter; mix well. Make a well in the center of dry ingredients. Stir just until moistened. Fold in blueberries. Fill greased muffin pan $^2/_3$ full. Bake at 425° for 20 to 25 minutes. Remove from oven immediately. Makes 18 muffins.

Down Here Men Don't Cook

The magnolia is not only the state flower, but is also the state tree. The mockingbird is the state bird.

Sausage Ring

2 pounds pork sausage	2 eggs, beaten
$^1/_4$ cup minced onions	$^1/_2$ cup milk
1 cup chopped apples	1 $^1/_2$ cups cracker crumbs
1 can apricot halves	

Sauté sausage in skillet. Add onions and apples; cook until tender. Drain off excess liquid. Stir in eggs, milk and cracker crumbs; combine thoroughly. Bake in a greased ring pan at 350° until set, about 30 minutes. Turn out onto heated platter. Arrange apricot halves filled with toasted nuts around sausage ring. Sprinkle with chopped parsley.

I Promised A Cookbook

French Breakfast Puffs

1 cup sugar, divided
1 egg
1/3 cup Crisco
1 1/2 cups sifted flour
1 1/2 teaspoons baking powder

1/2 teaspoon salt
1/4 teaspoon ground nutmeg
1/2 cup milk
1 teaspoon ground cinnamon
Melted butter

With mixer, cream 1/2 cup sugar, the egg and Crisco. Sift together flour, baking powder, salt and nutmeg. Add creamed mixture alternately with milk, beating well after each addition. Fill 12 greased muffin pans 2/3 full with batter. Bake at 350° for 20-25 minutes. When removed from oven, dip puffs, while hot, in melted butter and roll in mixture of cinnamon and remaining sugar. Freezes well. Serve hot or cold.

The Country Gourmet
(Mississippi Animal Rescue League)

Ham and Eggs Breakfast

8 slices white bread
2 or 3 slices ham, hickory
    smoked, 1/3-inch thick
Cheese, sliced
7 eggs

3 cups milk
1 1/2 teaspoons dry mustard
1 teaspoon salt
3 cups corn flakes
1/4 cup butter, melted

Preheat oven to 300°. Trim crust from bread. Butter 8x13-inch casserole. Lay 4 slices bread in dish. Place ham slices on top. Top with slices of cheese and more bread. Beat together eggs, milk, mustard and salt. Pour over bread. Refrigerate overnight. Crush corn flakes and sprinkle over top of casserole. Drizzle with butter. Bake for 1 hour.

This is excellent to fix the night before for house guests.

Giant Houseparty Cookbook

Creamed Bacon, Eggs, and Cheese
(Served on Toast or in Patty Shells)

4 tablespoons butter
3 tablespoons flour
1 1/4 cups half-and-half
1/4 pound American cheese, grated
4 hard-cooked eggs, cut into cubes

2 teaspoons dehydrated parsley flakes
Salt and pepper to taste
Dry toast or patty shells
Paprika
8 slices bacon, cooked, drained, and crumbled

Melt butter in saucepan over low heat; add flour, stirring until blended. Turn heat to medium; add half-and-half all at once; stir constantly until smooth and thick. Add cheese and stir until melted. Combine eggs and parsley flakes with mixture, adding salt and pepper. Serve on toast or in patty shells topped with paprika and crumbled bacon. Serves 4.

Accent One

Sausage-Grits Casserole

1 cup 3-minute grits
3 cups undiluted beef bouillon
1/2 teaspoon salt
1 pound hot sausage
2 sticks butter

4 beaten eggs
1 cup milk
1/2 cup grated sharp cheese — use half and sprinkle with remainder

Cook grits in bouillon and salt until thick, about 3 — 4 minutes. In skillet, cook sausage until well done, drain on paper towels. Add sausage to cooked grits, mixing thoroughly. Add remainder of ingredients to grits and sausage, again mixing thoroughly. Pour into greased casserole. Sprinkle with remaining grated cheese before cooking. This looks very soupy before cooking; it thickens as it bakes. Bake for 30 to 45 minutes at 350°. Serves 8.

Gardeners' Gourmet II

Oeufs Crevettes

For each serving:

1 teaspoon butter
3 or 4 shrimp, cooked and
  peeled
1 egg

Salt and pepper
1 tablespoon cream
1 tablespoon Swiss cheese,
  grated

Melt butter in ramekin or custard cup. Add shrimp. Break egg over shrimp. Season. Pour on cream and top with cheese. Bake at 400° for 8-10 minutes.

The Twelve Days of Christmas Cookbook

Curried Eggs

4 tablespoons butter
2 tablespoons finely chopped
  onion
1 tablespoon finely chopped
  bell pepper
2 tablespoons finely chopped
  celery
1 teaspoon curry powder

1 teaspoon salt
4 tablespoons flour
2 cups warm milk
Red pepper
2 tablespoons chili sauce
  (optional)
12 hard boiled eggs

Cook vegetables in butter 2 or 3 minutes, add other ingredients except milk and mix well; stir in milk and cook until thick. Slice eggs onto platter and pour sauce over them. Another way to serve this is to cut the eggs in half and arrange with cooked mushrooms in a casserole. Pour the sauce over them.

Gourmet of the Delta

Breakfast Casserole

5-10 slices bread, trimmed
1/2 pound Cheddar cheese,
  shredded

1 pound sausage, browned and
  drained
8-10 eggs, beaten

Grease 9x13-inch baking dish. Cover bottom of dish with bread slices. Sprinkle shredded cheese over bread; add sausage over cheese. Pour beaten eggs over the entire mixture. Cover and refrigerate overnight. Bake at 350° for 30 minutes or until center is set.

Mississippi Memories

Eggs for a Bunch at Brunch

EGG MIXTURE:

4 tablespoons margarine
1 cup cooked ham, diced
$^1/_2$ cup green onions, chopped

$^1/_2$ cup sliced mushrooms
12 eggs, beaten

Sauté ham, onions and mushrooms in margarine until onion is tender and the mushrooms are cooked. Add the eggs and cook over low heat until eggs form soft curds. While the ham and vegetables sauté, make the cheese sauce.

CHEESE SAUCE:

$^1/_4$ cup margarine
2 $^1/_2$ tablespoons flour
2 cups milk
1 cup (4-ounce) Cheddar
   cheese, shredded

Salt to taste
Dash of hot sauce or black
   pepper

Melt the butter in a 1-quart saucepan. Stir in the flour and cook and stir for a minute or so. Gradually add the milk, stirring constantly. Cook and stir until the sauce is smooth and thick. Add the cheese and stir until cheese is melted. Add pepper or hot sauce and salt to taste. Stir the cheese sauce in the egg mixture and spoon into a greased 13x9x2-inch baking dish.

TOPPING:

$^1/_4$ cup margarine, melted
2 $^1/_4$ cups soft bread crumbs

$^1/_8$ teaspoon paprika

Top with the bread crumbs tossed in the melted margarine. Sprinkle with paprika. Chill for several hours or overnight. Bake at 350° for 30 minutes. Serves 10. Can double. Must do ahead.

Standing Room Only

Cakes, Cookies, Candies

J.B. Coleman State Park near Iuka.

Fresh Apple Cake

1 1/2 cups Mazola oil
2 cups sugar
2 large or 3 small eggs
1 teaspoon salt
1 teaspoon soda

2 teaspoons baking powder
1 teaspoon vanilla
2 1/2 cups sifted flour
1 cup pecans, chopped
3 cups fresh apples, chopped

Put oil in large mixing bowl. Add sugar and eggs. Beat until creamy on low speed, electric mixer. Sift flour again with salt, soda, and baking powder. Add a small amount of flour mixture at a time to egg and sugar mixture, beating after each addition. When all the flour mixture has been added, remove bowl from electric mixer and fold in vanilla, apples and pecans by hand. Spread evenly in a 9x13-inch cake pan lined on bottom with waxed paper. Bake in 350° oven for about 55 to 60 minutes. Cook on cake rack.

Good served with orange or lemon sauce or whipped cream.

I sometimes mix 1/2 cup brown sugar, 2 tablespoons butter, 2 tablespoons cream and 1/2 cup grated coconut and put on cake just before taking from oven, just letting it stay in oven long enough to form a glaze.

Gourmet of the Delta

Hazel's Fresh Apple Cake

1 cup sugar
1/2 cup butter, softened
1 egg
1 cup mashed fresh apples
1 teaspoon soda

1 3/4 cups cake flour
1 cup seedless small raisins
1 cup chopped pecans
1 cup chopped dates
1/2 cup chopped bottled
  cherries

Preheat oven to 350°. Stir together with a spoon the sugar, butter, egg and apples. Add soda, flour, raisins, nuts, dates, and cherries. Bake in a greased loaf pan for 40 minutes. Allow to cool in pan.

Festival

Carrot Cake

2 cups all-purpose flour	1 teaspoon salt
2 cups sugar	1 cup Wesson oil
2 teaspoons baking soda	4 eggs
1½ teaspoons cinnamon	3 cups grated carrots

Preheat oven to 350°. Sift dry ingredients together, and add oil and eggs. Blend well. Add carrots and mix about 2 minutes. Pour into two 9-inch pans and bake about 25 to 30 minutes. Frost when cool.

ICING:

1 box confectioners' sugar, sifted	1 teaspoon vanilla
1 stick oleo	1 cup chopped pecans
1 (8-ounce) package cream cheese	

Blend sugar, oleo and cream cheese until smooth. Add vanilla and pecans.

Note: This recipe won a Blue Ribbon at the Jackson Country Fair.

Bouquet Garni

French Chocolate Cake

6 squares semi-sweet chocolate
2 egg yolks (well beaten)
1 cup buttermilk
$^1/_2$ cup butter
2 cups sifted brown sugar

3 cups all-purpose flour
1 $^1/_2$ teaspoons salt
1 $^1/_2$ teaspoons soda
1 cup very strong coffee
2 teaspoons vanilla

RUM GLAZE:
$^1/_4$ cup butter
$^2/_3$ cup sugar

$^1/_2$ cup rum

CREAM FILLING:
1 (6-ounce) package semi-sweet
   chocolate chips
1 (4-ounce) can evaporated
   milk

1 egg, beaten

TOPPING:
2 cups whipping cream

Shaved chocolate

Grease 2 (9-inch) pans; then line with waxed paper and flour pans. Melt semi-sweet chocolate in double boiler. Add egg yolks. Slowly stir in buttermilk. Mix well. Cook until thick. Cool. Cream together butter and brown sugar. Sift flour with salt and soda. Add this to butter mixture with the coffee. Add chocolate mixture and vanilla. Bake at 325° about 30 minutes. Mix ingredients for rum glaze. Cook over low heat until sugar is dissolved. Pour evenly over warm cakes. Let stand in pans until cool. Mix chocolate chips and evaporated milk. Stir over low heat until smooth. Do not boil. Add one whole beaten egg. Mix well and chill. (If sauce is too thin add a beaten egg yolk). To assemble: Remove cakes from pans and generously spread a layer of filling between layers and on top. Whip the cream and ice the entire cake. Shave chocolate over top of iced cake.

Temptations

Grandma Taylor's Marble Cake

LIGHT BATTER:
$1/2$ cup butter
1 cup sugar
2 cups flour
1 teaspoon cream of tartar

$1/2$ teaspoon baking soda
$1/2$ cup milk
1 teaspoon lemon extract
4 egg whites, beaten

Cream butter and sugar thoroughly. Sift together flour, cream of tartar and baking soda; add to creamed mixture alternately with milk, beating well after each addition. Add lemon extract and fold in egg whites.

DARK BATTER:
$1/2$ cup butter
1 cup sugar
4 egg yolks, beaten
1 teaspoon baking soda
$1/2$ cup buttermilk
2 cups flour

2 teaspoons ground cinnamon
2 teapoons ground allspice
2 teaspoons ground cloves
1 grated nutmeg
$1/2$ cup molasses

Cream butter and sugar thoroughly; add egg yolks. Stir baking soda into buttermilk. Sift together flour and spices; add to creamed mixture alternately with buttermilk. Add molasses and beat until smooth.

TO ASSEMBLE:
Thoroughly grease a 10-inch tube pan. Line the bottom of pan with wax paper and lightly grease the paper. Alternately pour in light and dark batters; bake at 325° for $1 1/2$ hours. Flavor improves after a day or two. The modern method of keeping the cake fresh is to spread with Cream Cheese Frosting.

CREAM CHEESE FROSTING:
$1/2$ cup butter, softened
1 (8-ounce) package cream
   cheese, softened

1 (1-pound) box confectioners
   sugar
1 teaspoon vanilla

Beat butter and cream cheese until well blended. Add sugar and beat until texture of whipped cream; add vanilla. Serves 16.

Taste of the South

Doberge Cake (Butter)

1/2 cup butter
1/2 cup shortening
2 cups sugar
1/2 teaspoon salt
4 eggs, separated

3 cups sifted flour
3 teaspoons baking powder
1/2 cup milk
1/2 cup water
1 teaspoon vanilla extract

Cream butter, shortening, salt, and sugar together until light and fluffy. Add egg yolks and blend until smooth. Sift flour and baking powder together and add milk and water alternately to creamed mixture. Beat until blended. Add vanilla and fold in the stiffly beaten egg whites.

Grease a 9-inch cake pan and line with wax paper, lightly greased. Pour 3/4 cup of batter into pan and spread evenly over bottom. Bake at 375° for 12 to 15 minutes, until lightly browned. Remove cake from pan, peel off paper, and cool on rack. Repeat baking process until batter is completely used. Should have 8 thin layers (1/4 to 1/2-inch thick). Put together with Chocolate Cream Filling. Frost top with Chocolate Icing.

CHOCOLATE CREAM FILLING:

2 cups sugar
10 tablespoons cornstarch
1 teaspoon salt
4 cups milk

4 (1-ounce) squares bitter
    chocolate
4 egg yolks, slightly beaten
2 teaspoons vanilla extract

Mix cornstarch, sugar, salt and milk in saucepan and heat, stirring. Cut up chocolate and soften over warm water. Add softened chocolate to hot mixture and boil over medium heat until thick. Remove from heat, slowly blend beaten egg yolks into hot mixture. Cook over low heat stirring until thick. Cool two minutes. Add vanilla. Chill until filling sets. Spread on cool cake layers, reserving top layer for icing or chocolate frosting.

CHOCOLATE ICING:

1 cup sugar
1 stick butter, creamed
4 tablespoons cocoa

1/4 cup hot milk
1/3 teaspoon vanilla extract

Blend ingredients into creamed butter adding hot water or hot milk until icing reaches spreading consistency.

My Mother Cooked My Way Through Harvard
With These Creole Recipes

Fudge Fantasy Cake

1 stick butter
$1/4$ cup sugar
1 cup brown sugar, firmly
   packed
2 eggs
3 ounces unsweetened
   chocolate, melted and cooled

1 teaspoon vanilla
2 cups cake flour
$1 1/2$ teaspoons baking powder
$1/2$ teaspoon salt
$1/2$ teaspoon soda
1 cup milk

Cream butter and sugars. Beat in eggs, one at a time. Blend in chocolate and vanilla. Sift together flour, baking powder, salt and soda. Beat in flour alternately with milk. Bake in two 8-inch, greased, floured cake pans 25-30 minutes at 350°. Frost with Chocolate Cheese Frosting. Too good to be true!

CHOCOLATE CHEESE FROSTING:

1 (3-ounce) package cream
   cheese, softened
3 tablespoons butter, softened
1 tablespoon milk
$2 1/4$ cups powdered sugar

1 ounce unsweetened
   chocolate, melted
1 teaspoon vanilla
Dash of salt

Cream together cream cheese, butter and milk. Gradually beat in sugar. Blend in chocolate, vanilla and salt.

The Seven Chocolate Sins

Amaretto Cake

1 cup butter
2 1/2 cups sugar
6 eggs
1 cup sour cream
1 teaspoon vanilla
1 teaspoon orange extract

1 teaspoon lemon extract
2 teaspoons almond extract
1/4 teaspoon baking soda
1/2 teaspoon salt
3 cups sifted cake flour
1/2 cup Amaretto di Saronno

Preheat oven to 325°. Have all ingredients at room temperature. Beat butter and sugar until creamy. Add eggs one at a time, beating well after each egg has been added. Add sour cream, beat, then add extracts, baking soda and salt. Gradually beat in flour that has been sifted three times and then measured. Add Amaretto and beat well. Pour into large greased bundt cake pan. Bake 1 hour and 15 minutes or until done. Turn out on wire rack and cool.

GLAZE FOR CAKE:

1 (8-ounce) jar orange
  marmalade
1/2 jar or about 4 ounces of
  apricot preserves

1/4 cup Amaretto di Saronno
1 cup chopped toasted almonds

Heat marmalade, preserves and Amaretto until melted. Drizzle on cooled cake then sprinkle with chopped toasted almonds.

Giant Houseparty Cookbook

Chocolate Heaven Cupcakes
A chocoholic's dream

FILLING:

1 (6-ounce) package cream
  cheese, softened
1/3 cup sugar

1 egg, beaten
1 (4-ounce) package chocolate
  chips

Beat cream cheese, sugar, and egg. Stir in chocolate chips. Set aside.

CONTINUED

CONTINUED

CAKE:

3 cups flour	2/3 cup cooking oil
2 cups sugar	2 cups water
1/2 cup cocoa	2 tablespoons vinegar
1/2 teaspoon salt	2 teaspoons vanilla
2 teaspoons soda	

Sift dry ingredients. Add oil and other liquids. This makes a thin batter. Spoon into miniature muffin tins lined with "midget" baking cups, pouring them 3/4 full. Drop 1/2 teaspoon filling into center of each. Bake at 350° 20-25 minutes, shifting pans occasionally so cream cheese mixture won't brown. Makes 5 dozen.

Hors D'Oeuvres Everybody Loves

Eggnog Cakes

3/4 cup butter, softened	1/4 teaspoon salt
1 1/4 cups sugar	3/4 cup milk
8 egg yolks	1 teaspoon vanilla
2 1/2 cups sifted flour	1/2 cup chopped nuts
3 teaspoons baking powder	1/2 box vanilla wafers, crushed

Cream butter and sugar well. Add egg yolks and blend well. Sift dry ingredients 3 times; add to sugar mixture alternately with milk and vanilla. Beat until smooth. Pour into 3 square pans lined with waxed paper. Bake 20 minutes at 350°. After cake cools, cut into small squares.

Dip squares of cakes on all sides with Whiskey Sauce and roll in mixture of chopped nuts and crushed vanilla wafers. Store in airtight container. Improves with age. Do not taste for 3 days. Freezes well.

WHISKEY SAUCE:

1 (1-pound) box confectioners' sugar, sifted	1 stick butter, softened
	1 cup bourbon

Cream butter and sugar. Add bourbon and mix well.

The Pick of the Crop

A Good Cake

1 box spice cake mix	1 cup water
1 package butterscotch instant pudding	1/2 cup strawberry preserves
	1/2 cup raisins
3/4 cup oil	1 cup canned coconut
4 eggs	1 cup chopped pecans

Preheat oven to 325°. Combine cake mix and pudding mix. Add oil, eggs, water, and preserves, beating as you add. Beat well. Add raisins, coconut, and pecans and mix until well blended. Pour into a well-greased bundt pan and bake for 1 hour. Leave in pan to cool.

SAUCE (optional):

1 cup powdered sugar	Juice of 1 1/2 lemons

Mix powdered sugar and lemon juice. After cooling cake about 10 minutes, punch holes in top of cake with a fork. Pour sauce over cake, letting it soak in.

Dixie Dining

Pina Colada Cake

1 (18 1/2-ounce) box white cake mix	1/3 cup rum (Puerto Rican light is best)
1 small (3-ounce) package vanilla instant pudding	1 cup coconut
4 eggs	1 small (8 1/4-ounce) can crushed pineapple (do not drain)
1/4 cup oil	
1/2 cup water	

Mix cake mix, pudding, oil, water and rum. Add eggs, one at a time, and beat well after each addition. Mix in pineapple. Then fold in coconut. Bake in a 350° oven for 30 minutes. Makes sheet or layer cake. See recipe for Pina Colada Frosting.

CONTINUED

CONTINUED

PINA COLADA FROSTING:

1 small can crushed pineapple (do not drain)

$^1/_3$ cup rum

1 small package vanilla instant pudding

1 (9-ounce) container Cool Whip

Coconut to taste

Mix crushed pineapple (not drained), $^1/_3$ cup rum and vanilla instant pudding. Beat until it thickens. Fold in 1 (9-ounce) container of Cool Whip. Frost cake and top with coconut.

The Country Gourmet
(Mississippi Animal Rescue League)

Lemon Jelly Cake

1 cup butter

2 cups sugar

3 cups flour

3 teaspoons baking powder

$^1/_2$ teaspoon salt

$^3/_4$ cup milk

1 teaspoon vanilla

6 egg whites, stiffly beaten

Cream butter and sugar, beating until light and fluffy. Add sifted dry ingredients alternately with milk. Add vanilla. Fold in stiffly beaten egg whites. Pour into 3 greased round 9-inch layer pans. Bake at 350° for 25 or 30 minutes, or until top springs back when touched. Cool on racks.

LEMON JELLY FILLING:

$^1/_2$ cup butter

1 cup sugar

6 egg yolks

Grated rind of 2 lemons

Juice of 2 lemons

Combine all ingredients in top of double boiler. Cook over hot water, stirring constantly until thick, about 20 to 25 minutes. Let get good and cool, then put in freezer for a few minutes to firm up a little more. Spread between layers of cake and ice top and sides with 7-minute icing. If you prefer, spread filling between layers and on top, and sprinkle with coconut. Ice sides with 7-minute icing.

Into the Second Century

Peach-Butter Cake

3/4 cup butter or margarine,
  softened
1 1/2 cups sugar
3 eggs
1 teaspoon vanilla
1 teaspoon lemon extract
3/4 cup buttermilk
1/2 teaspoon baking powder
1/2 teaspoon soda

1/4 teaspoon salt
1 teaspoon nutmeg
1 teaspoon cinnamon
2 tablespoons cocoa
1 1/2 cups all-purpose flour
3/4 cup chopped pecans,
  toasted
1 cup peach preserves

Cream butter and sugar until fluffy. Add unbeaten eggs. Add flavorings to milk, then add baking powder, soda, salt, nutmeg, cinnamon, and cocoa to flour. Add the milk alternately with the flour mixture to the creamed mixture. Stir in the pecans and mix well. Spoon into two 9-inch square pans which have been buttered and floured. Bake at 375° for 45 minutes. Cool, then spread peach preserves between layers for filling, and frost top and sides with Sea-Foam Peach Frosting.

SEA-FOAM PEACH FROSTING:
1 egg white
3/4 cup brown sugar, packed
Dash salt
3 tablespoons water

1/4 cup peach preserves
1/2 teaspoon vanilla
1/4 cup chopped pecans,
  toasted

Combine egg white, brown sugar, salt, water and peach preserves in top of double boiler. Beat 1 minute to blend, then place over rapidly boiling water and beat constantly for 7 minutes, or until frosting stands in peaks. Remove from water and add vanilla. Beat until thick enough to spread on cake. Sprinkle with pecans.

Come and Dine

Peaches and Cream Cake

1 package butter flavor cake
   mix
1 1/2 cups sugar
4 tablespoons cornstarch
4 cups chopped, fresh peaches
1/2 cup water

2 cups whipping cream
2-3 tablespoons powdered
   sugar
1 cup sour cream
Fresh, sliced peaches

Prepare cake according to package directions, using two 8-inch pans. Cool and split each layer.

Combine sugar and cornstarch in a saucepan; add peaches and water. Cook over medium heat, stirring constantly, until smooth and thickened. Cool mixture completely.

Combine whipping cream and powdered sugar in a medium mixing bowl; beat until stiff peaks form. Spoon 1/3 of peach filling over split layer cake and spread 1/3 cup sour cream over filling. Repeat procedure with remaining layers, peach filling, sour cream, ending with remaining cake layer. Frost with sweetened whipped cream and garnish with fresh peach slices. Yield: one 8-inch cake.

Festival

Mary McDonald's Sour Cream Coconut Cake

1 package butter yellow cake
   mix
1 1/2 cups sugar
2 (8-ounce) cartons sour cream

2 (6-ounce) packages frozen
   coconut, thawed
1 (8-ounce) carton whipped
   topping, thawed

Prepare cake mix in 2 layers. Cool and split both layers. Combine sugar, sour cream and coconut; chill for 30 minutes or so. (Reserve 1 cup sour cream mixture for frosting.) Spread cream mixture between layers. Combine the 1 cup mixture with whipped topping and ice cake. Refrigerate 3 days before serving. Cover cake well with heavy duty foil.

Hospitality Heirlooms

Deluxe Coconut Custard Cake

CUSTARD LAYER:
2 cups scalded milk
5 tablespoons cake flour
3/4 cup sugar
1/8 teaspoon salt

4 beaten egg yolks
1 teaspoon vanilla
1/2 cup coconut

Scald milk in saucepan. Combine flour, sugar, and salt in top of double boiler over medium heat. Add milk gradually, stirring constantly until thickened. Pour small amount of custard over egg yolks; add eggs to remaining custard in double boiler. Cook 2 to 5 minutes longer. Add vanilla and coconut. Set aside to cool.

CRUST LAYER:
1 cup flour
1 stick butter or margarine

2 tablespoons sugar
1/2 cup chopped nuts

While custard is cooling, combine the flour, butter, sugar, and chopped nuts. Spread 1n 13x9x2-inch Pyrex pan. Bake 15 minutes at 350°. Cool.

CREAM CHEESE LAYER:
1 (8-ounce) package cream
   cheese
2 cups powdered sugar

2 cups whipping cream,
   whipped

Mix cream cheese and powdered sugar; fold in 1 cup of the whipping cream. Pour mixture over cooled crust. Pour cooled custard mixture over cream cheese filling. Top with remaining 1 cup whipping cream. Refrigerate overnight. Cut into 3x2-inch serving pieces.

Waddad's Kitchen

Butterscotch Torte
(John Leslie)

John Leslie is serving his third term as Mayor of Oxford, Mississippi. His name appeared on the ballot at the time Oxford was voting on beer. Mayor Leslie likes to say that he beat beer by twenty-three votes, and that's something—on a hot day in June. (The following recipe was submitted by his wife, Elizabeth Leslie.) We served this at our farm and, not only did it serve a large number of people, but most everyone enjoyed it!

6 eggs, separated	1 teaspoon almond extract
1 1/2 cup sugar	2 cups graham cracker
1 teaspoon baking powder	crumbs
2 teaspoons vanilla	1 cup chopped nuts

Beat egg yolks well, slowly adding sugar, baking powder, and flavorings. Beat egg whites until stiff. Fold egg whites into yolk mixture. Add nuts and crumbs. Pour into 2 cake layer pans, greased and lined with wax paper. Bake at 325° 30-35 minutes. Cool about 10 minutes. Remove from pan. Frost when completely cooked.

WHIPPED CREAM FROSTING:
2 cups whipping cream,
   whipped with 3 tablespoons
   confectioners' sugar

Frost cake with this mixture and put Butterscotch Sauce on top.

BUTTERSCOTCH SAUCE:

1/4 cup water	1 egg
1/4 cup butter, melted	1/4 cup orange juice
1 cup brown sugar	1/2 teaspoon vanilla
1 tablespoon flour	

Mix water and butter. Blend in brown sugar and flour. Add well-beaten egg, orange juice, and vanilla. Mix well (I usually blend in blender to mix well). Bring to boil and cook until thick. Cool and pour on top of Whipped Cream Frosting.

The Great American Politician's Cookbook

Cheese Cake

1 (6-ounce) box zwieback
  crackers, crushed
1 1/4 cups sugar, divided
1/2 teaspoon cinnamon
1/4 cup butter, melted
4 eggs, separated

1 cup sour cream
1 teaspoon vanilla extract
2 tablespoons flour
1/4 teaspoon salt
1 pound cream cheese,
  softened

Combine crackers, 1/4 cup sugar, cinnamon, and butter; press into bottom of a 9-inch springform pan. Bake at 350° for 10 minutes and let cool. Beat egg whites until stiff with 1/4 cup sugar. Set aside. Without washing the beater, beat egg yolks until thick. Add sour cream and vanilla. Beat in 3/4 cup sugar, flour, salt, and cream cheese. Mix well and then fold in egg whites. Pour into springform pan. Bake at 350° for 50 to 55 minutes. Cool and chill. Top with Strawberry-Raspberry glaze if desired; or for an easy topping, use 1 can cherry or blueberry pie filling. Yield: 12 to 15 servings.

Note: For a different flavor, add teaspoon each of fresh lemon juice and lemon rind or fresh orange juice and orange rind.

STRAWBERRY-RASPBERRY GLAZE:

2 pints strawberries
1 (12-ounce) jar red raspberry
  jelly

1 tablespoon cornstarch
1/4 cup Cointreau
1/4 cup water

Wash and hull berries and let dry completely. Combine a little jelly with cornstarch in saucepan and mix well. Add remaining jelly, Cointreau and water and cook over medium heat, stirring frequently, until thickened and clear, about 5 to 10 minutes. Cool to lukewarm, stirring occasionally. Arrange berries pointed end up all over top of cake. Spoon glaze over berries, allowing some to drip down sides of cake. Return to refrigerator until glaze is set.

Vintage Vicksburg

Praline Cheesecake

1 cup graham cracker crumbs
3 tablespoon sugar
3 tablespoon margarine, melted
3 (8-ounce) package cream cheese, softened
1 1/4 cup firmly packed dark brown sugar
2 tablespoon all-purpose flour
3 eggs
1 1/2 teaspoon vanilla
1/2 cup chopped nuts
Whipped cream

Combine graham cracker crumbs, sugar and margarine, mixing well. Press in the bottom of a 9-inch springform pan. Bake at 350° for 10 minutes. Cool.

Combine cream cheese, brown sugar and flour; beat until smooth and fluffy. Add eggs, one at a time, beating well after each addition. Blend in vanilla and nuts. Pour over crust. Bake at 350° for 50-55 minutes. Cool. Serve with whipped cream.

Top Rankin Recipes

Chocolate Cheesecake

1 1/3 cups chocolate wafer crumbs
2 tablespoons sugar
1/4 teaspoon ground cinnamon
1/4 cup butter, softened
1 1/2 cups semisweet chocolate morsels
2 eggs
1/2 cup sugar
2 teaspoons rum
1 (8-ounce) carton sour cream
2 (8-ounce) packages cream cheese, cubed and softened
2 tablespoons butter, melted
Whipped cream
Chocolate leaves

Combine wafer crumbs, 2 tablespoons sugar, cinnamon, and 1/4 cup butter; mix well. Firmly press into bottom of a 10-inch springform pan; set aside. Melt chocolate morsels over hot water in top of a double boiler. Set aside. Combine eggs, 1/2 cup sugar, rum, and sour cream in container of an electric blender; process 15 seconds. Continue blending, and gradually add chocolate and cream cheese. Add melted butter; blend well. Pour cheese mixture into chocolate crust. Bake at 325° for 45 minutes or until cheesecake is set in center. Cool at room temperature for at least 1 hour. Chill at least 6 hours. Remove sides of pan. Garnish with whipped cream and chocolate leaves.

Temptations

Sour Cream Pound Cake
(Crusty Top)

1/4 teaspoon soda
3 cups flour
2 sticks butter or margarine
3 cups sugar

6 eggs
1 cup sour cream
1 teaspoon vanilla

Sift flour and measure; resift twice with soda. Set aside. Cream butter and add sugar slowly, beating constantly to cream well. Add eggs, 1 at a time, beating after each addition. Stir in sour cream. Add flour mixture, 1/2 cup at a time, beating well. Stir in vanilla and turn batter into well-greased and floured 10-inch tube pan. Bake in 325° oven about 1 1/2 hours or until cake is done. Place pan on rack to cool 5 minutes. Loosen cake around edge of pan and edge of tube with dull side of knife. Press toward pan rather than toward cake. This protects crust. Turn cake onto rack to cool completely. Serve plain. (One teaspoon lemon extract or 1/2 teaspoon almond flavoring may be used instead of vanilla.)

Bell's Best

Apple Cider Pound Cake

1 cup butter, softened
1/2 cup shortening
3 cups sugar
6 eggs
3 cups all-purpose flour

1/2 teaspoon baking powder
1/2 teaspoon salt
1 1/2 teaspoons apple pie spice
1 cup apple cider
1 teaspoon vanilla

Cream butter and shortening, add sugar, beating until light and fluffy. Add eggs one at a time, beating after each. Combine next four ingredients. Add to creamed mixture alternately with apple cider. Stir in vanilla. Pour batter in greased and floured 10-inch tube pan. Bake at 325° for 1 hour and 20 minutes. Cool in pan 10 to 15 minutes. Cool on rack.

Gardeners' Gourmet II

Brown Sugar Pound Cake

3 cups flour
1/2 teaspoon baking powder
1/4 teaspoon salt
3/4 cup butter (room
   temperature)
3/4 cup shortening
1 (1-pound) box light brown
   sugar

1 cup sugar
5 large eggs
1 cup milk
1 1/2 teaspoon vanilla
1 cup pecans, chopped

Into a large bowl sift together the flour, baking powder, and salt. In another large bowl cream the butter and shortening until light and creamy. Gradually add the brown sugar and sugar, mixing until light and creamy. Add eggs one at a time to the sugar, beating well after each addition. Add the dry ingredients alternately with the milk, ending with the dry ingredients, beating each addition just until blended. Stir in vanilla and nuts. Pour butter into a greased and floured 10-inch tube pan. Bake at 325° for 1 to 2 hours. Cool the cake upright for 10 minutes on a wire rack. Invert on rack and let cool. Serve unfrosted. Serves 12-14.

Natchez Notebook of Cooking

Turtle Cake

1 box chocolate cake mix
1 (14-ounce) package caramels
1 (6-ounce) can evaporated
    milk

1 cup chocolate chips
1 cup chopped pecans

Preheat oven to 350°. Grease and flour the bottom of a 9x13-inch baking pan. Mix the cake according to directions on box. Spread ¹/₂ of prepared cake batter into pan and bake for 20 minutes. In a saucepan, melt caramels and milk together. Pour caramel mixture over the hot cake layer, then sprinkle the chocolate chips and pecans over this. Spoon the remaining cake batter over the top and continue baking for 25 minutes.

Festival

Mississippi Mud Cake

2 sticks oleo margarine
2 cups sugar
4 eggs
2 tablespoons cocoa

1 ¹/₂ cups all-purpose flour
1 cup angel flake coconut
1 teaspoon vanilla
1 ¹/₂ cups chopped pecans

Cream 2 sticks of oleo margarine with 2 cups of sugar. Add remaining ingredients and beat well after each addition. Bake in 9x12-inch greased and floured pan for 30 to 40 minutes at 350°.

FROSTING:

1 jar marshmallow cream
¹/₂ cup canned milk
1 box powdered sugar

¹/₃ cup cocoa
1 teaspoon vanilla
1 stick margarine, softened

While cake is still warm spread with marshmallow cream and ice with mixture of remaining ingredients.

The Mississippi Cookbook

Kahlua Fudge Brownies

1 1/2 cups sifted flour
1/2 teaspoon baking powder
1/2 teaspoon salt
2/3 cup butter
2 (1-ounce) squares
   unsweetened chocolate

3 large eggs
2 cups sugar
1/4 cup plus 1 tablespoon
   Kahlua, divided
1/3 cup chopped pecans or
   walnuts

Resift flour with baking powder and salt. Melt butter with chocolate over low heat or over hot water. Beat eggs with sugar until light. Stir in chocolate mixture and 1/4 cup Kahlua. Add flour mixture and mix well. Stir in nuts. Turn into 9-inch square pan lined with greased aluminum foil. Bake at 350° for 30 to 40 minutes or until top springs back when touched lightly, or when sides begin to pull away from edge of pan. Do not overbake. Remove from oven and cool in pan. When cold, brush top with 1 tablespoon Kahlua. Let stand until thoroughly cold before cutting into bars. Makes 24. Can freeze.

Standing Room Only

Shortbread Toffee Squares

3/4 stick butter
4 tablespoons sugar
1 cup self-rising flour
1/2 stick butter
2 tablespoons sugar
1 (14-ounce) can condensed
   milk

1/4 cup pecans, chopped
1/2 teaspoon vanilla
4 ounces German sweet
   chocolate, melted in
   1 tablespoon water

Cream 3/4 stick butter with 4 tablespoons sugar. Blend in flour. Spread onto greased 8-inch square pan, and bake at 350° for 20 minutes. Mix together next 4 ingredients and cook, stirring until mixture leaves the sides of the pan. Add vanilla. Pour over shortbread. Cool. Spread melted chocolate over toffee. Cool. Cut into squares. Makes about 12.

The Twelve Days of Christmas Cookbook

Cream Cheese Streusel Brownies

$^1/_4$ cup margarine
1 (21.5-ounce) package Betty
   Crocker fudge brownie mix
1 cup chopped nuts
1 egg
$^1/_4$ cup vegetable oil
$^1/_4$ cup water

1 (8-ounce) package
   Philadelphia cream cheese
   (soft)
$^1/_4$ cup sugar
$^1/_2$ teaspoon vanilla
1 egg

Heat oven to 350°. Grease bottom of a 13x9-inch pan. Cut margarine into $^1/_2$ cup dry brownie mix until crumbly. Stir in the nuts and reserve. Mix remaining dry brownie mix, 1 egg, oil, and water. Spread in greased pan. Combine cream cheese, sugar and vanilla. Mix on medium speed until well blended. Blend in 1 egg. Spread over brownie mixture in pan. Sprinkle with reserved brownie mixture. Bake at 40 minutes at 350°. Cool completely before cutting into squares.

Family Secrets

Peanut Butter Fingers

1 cup plain flour
$^1/_2$ cup brown sugar, packed
   firmly
$^1/_2$ teaspoon soda
$^1/_4$ teaspoon salt
$^1/_2$ cup softened butter

$^1/_3$ cup crunchy peanut butter
1 egg
1 cup uncooked oatmeal
1 (12-ounce) package chocolate
   chips

TOPPING:
$^1/_2$ cup sifted powdered sugar
$^1/_2$ cup crunchy peanut butter

2-4 tablespoons milk

Mix flour, sugar, soda, salt, butter, peanut butter, egg, and oats. Press dough into greased 13x9x2-inch pan. Bake at 350°for 20 minutes. Remove and sprinkle chocolate chips over it. Let stand 5 minutes or until melted. Spread evenly. Combine sugar, peanut butter, and milk. Beat well. Drizzle over crust and chocolate. Cut into bars.

The Pick of the Crop

Knock You Nakeds

1 package German chocolate
  cake mix
1 cup nuts, chopped
$^1/_3$ cup evaporated milk

$^3/_4$ cup butter, melted
60 pieces caramel candy
$^1/_2$ cup evaporated milk
1 cup chocolate chips

Combine, and mix well cake mix, nuts, $^1/_3$ cup milk, and butter. Press half of mixture into the bottom of a greased 8 x 13-inch pyrex dish; bake at 350° for 8 minutes. Melt caramel candy in top of double boiler with half cup of milk. When caramel mixture is well mixed, pour over baked mixture. Cover with chocolate chips, and pour rest of dough on top of chips. Bake for 18 minutes at 350°. Cool before slicing. QUITE SIMPLY DIVINE! Yields 18-20 squares.

Great Flavors of Mississippi

Taffy Apple Cookies

$^1/_2$ pound plus 1 tablespoon
  butter or oleo
8 tablespoons powdered sugar

2 egg yolks
3 cups flour

Cream butter and powdered sugar. Add egg yolks and flour to form a dough. Pinch dough into small balls about 1 inch in diameter. Bake on ungreased cookie sheet for 12-15 minutes at 375° or until golden brown. While warm, insert round toothpicks in center of cookies.

TOPPING:
1$^1/_2$ (14-ounce) packages Kraft
  caramels

$^3/_4$ cup milk

Melt caramels and add milk. Mix. While caramel mixture is warm (I keep it over the hot water from a double boiler), dip cookies in and cover with caramel. Sprinkle with finely chopped nuts. Put into small candy-size paper cups. (I place them on waxed paper until they set and then put into paper cups.)

Family Secrets

Southern Sand Tarts

2 cups plain flour
1 (1-pound) box powdered
  sugar

1 ½ cups pecans, chopped
1 tablespoon vanilla extract
2 sticks oleo

Lay out oleo to reach room temperature. Sift together 2 cups of once-sifted flour and 7 tablespoons powdered sugar; blend flour and sugar with oleo. Add vanilla, mix well; add chopped pecans. Mix well. Place in covered bowl and refrigerate overnight or longer.

Roll chilled dough into neat balls. Place on lightly greased cookie sheet and bake at 325° for 20 – 25 minutes until slightly brown. (Do not overcook.)

Remove from oven. Leave on cookie sheet 7 – 10 minutes. Then gently roll all cookies at once in remainder of powdered sugar which has been sifted into a heavy paper bag. Cookies will absorb most all the sugar. Pour into container that can be sealed. Yields 110 – 118 cookies.

Down Here Men Don't Cook

Praline Cookies

24 whole graham crackers,
  broken where marked
1 cup brown sugar, packed
1 cup butter (or margarine or
  mixed half and half)

1 teaspoon vanilla
1 cup chopped pecans
1 (8-ounce) chocolate bar,
  optional

Line a 10x15-inch jelly roll pan with graham crackers fitted together, leaving no spaces between them. Break crackers to fit if necessary. In a saucepan, combine brown sugar and butter. Bring to a boil, stirring constantly, and boil just 2 minutes. Remove from heat; stir in vanilla and nuts. Pour syrup over crackers and bake 10 minutes at 350°. They should be bubbly. Cool slightly and cut into bars. Cool thoroughly and store in tightly covered container. If chocolate bar is used, melt bar and drizzle over cookies before cutting. Yield: 48 bars.

Into the Second Century

Sugar Cookies

1 cup sugar
3/4 cup oil
1 cup powdered sugar
1 cup softened butter or
  margarine
2 eggs

4 cups flour
1 teaspoon soda
1 teaspoon cream of tartar
1 teaspoon salt
1 teaspoon vanilla
Sugar

Cream sugar with oil and powdered sugar. Add softened butter, eggs and flour which has been sifted with soda, cream of tartar and salt. Mix well and add vanilla. Chill. Make 1-inch balls, flatten with bottom of shot glass on greased cookie sheet. Sprinkle with sugar and bake at 350° until light golden.

P.S. This makes a very big batch of cookies. I flatten mine and press the edges with the prongs of a fork. Edges brown and they are very pretty. I think they are really great!

Southern Legacies

Judy's Chocolate Crinkle Cookies
They look so pretty and taste like brownies

$1/2$ cup vegetable oil
4 ounces unsweetened
  chocolate, melted
2 cups granulated sugar
4 eggs

2 teaspoons vanilla
2 cups unsifted flour
2 teaspoons baking powder
$1/2$ teaspoon salt
1 cup confectioners' sugar

Mix oil, chocolate and granulated sugar. Blend in 1 egg at a time till well mixed. Add vanilla; stir in flour, baking powder and salt; chill overnight.

Preheat oven to 350°. Drop dough by teaspoon into confectioners' sugar—don't attempt to shape yet. Coat lightly with confectioners' sugar—this makes it crinkle. Pick up, roll into a ball, and roll again in confectioners' sugar. Place 2 inches apart on greased baking sheets. Bake 10-12 minutes. Do not overcook. They will be a little soft to the touch. Makes about 4 dozen small cookies.

Hors D'Oeuvres Everybody Loves

Cheese Cake Cookies

$1/3$ cup brown sugar (packed)
$1/2$ cup chopped walnuts or
  pecans
1 cup flour
$1/3$ cup melted butter
1 tablespoon vanilla
1 (8-ounce) package cream
  cheese

$1/4$ cup sugar
1 egg
1 tablespoon lemon juice
2 tablespoons cream
1 teaspoon vanilla
Powdered sugar

Mix first 5 ingredients until about like meal. Reserving one cup of mixture, spread in an 8-inch square cake pan (buttered). Bake at 350° for 12 minutes.

Put cream cheese in mixing bowl with sugar, egg, lemon juice, cream and vanilla. When well mixed, pour over cooked crust, sprinkle remaining crust mixture over top and bake for about 20-25 minutes. Cut in squares and sprinkle with powdered sugar.

Southern Legacies

Almond Lace Cookies

1 (2⅞-ounce) package sliced
   almonds, pulverized
½ cup butter

½ cup sugar
1 tablespoon flour
2 tablespoons milk

Blend ingredients in a skillet over low heat. Remove from heat. Grease and flour Teflon or Silverstone cookie sheets. Drop half teaspoonfuls of mixture at least 4 inches apart on cookie sheets. Bake at 350° for 4-6 minutes or until lightly browned. Remove from oven; cool 1½-2 minutes. Roll each cookie around the handle of a wooden spoon. Cool on wire racks. If cookies become too stiff before rolling is completed, return to oven for a minute to reheat. Cookies will keep 2 weeks in moisture-proof container.

Taste of the South

Near Fatal Drops

1 stick butter
½ cup light cream
1 cup sugar
1¼ cups flour
¼ teaspoon baking powder
¼ teaspoon salt

6 ounces chocolate chips
¾ cups maraschino cherries,
   drained and chopped
1 cup almonds, slivered
½ teaspoon almond extract

Melt butter with cream and sugar. Cook over low heat until sugar dissolves. Sift together flour, baking powder and salt. Mix together in a bowl chocolate chips, cherries and half the flour mixture. Add the hot, melted mixture and mix well. Stir in rest of flour mixture and extract. Drop by spoonsful onto greased cookie sheet and bake for 15-20 minutes at 325°. Makes about 5 dozen.

The Seven Chocolate Sins

Romantic Raspberry Chocolate Meringues
Versatile because of Jello base—try experimenting with other flavors

3 egg whites
1 1/2 ounces raspberry Jello
3/4 cup sugar
1/8 teaspoon salt
1 teaspoon white vinegar

1 (6-ounce) package
   semisweet chocolate chips
1/2 cup pecans or walnuts,
   finely chopped

Beat egg whites until they begin to get stiff. Add gelatin gradually, blending thoroughly. Add sugar a little at a time; beat until stiff peaks form. Beat in salt and vinegar. Fold in chocolate chips and nuts. Drop by half full teaspoon on foil-lined baking sheets. Bake 20 minutes at 250°. Turn off heat and leave in oven 3 hours without opening door. To garnish, you may dip the tops in a little melted chocolate, or before baking, add a little shaved chocolate or a chocolate chip to top of cookie. These will hold their shape. Makes approximately 80.

Hors D'Oeuvres Everybody Loves

Praline Cookies
(Meringues)

2 egg whites, beaten frothy
2 cups well packed brown
   sugar

3 cups whole pecans
2 teaspoons vanilla

Add sugar, nuts, and vanilla to frothy egg whites. Drop by spoonfuls on greased, foil covered cookie sheet. Pre-heat oven to 400°. Place cookies in oven. Cut off heat and leave for 8 minutes. Remove from oven and allow to cool. Yields 4-6 dozen.

The Pilgrimage Garden Club
Antiques Forum Cookbook

Peanut Kisses

1 cup shortening	1 cup peanut butter
1 cup white sugar	2¼ cups sifted flour
1 cup brown sugar	2 teaspoons baking soda
2 eggs	½ teaspoon salt
½ teaspoon vanilla	¾ pound Hershey's Kisses

Cream together shortening, sugars, eggs. Add vanilla and stir in peanut butter. Sift dry ingredients and stir into creamed mixture. Shape into balls, about 1 teaspoon each, and put on ungreased sheet. Press Kisses in center so dough will form over edge. Bake 10-12 minutes in 350° oven.

Bell's Best

Divinity Fudge

2 cups sugar	2 egg whites
½ cup corn syrup	1 cup pecans, choppped
½ cup hot water	1 teaspoon vanilla

Boil together sugar, syrup and water until it forms a hard ball when dropped in cup of cold water. Pour the hot syrup over beaten whites of the eggs, beating vigorously all the time. Add vanilla and nuts. Continue beating until it is too stiff to beat any more and spread on a buttered platter and cut into squares. Instead of spreading on the platter, it can be dropped by the spoonful onto the buttered platter or a cookie tin.

DAR Recipe Book

Microwave Peanut Brittle

1 cup sugar
1/2 cup light corn syrup
1 cup raw peanuts
1/4 teaspoon salt

1 tablespoon butter
1 teaspoon vanilla extract
1 teaspoon soda

Combine sugar, corn syrup, peanuts and salt in a 2-quart casserole. Mix well. Microwave at high 8-9 minutes. Mixture will be light brown in color. Add butter and vanilla. Blend thoroughly. Microwave at high 1-3 minutes or until mixture reaches the hard crack stage (300°). Stir in soda quickly. Pour onto greased slab or cookie sheet. Let cool at least 1 hour. Break into small pieces. Store in airtight container. Yield: 1 pound. Total cooking time: 9-12 minutes.

Note: Roasted salted peanuts may be used and added as the last ingredient. Omit salt if peanuts are salted.

Bell's Best 2

Pies and Desserts

Historical lighthouse, still in use, overlooking Biloxi Beach.

Lemon-Crusted Fresh Blueberry Pie

LEMON PASTRY:

2 cups sifted flour
1 teaspoon salt
$^1/_2$ teaspoon grated lemon peel

$^2/_3$ cup shortening
4-6 tablespoons cold water
1 tablespoon lemon juice

Sift together flour and salt; stir in lemon peel. Cut in shortening with pastry blender until pieces are the size of small peas. Mix together water and lemon juice. Sprinkle 1 tablespoon liquid over part of flour mixture. Gently toss with fork; push to side of bowl. Sprinkle next tablespoon liquid over dry portion; mix lightly; push to moistened part at side of bowl. Repeat with remaining liquid until all flour mixture is moistened. Divide dough into 2 portions and form each portion into a ball. Flatten pastry balls 1 at a time, on lightly floured surface. Roll from center to edge until dough is $^1/_8$-inch thick.

PIE:

1 recipe lemon pastry
4 cups fresh blueberries
$^3/_4$-1 cup sugar
3 tablespoons flour
$^1/_2$ teaspoon grated lemon peel

Dash of salt
1-2 teaspoons lemon juice
1 tablespoon butter or
   margarine

In mixing bowl, combine blueberries, sugar, flour, lemon peel, and salt. Line a 9-inch pie plate with pastry; pour in filling. Drizzle with lemon juice and dot with butter or margarine. Adjust top crust, cutting slits or decorations for escape of steam. Seal and flute edges. If desired sprinkle top crust with additional sugar. Bake at 400° for 35 to 40 minutes. Yield: 8 servings.

Vintage Vicksburg

Blueberry Cream Pie

1 can blueberries
$1/4$ cup sugar
2 tablespoons flour
$1 1/2$ tablespoons lemon juice
$1/4$ teaspoon cinnamon
1 (3-ounce) package cream
    cheese

$1/2$ cup powdered sugar
1 teaspoon vanilla
$1/2$ pint whipping cream
1 (9-inch) baked pie shell

Drain blueberries. Combine juice with sugar, flour, lemon juice and cinnamon. Boil until thick, stirring constantly. Cool and add blueberries. Cream cream cheese, powdered sugar and vanilla. Whip whipping cream until stiff. Stir together whipped cream and cream cheese combination. Spread into pie shell. Spoon blueberry mixture over top and chill overnight.

Madison County Cookery

Sunrise Cherry Pie
A very pretty pie

1 (8-ounce) can crushed
    pineapple (in heavy syrup)
1 (8-ounce) package cream
    cheese, softened
1 teaspoon vanilla

1 can cherry pie filling
$1/4$ cup sugar
1 cup heavy cream
1 graham cracker crust

Drain pineapple and reserve 2 tablespoons juice. Combine cream cheese, vanilla, and juice; mix until well blended. Stir in $1/4$ cup pineapple and $1/2$ cup pie filling. Gradually add sugar to cream in small mixing bowl, beating until soft peaks form. Fold into cheese mixture. Pour into crust. Top center with remaining pie filling, and circle outer edge of pie with remainder of pineapple. Chill until firm.

Natchez Notebook of Cooking

Blackberry Trifle
(Aunt Fannie's)

1 cup blackberry jam
1 cup sugar
1 cup buttermilk
$^{1}/_{2}$ cup butter
2 tablespoons flour

4 eggs, separated
1 teaspoon vanilla
1 (9-inch) unbaked pie shell
4 tablespoons sugar

Preheat oven to 350°. Mix jam, sugar, buttermilk, butter, flour, egg yolks and vanilla well. Pour into unbaked pie shell. Bake about 40 minutes. Beat the 4 egg whites until stiff, adding 4 table-spoons of sugar gradually. Spread meringue on top of pie and return to oven to brown lightly.

(At the age of 102, "Aunt Fannie" Smith is the only living person who attended the first Neshoba County Fair in 1889, which she remembers vividly.)

Giant Houseparty Cookbook

French Coconut Pie

$^{1}/_{2}$ cup butter, softened
1 $^{1}/_{2}$ cups sugar
3 eggs, slightly beaten
1 tablespoon vinegar
1 teaspoon coconut extract

1 teaspoon vanilla extract
Pinch of salt
1 (6-ounce) package frozen
   coconut
1 (9-inch) pie shell, unbaked

Cream butter and sugar. Add eggs and beat slightly. Add vinegar, coconut, extracts, and salt. Mix well. Add frozen coconut and mix. Pour into a 9-inch unbaked pie shell. Bake at 325° for 40 to 50 minutes. 6 to 8 servings.

Temptations

Chess Pie

1 cup sugar
²/₃ stick butter
3 eggs
Nutmeg

2 tablespoons milk
2 tablespoons corn meal
2 teaspoons vinegar
1 teaspoon vanilla

Cream sugar and butter; add remaining ingredients. Bake at 400° for 10 minutes, then at 300° for 30 minutes.

Bell's Best 2

Chocolate Pie
(This has been the best seller at our restaurant—have it every Friday)

2 tablespoons cocoa
1½ cups sugar
Scant ½ cup flour

1 cup milk
3 egg yolks
½ stick oleo

Cook until thick and bubbly. This will become thick very quickly. Add 1 teaspoon vanilla extract and beat with whip until smooth. Pour into cooked Butter Crust pie shell. Top with meringue and brown.

BUTTER CRUST:
1 stick melted oleo   1½ cups flour

Mix together. Pat into pie pan. Bake in 350° about 7 minutes. Do not over brown; if you get this crust too brown it makes the butter taste burnt.

Seasoned With Love

Rum Pie

2 cups milk
$^{1}/_{2}$ cup sugar
1 $^{1}/_{4}$ tablespoons cornstarch
4 eggs, separated
$^{1}/_{4}$ cup cold water
1 teaspoon gelatin
4 tablespoons confectioners'
    sugar

1 tablespoon rum
1 graham cracker pie crust,
    chilled
$^{1}/_{2}$ pint whipping cream,
    optional

Scald milk in top of a double boiler. Mix the sugar and cornstarch; add $^{1}/_{4}$ of the cup of milk from the double boiler to sugar mixture to make a paste. Add egg yolks and beat together. Pour this mixture into the hot milk in the double boiler and cook for 10 minutes, or until custard coats the spoon.

Soak gelatin in cold water and add to the above custard while it is hot, stirring until dissolved. Chill until thoroughly set, then beat until spongy. Fold in meringue made from the beaten egg whites, and the confectioners' sugar. Add rum and pour into chilled graham cracker crust and return to refrigerator to thoroughly chill before serving. This may be served topped with whipped cream or plain. If whipped cream is used, add one teaspoon of rum to whipped cream.

DAR Recipe Book

Individual Pecan Pies

3 eggs, well beaten
$^{1}/_{2}$ cup sugar
1 cup white corn syrup
$^{1}/_{4}$ cup melted margarine
1 heaping tablespoon flour

1 cup pecans, chopped
1 teaspoon vanilla
Dash salt
Pastry for 9-inch pie shell

Blend first five ingredients well; add pecans, vanilla and salt. Pour into unbaked individual tart shells. Bake at 350° until firm and lightly browned.

To cut out tart shells, use fluted cookie cutter and place in muffin tins. Fills 12 (3-inch) tarts (bake for 30 minutes). Fills 36 (1$^{3}/_{4}$-inch) tarts (bake for 15 minutes). Fills 1 (9-inch) pie (bake for 45 minutes).

I Promised A Cookbook

Down in Dixie Bourbon Pie

1 box chocolate wafers,
  crushed
1/4 cup butter or margarine,
  melted

21 marshmallows
1 cup evaporated milk
1 cup heavy cream
3 tablespoons bourbon

Mix chocolate wafer crumbs and melted butter. Pat into bottom and sides of a 9-inch pie pan. Bake at 350° until set, about 15 minutes. In saucepan, heat marshmallows and milk until marshmallows melt and mixture is smooth. Do not boil. Remove from heat. Whip cream until stiff. Fold into marshmallow mixture. Add bourbon and pour into cooled chocolate crumb crust. Refrigerate 4 hours or until set. Additional whipped cream and chocolate crumbs make an attractive garnish. Yield: 6 to 8 servings.

Vintage Vicksburg

Black Bottom Pie

1/2 cup sugar plus 2 teaspoons
  flour
1 tablespoon cornstarch
2 cups milk, scalded
4 beaten egg yolks
1 teaspoon vanilla
1 (6-ounce) package semi-sweet
  chocolate pieces, melted
1 (9-inch) pie shell, baked

1 tablespoon unflavored
  gelatin
1/4 cup cold water
Bourbon to taste (1/2 cup)
4 egg whites
1/2 cup sugar
1 cup heavy cream, whipped
Chocolate pieces, grated for
  garnish

Combine sugar, flour and cornstarch. Slowly add scalded milk to beaten egg yolks. Stir in sugar mixture. Cook and stir in top of double boiler until the custard coats a spoon. Add vanilla. To 1 cup of the custard add the melted chocolate. Pour in bottom of cooled pie shell. Chill. Soften gelatin in cold water and add to remaining hot custard. Stir until dissolved. Chill until slightly thickened. Beat egg whites, adding sugar gradually until mixture stands in peaks. Fold in custard-gelatin mixture to which bourbon has been added. Pour over chocolate layer and chill until set. Garnish with whipped cream and chocolate pieces grated on top.

The Gulf Gourmet

Sweet Potato Pie

My granddaughter, Denise, loves this pie, and she doesn't even like sweet potatoes very much. It's delicious with a scoop of home-made vanilla ice cream on top.

FILLING:

2 cups mashed, cooked sweet
   potatoes
6 tablespoons unsalted butter,
   softened
2 eggs, beaten
1/3 cup granulated sugar
1 teaspoon vanilla extract

1/2 teaspoon cinnamon
1/2 teaspoon freshly grated
   nutmeg
1/4 cup evaporated milk
1 (9-inch) deep-dish pie shell,
   partially baked

Preheat the oven to 350°. In a bowl mash together the sweet potatoes and the softened butter. Add the eggs, sugar, vanilla, cinnamon, nutmeg, and evaporated milk and stir well until smooth. Pour into pie shell; and smooth the top.

TOPPING:

3 tablespoons unsalted butter,
   melted
1/2 cup tightly packed light
   brown sugar

1/3 cup all-purpose flour
2/3 cup finely chopped pecans

In a small bowl, combine the melted butter, brown sugar, flour, and pecans. Stir to blend; the mixture will be crumbly. Sprinkle the topping over the pie.

Bake the pie on a cookie sheet 25 to 35 minutes.

Aunt Freddie's Pantry

Elegant Pumpkin Pie

1 (9-inch) pastry shell
3 eggs, well beaten
1/2 cup dark brown sugar,
   firmly packed
1 teaspoon salt
1/2 teaspoon cinnamon
1/2 teaspoon nutmeg

1/2 teaspoon ginger
1/4 teaspoon cloves
2 cups strained, cooked
   pumpkin
1 1/2 cups milk, scalded
1/2 cup thick cream

Line 9-inch pie pan with pastry and make fluted standing rim. Combine eggs, sugar, salt and spices; gradually stir in milk, cream and pumpkin (the canned variety of strained pumpkin is ideal). Turn into uncooked pastry-lined pie plate and bake in hot oven 450° 10 minutes. Reduce heat to moderate 350°, and bake 20 to 25 minutes longer, or until knife comes out clean when carefully inserted in custard.

This pie is delicious plain or may be covered with meringue or sweetened whipped cream.

Gourmet of the Delta

Pumpkin Pie

2 tablespoons butter
3 eggs
1/4 teaspoon ginger
1/2 teaspoon cinnamon
1 cup evaporated milk
3/4 cup granulated sugar

1/2 teaspoon salt
1/4 teaspoon nutmeg
1 cup canned pumpkin
1/4 cup bourbon whiskey
Unbaked pie shell

Soften butter with mixer then add ingredients one by one. Mix until well blended. Pour into pie shell and bake 10 minutes at 450°. Lower oven to 325° and continue baking for 35 minutes or until knife stuck into center comes out clean.

DAR Recipe Book

Carolyn's Pecan Pie

3 eggs
Dash of salt
1 tablespoon flour
1/2 cup sugar
1 cup maple/butter flavored
   pancake syrup

1/4 cup butter, melted
1 cup pecan halves or 1 1/2 cups
   crushed pecans
1 unbaked (9-inch) pie shell

Beat eggs thoroughly with sugar, salt, flour and melted butter. Add syrup and pecans; pour into unbaked pie shell. Bake at 350° for 45 to 50 minutes or until knife inserted in center comes out clean. Cool.

Note: The secret to this delicious, rich dessert is the maple/butter flavored syrup.

Mississippi Memories

Good Intentions Pie

1 Chocolate Wafer Crust
1 (3 1/2-ounce) package instant
   vanilla pudding
1 3/4 cups milk
1 cup strawberry or raspberry
   yogurt

1 tablespoon strawberry or
   raspberry jam
1 (9-ounce) container whipped
   topping
1/2 ounce semi-sweet
   chocolate, shaved

Prepare instant pudding with milk. Thoroughly blend yogurt and jam into pudding. Fold in whipped topping. Pour into crust, top with chocolate, and chill 4 hours. May be frozen.

CHOCOLATE WAFER CRUST:

1 cup chocolate wafer crumbs
   (18 Famous Chocolate
   Wafers)

3 tablespoons butter, melted

Mix crumbs and butter and press into 9-inch pie pan. Bake about 5 minutes in 350° oven.

The Seven Chocolate Sins

Lemon Tarts

1 1/2 cups sugar
1/3 cup cornstarch
Grated rind of 2 lemons
2 cups boiling water
4 eggs, separated

1 tablespoon butter
1/3 cup lemon juice
1/8 teaspoon salt
1/2 cup sugar
Individual pie shells

Combine sugar, cornstarch and lemon rind. Add boiling water. Cook until thickens. Cook slowly for 5 minutes. Beat egg yolks; add a small amount of above mixture to yolks. Then pour yolks into sugar mixture. Add butter, lemon juice and salt. Cook slowly for 5 minutes. Pour into individual pie shells. Cover with meringue made of 4 egg whites and 1/2 cup sugar. Bake at 325° for 15 minutes.

Inverness Cook Book

Persian Pastries

2 cups dried apricots
2 cups water
1 1/2 cups plus 2 tablespoons
   sugar
3 cups flour
3 tablespoons powdered sugar
1/2 teaspoon salt

2 sticks butter
1/2 cup warm milk
1 package dry yeast
1 egg, slightly beaten
2 ounces semi-sweet chocolate,
   melted
1 teaspoon vanilla

Cook apricots in water and sugar until tender. Sift together flour, powdered sugar and salt. Cut in butter. Dissolve yeast in warm milk. Mix egg into milk. Blend in cooled chocolate. Add vanilla. Add milk mixture to flour mixture and stir until dampened. Roll out pastry very thin. Cut into 2-inch squares. Put 1/2 teaspoon apricots in center. Fold over and pinch corners. Bake on greased baking sheet about 15 minutes at 400°. Dust with powdered sugar.

The Seven Chocolate Sins

Apple Pan Dowdy

$^1/_2$ (18-ounce) box yellow
   cake mix
2 cans sliced apples that have
   been cooked with 1 cup

sugar, $^1/_2$ stick oleo and 2
   teaspoons cinnamon
1 small package vanilla wafers

Put $^1/_2$ box cake mix on bottom of pan. Put apples (juice and all). Stir together. Crush vanilla wafers and put on top. Cook at 350° for about 20 minutes. Serve warm topped with Cool Cream Topping below.

COOL CREAM TOPPING:
1 box instant vanilla pudding
   and pie filling (fixed as
   directed on box)

1 can condensed milk
1 (9-ounce) carton Cool Whip

Mix together. This topping can be kept in refrigerator for weeks.

Seasoned With Love

Apple Spoon-Ups

2 cans apple pie filling
1 teaspoon cinnamon
1 can crescent-shaped dinner
   rolls

1 $^1/_2$ cups sour cream
1 cup brown sugar

Spread apple pie filling in 13x9-inch pan. Sprinkle with cinnamon. Unroll crescent rolls and place over apples. Combine sour cream and brown sugar. Spread over roll dough. Bake at 375° for 40 to 45 minutes. Serve warm.

The Pick of the Crop

Apple-Cheese Casserole

1 stick oleo
1/2-1 cup sugar
1/2 pound Velveeta cheese

3/4 cup flour
1 can sliced apples (not pie
   filling)

Cream together oleo and sugar; mix with Velveeta cheese and flour. Pour sliced apples in buttered casserole. Spread cheese mixture on top. Bake at 350° for 30 minutes.

Tasting Tea Treasures

Berry Cobbler

1/4 cup soft butter
1/2 cup sugar
1 egg
1 cup flour
2 teaspoons baking powder

1/4 teaspoon salt
1/2 cup milk
1 1/2 cups blackberries or
   raspberries
1 cup berry juice

Cream together until light and fluffy the butter, sugar and egg. Sift together the flour, baking powder, salt. Mix alternately with 1/2 cup milk the dry mixture with sugar-shortening mixture. Beat until smooth. Sprinkle 1/2 cup sugar over berries. Pour batter into 11 1/2 x 7 1/2 x 1 1/8-inch greased pan or 10-inch casserole. Bake 45 minutes in 375° oven. During baking, the fruit and juice will go to bottom and a cake-like layer forms on top. Serves 6. Serve with cream.

Bell's Best

Caramel Dumplings

1 1/2 cups light brown sugar
1/8 teaspoon salt
2 tablespoons butter or
   margarine

1 3/4 cups boiling water

Mix all ingredients together in a large saucepan, and boil gently while mixing dough.

DOUGH:
3/4 cup all-purpose flour
1 teaspoon baking powder
1/4 cup sugar
Dash salt
1 tablespoon butter or
   margarine

1/4 cup milk
1/2 teaspoon vanilla
Whipped cream (optional)

In a mixing bowl, mix together the flour, baking powder, sugar, and salt. Cut in the butter; then add the milk and vanilla. Mix well and drop by teaspoons into sauce. Cover tightly and continue to cook slowly for 20 minutes, without removing lid. Serve in dessert dishes, topped with whipped cream.

Come and Dine

Lemon Mousse

1 cup sugar
2 tablespoons lemon juice

3/4 teaspoon grated lemon rind
2 cups heavy whipping cream

Mix together sugar and lemon juice. Add rind. Whip whipping cream and fold most of it into other mixture. Pour into parfait glasses and freeze. Remove minutes before serving and top with remaining whipped cream.

Tasting Tea Treasures

Chocolate Mousse de Cacao

2 cups whipping cream,
  divided
1 (12-ounce) package
  semisweet chocolate chips
2 teaspoons vanilla
1/8 teaspoon salt
5 large eggs, separated
1 envelope unflavored gelatin

1/4 cup créme de cacao
2 (3-ounce) packages
  ladyfingers, split
1/2 cup whipping cream,
  whipped and flavored with
  1-2 tablespoons créme de
  cacao, optional

Heat 1 cup whipping cream just to boiling point. Combine chocolate chips, vanilla and salt in a blender or a food processor; mix for 30 seconds. Add heated cream and continue mixing for 30 seconds more or until chocolate is completely melted. Add egg yolks and mix about 4 seconds. Soften gelatin in créme de cacao and stir into chocolate mixture. Beat egg whites until stiff and fold into chocolate mixture. Beat 1 cup whipping cream until stiff and fold into chocolate mixture. Line the sides and bottom of a 9-inch springform pan with ladyfingers; pour chocolate mixture into pan. Chill 6-8 hours; slice and serve. If desired, top with dollop of whipped cream flavored with créme de cacao. Serves 16.

Taste of the South

Lemon Cup Cake Pudding "Quickie"

2 1/2 tablespoons flour
3/4 cup sugar
1/4 teaspoon salt
1 tablespoon butter

2 eggs, separated
Grated lemon peel
1/4 cup lemon juice
1 cup sweet milk

Combine flour, sugar and salt with softened butter. Add egg yolks, lemon rind and juice, milk and stir. Fold in stiffly beaten egg whites. Pour into casserole and place it in a pan of warm water. Bake about 35 minutes at 350°. Will form a delicate cake-top layer with a custard sauce. Serve warm or chilled. Serves 6.

Gourmet of the Delta

Hotel Natchez Bread Pudding with Bourbon Sauce

The cooks of Natchez learned the secret of bread pudding: stale French bread and a good whiskey sauce. During the Yankee occupation of the city, many a Northern heart was stolen by this treat.

1 loaf French bread	3 tablespoons vanilla
1 quart milk	¹/₂ cup chopped pecans
3 eggs	1 cup raisins
2 cups sugar	1 tablespoon oleo

Soak bread in milk and work with back of a wooden spoon until it is well mixed. Add beaten eggs, sugar, vanilla, pecans, and raisins and combine well. Pour melted oleo in bottom of a heavy 7 x 11-inch oblong cake pan. Bake at 350° for 1¹/₂ hours or until very firm. Cool. Slice into squares. Top with Bourbon Sauce.

BOURBON SAUCE:

¹/₂ cup butter	3 tablespoons bourbon
1 cup sugar	whiskey
1 egg	

Cream butter and sugar together and cook in the top of a double boiler until the mixture is very hot and the sugar dissolves. Pour into a blender and add egg at top speed so that egg doesn't scramble. Cool. Add bourbon just before serving. Spoon sauce over bread pudding. Heat under broiler. Serves 8-10.

Cook with a Natchez Native

Brandy Alexander Soufflé

2 ounces unflavored gelatin
1/2 cup cold water
1 1/2 cups hot water
4 eggs, separated
3/4 cup sugar
1 (8-ounce) package cream
   cheese, softened

3 tablespoons créme de cacao
3 tablespoons brandy
1/4 cup sugar
1 cup heavy cream, whipped
Chocolate curls (optional)
Chocolate shavings (optional)

Cut a piece of aluminum foil to fit around a 1 1/2-quart souffle dish, allowing a 1-inch overlap; fold lengthwise into thirds. Lightly oil one side of the foil; wrap around outside of dish, oiled side against dish, allowing it to extend 3 inches above rim to form a collar. Secure with freezer tape.

Soften gelatin in cold water; stir. In a separate 2 1/2- quart casserole, microwave 1 2/ cups hot water at High for 5-9 minutes till boiling. Add gelatin mixture, stirring to dissolve. Beat egg yolks until thick and lemon colored; gradually add 3/4 cup sugar, beating well. Gradually stir in about 1/4 of the hot gelatin mixture; then stir into remaining hot mixture. Microwave at High 2-3 minutes or until thickened, stirring after 2 minutes.

Beat cream cheese until smooth; gradually add yolk mixture, beating well. Stir in creme de cacao and brandy; chill until slightly thickened.

Beat egg whites until foamy; gradually add 1/4 cup sugar, beating until stiff peaks form. Gently fold whipped cream and beaten egg whites into cream cheese mixture. Spoon mixture into collared souffle dish; chill until formed. Serve in champagne glasses. Garnish with chocolate curls and shavings. Serves 8-10.

The Country Mouse

Tres Elegant Chocolate Ice Box Cake

2 dozen lady fingers
3 bars Baker's German Sweet
    Chocolate
3 tablespoons sugar
3 tablespoons hot water

6 eggs
1 cup ground pecans
3/4 cup tiny marshmallows
1 pint whipping cream
Red cherries and whole pecans

Grease spring form pan lightly. Split lady fingers, making 1 layer on the bottom, breaking a few to fill up gaps. Stand lady fingers around pan, cake side to outside. Put chocolate, water and sugar in the top of a double boiler, stirring until it is melted and smooth. Take off fire. Add 1 egg yolk at a time, beating after each addition. Cook until thick. Cool. Beat egg whites stiff and fold into chocolate mixture. Add nuts and marshmallows. Pour into spring form pan. Put in refrigerator overnight. When ready to serve, put whipped cream on top of cake and decorate with cherries, whole pecans and grated ones, too. This cake freezes the best, even with cream on top. Take rim off before serving. This is a beautiful dessert.

The Country Gourmet (Miriam G. Cohn)

Strawberry Angel Pie

3/4 cup sugar
4 tablespoons cornstarch
1 1/2 cups boiling water
3 egg whites
3 tablespoons sugar

1 teaspoon vanilla flavoring
1 package frozen strawberries
10 individual baked tart shells
    or meringue shells
1 cup whipping cream

Combine sugar and cornstarch. Bring 1 1/2 cups water to a boil; stir sugar mixture into boiling water and cook, stirring constantly, until clear. Pour slowly into well-beaten egg whites beaten with 3 tablespoons sugar. Add vanilla. Fold in 2 tablespoons strawberries; pour mixture into baked tart shells or meringue shells. Cool. Serve with whipped cream and remaining strawberries. If fresh strawberries are in season, garnish each serving with one or two.

I Promised A Cookbook

Cherry Puffs

1 (8-ounce) can refrigerated
  crescent dinner rolls
1 (3-ounce) package cream
  cheese, softened
2 tablespoons powdered sugar

2 tablespoons finely chopped
  pecans
1 (10-ounce) bottle maraschino
  cherries, drained

On a cutting board, separate crescent dough into 4 rectangles, pressing perforations to seal. Cut each into 8 squares. Combine cream cheese, powdered sugar, and pecans. Spread each square of dough with cream cheese mixture. Place a cherry on each. Fold corners of dough over cherry to cover, and press edges to seal. Place, seam-side down, on ungreased cookie sheet. Bake at 375° for 15 minutes. Cool, then spread with Glaze.

GLAZE:

3/4 cup powdered sugar
1 tablespoon milk
1 tablespoon cherry juice

1/2 teaspoon vanilla
2 drops red food color
  (optional)

Combine all ingredients and mix until smooth. Spread over cooled cookies. Store in covered container in refrigerator. Yield: 32 puffs.

Come and Dine

Charlotte Russe

2 envelopes Knox gelatin	1 cup sugar
1/2 cup cold water	1 teaspoon vanilla
2 cups milk	2 cups cream, whipped
6 egg yolks	

Soften gelatin in cold water. Scald milk and stir into it egg yolks and sugar beaten together. Cook in double boiler until it thickens. Before removing from fire add gelatin and dissolve. Add vanilla, Cool and fold in whipped cream. This is good flavored with whiskey and may be poured over molds lined with ladyfingers. For chocolate charlotte, add two squares melted chocolate.

DAR Recipe Book

Polar Creams

2 (8-ounce) boxes semi-sweet chocolate	1/2 cup crushed Heath bars
2 tablespoons butter	1/2 cup blanched, slivered almonds, toasted
2 eggs	1 teaspoon vanilla
1 cup brown sugar	1 cup whipped cream
2/3 cup butter, melted	

Melt chocolate with butter and pour in muffin cups. Paint chocolate up sides of cups. Chill thoroughly. Beat eggs until thick and light. Add sugar, blending until dissolved. Add butter, candy, almonds and vanilla. Fold in whipped cream. Spoon into chocolate shells and freeze. Peel off muffin cups and let set for 10 minutes.

Tasting Tea Treasures

Frozen Lemon Pie

3 egg yolks, well beaten
Juice and rind of 1 lemon
2/3 cup sugar
1/2 teaspoon salt

1 cup heavy cream, whipped
3/4 cup crushed vanilla wafers
3 egg whites, beaten stiff

Combine in the order given, the first four ingredients and cook in saucepan until the consistency of custard, stirring constantly. Cool. Fold in beaten egg whites and then whipped cream.

Sprinkle vanilla wafer crumbs in long pyrex dish. Pour mixture on top of crumbs. Then sprinkle light coating of crumbs on top. Cover with plastic wrap and freeze. Cut in squares to serve.

Garnish with fresh strawberries, fresh sliced peaches, or a cherry. Serves 8.

Pineapple Gold

Frosty Strawberry Squares

1 cup sifted flour
1/4 cup brown sugar
1/2 cup chopped walnuts or
   pecans
1/2 cup butter, melted
2 egg whites
1 cup sugar
2 cups sliced fresh

strawberries or
   1 (10-ounce) package frozen
   strawberries, partially
   thawed
2 teaspoons lemon juice
1 teaspoon almond extract
1 cup heavy cream, whipped

Stir together first four ingredients. Spread evenly in shallow pan. Bake 20 minutes in 350° oven, stirring occasionally. Sprinkle 2/3 of this crumbed mixture in a 13x9x2-inch baking pan. Combine egg whites, sugar, berries, lemon juice, and almond extract in a large bowl. Beat at high speed until stiff peaks form—about 10 minutes. Fold in whipped cream. Top with remaining crumbed mixture. Freeze 6 hours or overnight. Cut in squares. Top with fresh straw-berries. Yield: 15 squares.

Variation: May also be made with frozen peaches.

The Mississippi Cookbook

French Pears

8 fresh, ripe, large pears
1 (8-ounce) package cream
  cheese

$^1/_2$-1 cup chopped pecans
2 tablespoons to $^1/_4$ cup
  powdered sugar

Carefully peel pears. Slice in half lengthwise and remove core. Do not break pear in the process. Set aside. Mix remaining ingredients according to taste. The mixture should have enough nuts to look pretty and provide enough crunch and enough powdered sugar to be slightly sweetened. Carefully stuff mixture into each pear half. Put stuffed pear halves together to form each whole pear again and wrap individually with plastic wrap. Store in covered container in refrigerator until serving time, preferably serve within 12 hours. To serve, place one pear in stemmed sherbet glass, pour warmed Chocolate Sauce over top, and sprinkle with crushed pecans, if desired.

CHOCOLATE SAUCE:

1 stick good margarine
4 squares semi-sweet baking
  chocolate

3 cups sugar
1 large can evaporated milk
1 teaspoon vanilla

In double boiler melt margarine and chocolate. Gradually add sugar. Stir constantly and blend well. Add canned milk. Blend well. Cook 10 minutes or until chocolate forms soft ball (has some body) when small amount is dropped in cup of cool water. Remove from heat. Stir in 1 teaspoon vanilla. Cool. Serve warm over pears. Store in refrigerator.

The Gulf Gourmet

Sherried Strawberries

4 egg yolks
1 cup sugar
2-4 tablespoons sherry

1 cup whipped cream
2 boxes strawberries (sliced
    in half)

Combine yolks and sugar in double boiler, stirring constantly for about 15 minutes. Remove from flame and add sherry. Chill. When cold, add 1 cup whipped cream and chill until ready to serve. Just before serving combine sherried mix with strawberries. Serves 8.

Best of Bayou Cuisine

University Club Sauce for Fresh Strawberries

8 ounces raisins
2 ounces brandy
$^{1}/_{2}$ cup sugar
16 ounces sour cream

1 teaspoon cinnamon
Dash of nutmeg
Fresh strawberries

Purée raisins and brandy in blender. Stir in sugar, sour cream, cinnamon and nutmeg. Pour over fresh chilled strawberries.
    Note: Can be done the day before.

Tasting Tea Treasures

Raspberry Cognac Sauce

1 (12-ounce) jar red raspberry
    jelly or preserves
1 tablespoon corn starch

$^{1}/_{4}$ cup water
$^{1}/_{4}$ cup cognac

If using preserves heat and put through sieve to remove seeds. Mix corn starch and water with fingers. Place all ingredients in saucepan and cook over medium heat, stirring frequently until thickened and clear, about 5 minutes. Pour and refrigerate. Use on cheesecake, pound cake or ice cream as well as bread pudding.

Into the Second Century

Cherries Jubilee
(William Winter)

William Winter was Governor of Mississippi. A Democrat, he served from 1979 to 1983. (The following recipe was submitted by his wife, Elise Winter.)

1 (1-pound) can (2 cups) dark, pitted sweet cherries
1/4 cup sugar
2 tablespoons cornstarch

Cherry syrup
1/4 cup brandy, kirsch or cherry brandy
Vanilla ice cream

Drain cherries, reserving syrup. In a saucepan, blend sugar and cornstarch, gradually stir in reserved syrup, mixing well. Cook and stir over medium heat until mixture thickens and bubbles. Remove from heat; stir in cherries. Turn into heat-proof bowl or top pan or a chafing dish. (Be sure bottom of chafing dish is filled with hot water; keep hot over flame.) Heat brandy or kirsch in a small metal pan with a long handle. (If desired, pour heated brandy into a large ladle.) Carefully ignite heated brandy and pour over cherry mixture. Stir to blend brandy into sauce and serve immediately over ice cream. Makes 2 cups.

Note: The Governor is really not a cook—in fact, he's the sort of person who hardly knows where the kitchen is!

He first discovered cherries jubilee at a lovely old restaurant in New Orleans years ago and on rare occasions he likes to try his hand at it. Even though he dribbles cherry juice all over the kitchen, that doesn't slow him down a bit. He's very fond of ice cream and even if the kirsch doesn't ignite or the cherries aren't quite sweet enough, it's still a success in his book! With a Dagwood smile, he serves it up in style to an admiring family proud of his latest accomplishment.

The Great American Politician's Cookbook

Peach Buttermilk Ice Cream

1 tablespoon unflavored
   gelatin, (1 envelope)
1¼ cups sugar, divided
2 cups buttermilk
1 egg, beaten

¼ teaspoon salt
4 cups whipping cream
1 tablespoon vanilla extract
2 cups fresh peaches, mashed

In saucepan combine gelatin, 1 cup sugar and buttermilk. Dissolve gelatin mixture over low heat, stirring occasionally. Gradually add hot mixture to egg, stirring constantly. Stir in salt, cream and vanilla. Combine mashed peaches and ¼ cup sugar; add to mixture. Chill and churn-freeze.

Note: If fresh peaches are not available, mashed, canned freestone peaches may be used. Do not add sugar to peaches. Regular milk may be substituted for buttermilk in the recipe. Yield: approximately 3 quarts.

Giant Houseparty Cookbook

Ice Cream
(John Leslie)

John Leslie, Mayor of Oxford.

6-8 whole eggs
2 cups sugar
2 heaping tablespoons
   cornstarch
2 quarts milk

Dash of salt
1 large can Pet milk
1 cup whipping cream
1 tablespoon vanilla

Blend eggs, 1 cup sugar, conrstarch in blender. Add to 2 quarts milk. Add another cup sugar and salt.

Place mixture in heavy pan (I use bottom of pressure cooker) and cook until mixture coats spoon. (It should not boil.) Take off heat. When cooled, add Pet milk, cream, and vanilla. Place in electric or hand freezer and freeze until hard.

The Great American Politician's Cookbook

Raspberry Sorbet

2 cups water
1 cup sugar
1 (10-ounce) package frozen
    raspberries

$1/3$ cup lemon juice
Pinch of salt
1-2 tablespoons Kirsch

Combine water and sugar in saucepan. Stir over high heat to dissolve the sugar. Bring to a boil; reduce heat and let boil for 5 minutes without stirring. Remove from heat and let cool at room temperature.

Strain juice from berries to make $2/3$ cup; discard berries. Stir in lemon juice and salt. Pour into a shallow 9-inch square metal pan. Place in freezer and freeze until firm throughout. Remove from freezer. Break up with a wooden spoon; beat with mixer or in food processor until free of lumps. Stir in Kirsch. Freeze until firm again. Yield: 6 servings.

Vintage Vicksburg

Pickles, Jellies, Sauces

Marine Life—one of many attractions on Mississippi's Gulf Coast.

Summer Squash and Zucchini Pickles

Pretty yellow summer squash and green zucchini taste so good and they seem to grow like weeds. Remember, the smaller the squash, the tastier it will be. I save all the small ones for pickling. If you like, you can substitute Jerusalem artichokes for the squash; just use brown sugar and add four red hot peppers.

8 cups sliced yellow squash or zucchini	Salt
2 large onions, thinly sliced	2 cups cider vinegar
4 medium red or green bell peppers, seeded and sliced into rings	2 cups sugar 2 teaspoons yellow mustard seed 2 teaspoons celery seed

In an earthenware crock or a stainless-steel, glass, or enameled container, arrange a layer of the squash, onions, and peppers and salt the layer liberally. Continue adding layers and salt. Cover and set aside for 1 hour. Drain off the liquid but *do not rinse.*

In a large pot, bring the vinegar, sugar, mustard seed, and celery seed to the boil over moderately high heat. Add the vegetables and bring back to the boil. Count to 10; remove from heat. Ladle into hot sterilized pint jars, fill to ¼ inch from the top, and seal. Process for 5 minutes in a boiling water bath, if desired. Makes about 6 pints.

Aunt Freddie's Pantry

Green Tomato Pickles

I soak these sliced green tomatoes in pickling lime because it acts as a firming agent—the slices hold their shape much better after this treatment. Serve these pickles with old-fashioned pimiento and cheese sandwiches or chicken sandwiches.

1 cup pickling lime (calcium hydroxide)*	5 pounds (10 cups) sugar
7 pounds green tomatoes	1 (1.12-ounce) box pickling spice, tied in a double thickness of cheesecloth
2 quarts cider vinegar	

CONTINUED

CONTINUED

In an earthenware crock or large glass jar, dissolve the pickling lime in 1 gallon of water. Wash the green tomatoes and slice them 1/4-inch thick. Soak the slices in the lime overnight.

Next day, wash the tomato slices several times; try not to break the slices. Place the tomatoes in a large pot and add the vinegar, sugar, and pickling spice. Bring to the boil over moderate heat, reduce the heat to low, and cook until tender, about 10 minutes. Remove the bag of spices, pack in hot sterilized jars, and seal. Makes 8 to 10 pints.

*Available at most drugstores.

Aunt Freddie's Pantry

Corn Relish

My family loves this corn relish so much that it's hard to keep on hand. You can serve it just anytime at all—it's so versatile, it goes with almost everything. My nephew, Lee, likes to serve it alongside steamed greens (beet, turnip, or kale) sprinkled with vinegar.

20 ears of corn
1/4 cup salt
2 1/2 cups sugar
1 (1.12-ounce) tin dry mustard
1 tablespoon turmeric
2 quarts white vinegar
1 medium cabbage, sliced
   (about 3 cups)
1 1/2 cups chopped green bell
   pepper
1 1/2 cups chopped sweet red
   pepper
6 large onions, chopped
1 (4-ounce) jar pimientos,
   drained and chopped
4 red hot peppers, seeded and
   chopped
6-8 celery ribs, chopped (about
   2 cups)

Cut the corn off the cobs. In a large pot, combine the salt, sugar, dry mustard, turmeric, and vinegar. Bring to the boil over moderate heat. Add all of the vegetables, reduce the heat, and simmer for 45 minutes.

Pack into hot, sterilized jars and fill with liquid, leaving 1/4 inch of headspace, and seal. Process for 15 minutes in a boiling water bath, if desired. Makes about 10 pints.

Aunt Freddie's Pantry

Pear Preserves

Pear preserves are soothing to eat with breakfast toast on a hot summer morning. If you like, add a stick of cinnamon and cook it with the pears.

16 cups peeled, sliced pears   **Juice of 1 lemon**
2 pounds (4 cups) sugar   **2 cups water**

Place the pears, sugar, and lemon juice in a large pot and add 2 cups of water. Cook over moderate heat until the pears are tender and the syrup is thick.*

Ladle the preserves into hot, sterilized jars and seal. Process for 5 minutes in a boiling water bath, if desired. Makes 8 to 10 half pints.

*I like to add about 3 drops of red food coloring because it makes the pears look more appetizing.

Aunt Freddie's Pantry

Ponder Preserves

Rind of 1 large watermelon   **8 or more whole cloves**
   (25-30 pound)   **16 sticks cinnamon**
Salt water (4 tablespoons salt   **A little mustard seed**
   to 1 quart water)   **Food coloring, optional**
8 cups sugar
4 cups vinegar

Peel and remove all green and pink from watermelon rind, leaving only the white part. Cut in 1-inch cubes and soak overnight in salt water. Drain, cover with fresh water and cook until almost tender. Drain again.

Mix vinegar and sugar in large pot, stirring until sugar dissolves. Tie spices in a cheese-cloth bag; add to syrup, heat to boiling and allow to set for 15 minutes. Add the rind and cook until transparent. Add green or red food coloring before the end of boiling if desired. Pack boiling hot into sterilized jars and seal at once. Makes 5-6 pints. Must do 6 weeks ahead.

Standing Room Only

Raspberry Fig Preserves

2 or 3 pounds ripe figs
2 tablespoons baking soda
3 cups sugar
1 box Sure Jell

1 (3-ounce) package raspberry
Jello
3 tablespoons lemon juice
1 tablespoon red food coloring

Wash figs with soda. Rinse several times to be sure all soda is removed. Peel and mash figs in order to have 3 cups. Put mashed figs, Sure Jell, sugar, Jello and lemon juice in large pot. Cook over medium heat, stirring, and only let it boil for 3 minutes. Add red food coloring. Pack into sterilized jars and seal. Makes six 1/2-pints.

The Country Gourmet (Miriam G. Cohn)

Mrs. McKenzie's Wine Jelly

3/4 cup water, room
temperature
1 box Mrs. Wages Home-Jell
powdered fruit pectin

1 (25.4-ounce) bottle wine
(Red, Sweet White or Rose)
4 1/2 cups sugar

In a large enamel kettle, using a wooden spoon, stir pectin into the water until dissolved. Bring to a boil over high heat; boil 1 minute, stirring constantly. Add wine, then sugar, stirring constantly, reducing heat to medium. Cook for 5 or 6 minutes to dissolve sugar. Do not boil. Remove from heat, skim with metal spoon as necessary. Quickly pour into hot sterile glasses. Cover with hot paraffin or use seal-type lids and rings. Chill before serving. Delicious with meats.

Note: For a milder flavor, add water to wine for total not to exceed 32 fluid ounces. A few drops of red food coloring added during final cooking stage enhances the color when using red wine.

Dixie Dining

Cranmerry Berry Ice

1 package cranberries
1 cup water
1/2 cup orange juice
1/3 cup lemon juice

Sugar to taste
1 (8-ounce) bottle ginger ale
2 teaspoons grated orange rind

Cook cranberries with water until tender. Put through sieve, getting as much of the pulp as possible. Add orange juice, lemon juice and sweeten to taste. Add ginger ale and grated orange rind. Freeze. Several hours before serving, put in electric mixing bowl or food processor and beat until smooth. Fill sherbet cups and refreeze. Serve with meal instead of cranberry sauce.

Note: This means Christmas to my family. I dreamed this recipe up on Christmas and it is a favorite, not only for our family, but for many of our friends. Nick named it when he was three years old. He couldn't pronounce it very well but he surely could eat it, and still can!

Southern Legacies

Holiday Relish

1 pound fresh cranberries
2 apples (Rome variety)
2 oranges

1 lemon
2 1/2 cups sugar

Wash and sort cranberries, removing stems and soft berries. Peel, core and quarter apples. Cut oranges and lemons into quarters, removing seeds and pithy centers. Put cranberries, apples, oranges and lemon through food chopper, using the medium blade. Add sugar, stirring until all ingredients are evenly mixed. Chill before serving. Store in refrigerator. Makes 1 1/2 quarts.

Note: Delicious with turkey or baked ham. This is a thanksgiving and Christmas tradition in my family.

Dixie Dining

Pickled Eggs

1 1/2 dozen hard-cooked eggs
1 medium-size onion
1 3/4 cups white vinegar
3/4 cup water
3 tablespoons brown sugar
1/2 teaspoon salt

1/4 teaspoon garlic salt
5 peppercorns
1 whole clove
Few dill seeds
Piece of ginger root

Prepare, peel and cool eggs. Thinly slice 1 medium onion. Put onion slices into a saucepan and add other ingredients. Set over medium heat and bring to boil. Reduce heat; simmer about 5 minutes. Put the eggs into 2 (1-quart) screw-top jars. Pour one half of the vinegar mixture into each jar. Cover, cool, and set in refrigerator. Before serving, let eggs stand for several hours.

Inverness Cook Book

Curry Sauce for Raw Cauliflower and Shrimp

1 pint thick homemade
    mayonnaise
1 tablespoon celery seed
2 small pods garlic, mashed or
    grated very fine
1 tablespoon prepared
    horseradish

2 teaspoons curry powder
3 or 4 teaspoons Lea and
    Perrins
Lemon juice to taste
2 teaspoons prepared mustard

Mix ingredients and chill.

DAR Recipe Book

Special Mustard Sauce

3/4 cup dry mustard
1 cup vinegar

2 eggs
1 cup sugar

Combine mustard and vinegar. Let stand overnight. Beat eggs and sugar. Mix with mustard mixture. Cook in double boiler 20 minutes, stirring frequently until thickened.

Special Menus for Very Special Occasions

Barbecue Sauce

You can use this barbecue sauce two ways: Either mix in the oil that comes to the top when you cook this sauce and brush meat or chicken with it, or do what I do and brush them with just the oil (which will have absorbed all those good flavors) and serve the thick tomatoey sauce separately with chunks of French bread to dip it in.

1 cup full-flavored vegetable
  oil (preferably peanut)
2 cups chopped celery
2 cups chopped onions
1/2 cup chopped green bell
  pepper

2 cloves garlic, minced
1 cup cider vinegar
1 teaspoon dry mustard
1 (35-ounce) can peeled
  tomatoes with their juice

In a large saucepan, heat the oil over moderate heat. Sauté the celery, onions, bell pepper, and garlic until tender, about 10 minutes. Add the vinegar, dry mustard, and tomatoes with their juice, breaking the tomatoes up with a wooden spoon. Cook over low heat for at least 30 minutes, until thick and flavorful. Refrigerate if not using at once. Will keep at least a month. Makes about 4 cups.

Aunt Freddie's Pantry

Tomato Chili Sauce

24 large tomatoes
8 large onions
4 hot peppers
2 tablespoons salt

3 sticks whole cinnamon
2 cups brown sugar
4 cups cider vinegar

Scald tomatoes and slip peelings off. Cut up. Chop onions and peppers. Put all ingredients in large pan and cook down until thick. This takes several hours. Do not let burn. Remove sticks of cinnamon. Makes 7 pints.

The Cook's Book

Index

The International Ballet Competition is held in Jackson, one of four cities in the world sanctioned to hold this prestigious event.

Catalog of
Contributing
Cookbooks

Old bridge crossing the mighty Mississippi River at Vicksburg.

CATALOG OF CONTRIBUTING COOKBOOKS

All recipes in this book have been submitted from the cookbooks shown on the following pages. Individuals who wish to obtain a copy of a particular book can do so by sending a check or money order to the address listed. Prices are subject to change. Please note the postage and handling charges that may be required. State residents add applicable sales tax. Retailers are invited to call or write to the same address for wholesale information. Some of these contributing cookbooks may have gone out of print since the original publication of this book. Quail Ridge Press is proud to preserve America's food heritage by keeping many of their recipes in print.

ACCENT ONE
by Frank Simpson, Jr.
Bentonia, MS

Accent One is an anthology of original, traditional and contemporary recipes from files of family and friends. Although there are some excellent processed foods and canned soups on the market today, we omit them from our preferred recipes, advising use of homemade bases and sauces in tribute to our mother's and grandmother's cooking.

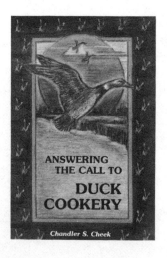

ANSWERING THE CALL TO DUCK COOKERY
by Chandler S. Cheek
Biloxi, MS

Answering the Call to Duck Cookery is a fun to read, multi-tested treatment of recipes and techniques which make wild and domestic duck and the dishes that go with them delightful and well within the reach of the interested beginner. Currently out of print.

AUNT FREDDIE'S PANTRY

by Freddie Bailey
400 So. Commerce
Natchez, MS 39120   601-442-9974

Aunt Freddie's Pantry includes recipes for all sorts of sweet and savory pantry items, as well as treasured recipes for foods that go particularly well with them. There are 45 recipes in all, and the book is illustrated with charming photographs of Aunt Freddie and her jelly kitchen.

$7.95 Retail price
$1.50 Postage and handling

Make check payable to Bailey's Jelly Kitchen
ISBN 0-517-55300-7

BEST OF BAYOU CUISINE

St. Stephens Episcopal Church
P O Box 1005   601/887-4365
Indianola, MS 38751   or 800/343-1583

Originally published in 1970, *Bayou Cuisine* sold nearly 100,000 copies and is considered a classic cookbook on the special cuisine of the Mississippi Delta. This new version includes only the most popular recipes from the original edition plus nearly 100 new recipes that feature the cooking skills of a new generation of Delta cooks.

$14.95 Retail price
$3.00 Postage and handling

Make check payable to Bayou Cuisine

BELL'S BEST

Telephone Pioneers of America
P O Box 811 (110 Landmark Center)
Jackson, MS 39205   601/961-1993

In 792 pages, *Bell's Best* features 2002 recipes from employees and their families of BellSouth Telephone Company in Mississippi. The Pioneers (over 500,000 in the United States and Canada and over 4,000 in Mississippi) are non-profit and monies are designated to charitable activities and community service projects.

$10.00 Retail price
$2.00 Postage and handling

Make check payable to Telephone Pioneers

BELL'S BEST 2

Telephone Pioneers of America
P O Box 811 (110 Landmark Center)
Jackson, MS 39205   601/961-1993

Over 1800 recipes in 690 pages, a companion book to *Bell's Best,* our first edition. Over 111,000 copies sold to date. Recipes collected from Bell System employees in the state of Mississippi. Proceeds to charitable projects adopted by the Pioneer organization.

$10.00   Retail price
  $2.00   Postage and handling
Make check payable to Telephone Pioneers

BOUQUET GARNI

Pascagoula-Moss Point Junior Auxiliary
Pascagoula, MS

Bouquet Garni is a collection of 650 outstanding recipes contributed to the book by our membership. Twice tested, each recipe is excelled by the next. Seafood and Gulf Coast cuisine are predominant. Excellent sketches of Jackson County historical sites and other points of interest appear throughout. A must for collectors. Currently out of print.

COME AND DINE

by Naomi Fonville
Lumberton, MS

Come and Dine is a Menu-Cookbook by former home economist Naomi Fonville. It has 155 pages of household hints and enticing recipes for preparing complete meals, and includes 26 menus, plus 153 recipes for breakfast, lunches, dinners, family meals, holiday affairs and parties.

THE COOK'S BOOK

Calvary Episcopal Church
Cleveland, MS

Cooks and critics alike have enjoyed *The Cook's Book* through its three editions. With over 700 recipes contributed by 400 cooks, *The Cook's Book* features recipes from the everyday to the gourmet in 14 sections including three unique sections—outdoor, diet and beverage. It was "written by cooks for cooks." Currently out of print.

COOK WITH A NATCHEZ NATIVE

by Bethany Ewald Bultman
Myrtle Bank Publishers
Natchez, MS

Cook with a Natchez Native includes a brief tracing of the origin of cuisine that is typically Natchez-Indian, Spanish, Mediterranean, French, English, Irish, Scotch and the American "melting pot." Each recipe is preceded by a paragraph of history or description of the food selection in the charming flavor of the Old South.

THE COUNTRY GOURMET

by Miriam G. Cohn
P O Box 13077
Alexandria, LA 71315   318/445-6590

The Country Gourmet has 200 pages and 500 recipes. Miriam has been collecting recipes for 30 years— these have been tried and retried, the ingredients measured and re-measured, the directions written and rewritten. Consequently, this is a personal collection of delicious goodness from a Mississippi kitchen that is so explicit, a beginning cook can produce masterpieces!

$12.00 Retail price
 $2.00 Postage and handling

Make check payable to Miriam G. Cohn

271

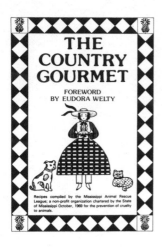

THE COUNTRY GOURMET
Mississippi Animal Rescue League
Jackson, MS

This Mississippi Animal Rescue League operates solely on private contributions with no city, county or state aid. No animal is ever turned away from the League. All proceeds from the sale of this cookbook goes toward maintaining the League, a non-profit corporation. A cookbook for animal lovers who like good food! Currently out of print.

THE COUNTRY MOUSE
by Sally Walton and Faye Wilkinson
Quail Ridge Press
P O Box 123   601/825-2063
Brandon, MS 39043   or 800/343-1583

When the country mouse visits the city mouse, they dine on quick, easy, usually microwave cheese dishes that fit the fast-paced lifestyle of the city. And each chapter continues the delightful visits of the country mouse while presenting a marvelous collection of cheese recipes for all occasions and tastes. Cheesylicious!

$5.95   Retail price
$3.00   Postage and handling

Make check payable to Quail Ridge Press

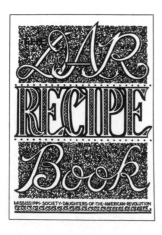

DAR RECIPE BOOK
Daughters of the American Revolution,
Mississippi State Society
Brandon, MS

A fantastic collection of Mississippi cuisine. Tested, tasty and reliable recipes. Special sections: Pre-planned menus, antebellum "receipts" of Old Natchez, Pink Tea Menu of a Mississippi First Lady, Mississippi game treats. Useful for brides and gourmet cooks. Truly a taste of the Old South. Currently out of print.

DIXIE DINING

GFWC-Mississippi Federation of Women's Clubs
2407 North State Street
Jackson, MS 39216   601/366-2652

Dixie Dining has 550 recipes submitted by club-women from all over Mississippi. In addition to many Southern-style, family recipes, it features a "Cooking for a Group" section and numerous microwave recipes. Chapter openings have photographs of table settings taken at various places of interest throughout Mississippi.

$9.00 Retail price
$1.25 Postage and handling

Make check payable to Mississippi Federation of Women's Clubs

ISBN 0-939114-41-0

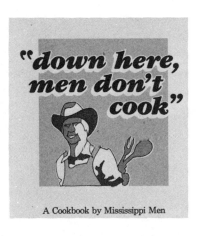

A Cookbook by Mississippi Men

DOWN HERE MEN DON'T COOK

Southern Images
Jackson, MS

More than 200 Mississippi men who love to cook contributed everything from Perfect Boiled Eggs to venison specialties and gourmet originals. Inspired by a male state official's assertion to Geraldine Ferraro that "Southern men can't cook," this book debunks the myth. It is eminently readable and a sought-after collector's item. Currently out of print.

FAMILY SECRETS

by Denise Wilson
1913 McClain
Greenville, MS 38701   662/378-9624

Family Secrets is a spiral-bound collection of 300 recipes from the author's family and her husband's family. The recipes are varied with "old family favorites" to the more contemporary ones. *Family Secrets* has been widely accepted, having been published for less than one year and already in its 3rd printing.

$7.00 Retail price
$3.00 Postage and handling

Make check payable to Family Secrets

FESTIVAL COOKBOOK

Humphreys Academy Patrons
P O Box 179
Belzoni, MS 39038   662/247-1572

Festival Cookbook is named for this time of celebration of one of America's newest food industries—catfish! Over 600 recipes in 347 pages with a special section on catfish, plus interesting "catfish facts" and artwork by local artists. Not *just* a catfish cookbook, but also favorite recipes of Delta cooks.

$11.95 Retail price
 $1.00 Postage and handling

Make check payable to Festival Cookbook
ISBN 0-9610058-0-7

The Garden Clubs of Mississippi, Inc.

GARDENERS' GOURMET II

Garden Clubs of Mississippi, Inc.
Yazoo City, MS

Gardeners' Gourmet is a collection of recipes from members of the Garden Clubs of Mississippi, from the Tennessee border to the Mississippi Gulf Coast. Artwork is by Bill Garbo and it was edited by Mrs. L. A. Gray, Jr. There are over 1,000 recipes in 268 pages. Currently out of print.

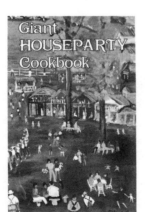

GIANT HOUSEPARTY COOKBOOK

Philadelphia-Neshoba County Chamber of Commerce
P O Box 51
Philadelphia, MS 39350   601/656-1742

Giant Houseparty was the result of a project by the Philadelphia Rotary Club, which for many years distributed mimeographed recipe booklets at annual pancake suppers. *Giant Houseparty* has plenty good eating in its 388 pages, including a section of famous Neshoba County Fair recipes (over 700 in all!).

$16.95 Retail price
 $3.00 Postage and handling

Make check payable to Giant Houseparty

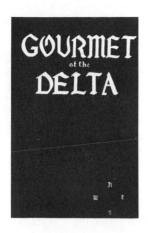

GOURMET OF THE DELTA

St. Paul's Episcopal Churchwomen
Box 25
Hollandale, MS 38748   662/827-2655

Gourmet of the Delta features recipes compiled by St. John's Women's Auxiliary in Leland and St. Paul's Women's Auxiliary in Hollandale. Now with 268 pages, it has been reprinted and supplemented many times.   Each chapter opening has a dinner party menu beneath a drawing of a home or place of interest in the Delta.

$7.50   Retail price
$1.00   Postage and handling

Make check payable to Gourmet of the Delta

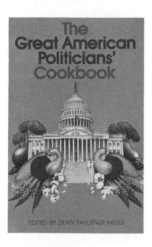

THE GREAT AMERICAN POLITICIAN'S COOKBOOK

Yoknapatawpha Press
Oxford, MS

Over 350 delicious recipes by Mayors, Governors, Congressmen, Senators and Presidents. It was edited by Dean Faulkner Wells (William Faulkner's niece) and contains not only good recipes, but interesting and humorous reading throughout.   240 pages. Currently out of print.

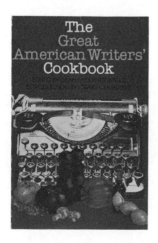

THE GREAT AMERICAN WRITERS' COOKBOOK

Yoknapatawpha Press
Oxford, MS

Here are 200 recipes from 175 American writers, edited by Dean Faulkner Wells and including a foreword by Craig Claiborne. *Writer's Digest* says, "*The Great American Writers' Cookbook* will keep you laughing all the way to the kitchen." 224 pages. Currently out of print.

GREAT FLAVORS OF MISSISSIPPI

Southern Flavors, Inc.
P O Box 922
Pine Bluff, AR 71613   870/536-8221

Clarksdale Press Register calls this cookbook a winner and says your kitchen counter will nominate it for the best-seller list! *Jackson Daily News* says it's the flavor of Mississippi that the editors of this cookbook savor. Peppered throughout the 160 pages are Mississippi Facts, Festivals, Notables and Real Mississippi Folks Facts. Easy-to-use flip-card trim size.

$8.95   Retail price
$1.55   Postage and handling

Make check payable to Great Flavors of Mississippi

THE GULF GOURMET

Westminster Academy
5003 Lawson Avenue
Gulfport, MS 39507   228/868-1312

The Gulf Gourmet presents selected recipes from the Mississippi Gulf Coast. In its 7 x 10-inch, full-color cover format, it features over 500 tested recipes with easy-to-read uniform directions. It also features beautiful area photographs throughout the book and an informative "Notes From Times Past" historical sketch.

$14.95   Retail price
$3.00   Postage and handling

Make check payable to Westminster Academy
ISBN 0-9611062-0-4

HORS D'OEUVRES EVERYBODY LOVES

by Mary Leigh Furrh and Jo Barksdale
Quail Ridge Press
P O Box 123   601/825-2063
Brandon, MS 39043   or 800/343-1583

Exquisite hors d'oeuvre recipes in 19 party menus ranging from baby showers to tailgate picnics. Craig Claiborne (*New York Times*) says: "This is an enormously imaginative, highly creative and inspiring book for anyone looking for new and appetizing ideas. It's fun to browse through and a nice addition to the kitchen."

$5.95   Retail price
$3.00   Postage and handling

Make check payable to Quail Ridge Press
ISBN 0-937552-11-9

276

HOSPITALITY HEIRLOOMS
South Jackson Civic League
P O Box 8481
Jackson, MS 39204   601/373-3848

It was the intention of the South Jackson Civic League to record our community's culinary and historical heritage by presenting in *Hospitality Heirlooms* cherished recipes and landmarks worthy of preservation. It is our hope that you will discover that our heirlooms will be yours in years to come. The book has 282 pages and 765 recipes.

  $10.00 Retail price
  $1.75 Postage and handling

Make check payable to South Jackson Civic League

INTO THE SECOND CENTURY
French Camp Academy
French Camp, MS

One hundred ninety pages featuring pictures and narratives telling the unique history and mission of French Camp Academy, as well as 322 favorite recipes of alumnae and supporters. This Limited Centennial Edition commemorates 100 years of providing a Christian school/home for children with problems, not of their own making. Currently out of print.

INVERNESS COOK BOOK
All Saints Episcopal Guild
P O Box 15
Inverness, MS 38753   662/265-5794

The *Inverness Cook Book* is a 200-page book in its fourth printing of "Southern-cooking" recipes compiled by members of All Saints Episcopal Church. There is a brief history of the church along with numerous drawings of many of the lovely homes in Inverness.

  $10.00 Retail price
  $1.50 Postage and handling

Make check payable to All Saints Episcopal Guild

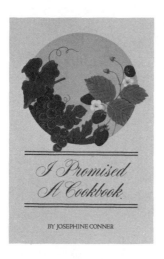

I PROMISED A COOKBOOK

by Josephine M. Conner

I Promised A Cookbook provides 475 favorite recipes within its 318 pages from the hundreds of parties Josephine Conner catered over the past half-century in the Mississippi Delta. The four special divisions list a variety of menus with the recipes immediately following each menu. Also included are some of Josephine's suggestions and comments. Currently out of print.

JUST A SPOONFUL

by Phyllis Harper
2720 Lawndale Drive   662/8742-2611
Tupelo, MS 38801   or 662/840-5555

500 recipes from *Northeast Mississippi Daily Journal's* longtime food columnist. Gourmet Sam Woodward of Big Spring, Texas wrote: "A compendium of wit and wisdom liberally mixed with genuinely fine country cuisine . . . a slice of Americana that can never again be—except in the minds, hearts and kitchens of the reader . . . a cookbook collector's kitchen staple."

$8.95   Retail price
$2.00   Postage and handling

Make check payable to *Just A Spoonful*
ISBN 0-9615704-0-7

MADISON COUNTY COOKERY

Madison County Chamber of Commerce
Canton, MS

With 786 recipes in 18 special sections—including microwave—*Madison County Cookery* features Southern cuisine at its finest, from "down-home" cooking to special party dishes. Illustrated with sketches of historic Madison County and the famous Canton Flea Market, it also includes favorite recipes from Flea Market artists and craftsmen. Currently out of print.

THE MISSISSIPPI COOKBOOK

University Press of Mississippi
3825 Ridgewood Road
Jackson, MS 39211   601/432-6205

The Mississippi Cookbook, with over 1,000 of Mississippi's most popular recipes, was compiled by the Home Economics Division of the Mississippi Cooperative Extension Service. Its 476-page eighth edition is now spiral-bound and features a special section of Governor's "Mansion Favorites." This is an outstanding book which preserves the state's culinary heritage.

$17.95 Retail price
$ 4.00 Postage and handling

Make check payable to University Press of Mississippi

ISBN 0-87805-3816

MISSISSIPPI MEMORIES, SECOND SERVINGS

American Cancer Society, Mississippi Division, Inc.
Jackson, MS

This delightful, spiral-bound, 190-page cookbook will make a treasured memory of every meal you cook! From Invited Guests (restaurateurs) to Mississippi Dignitaries and Old Family Favorites; from Appetizers to Desserts, every recipe reflects the fine culinary heritage of our state. A donation to a good cause. Currently out of print.

MY MOTHER COOKED MY WAY THROUGH HARVARD WITH THESE CREOLE RECIPES

by Oscar Rogers, Jr., Office of the President
5932 Holbrook Drive
Jackson, MS 39206   601/981-1370

A collection of more than 200 of the best recipes that can be found anywhere, with a moving tribute by a son to his mother for her work and sacrifice that enabled him to receive two advanced degrees from Harvard University. Mrs. Walter Tillman, his mother, prepared delicious creole dishes for the leading families of Natchez and New Orleans.

$5.95 Retail price
$3.00 Postage and handling

Make check payable to Claflin College

NATCHEZ NOTEBOOK OF COOKING
Trinity Episcopal Day School
Natchez, MS

Recipes for this cookbook have been collected from the files of parents, grandparents, relatives or close friends of current Trinity school students. In an effort to sponsor a truly fabulous cookbook, many people searched their files to find just the right tried-and-true recipe. We tested them all and hope you agree! 155 pages. Currently out of print.

THE PICK OF THE CROP TWO
North Sunflower Academy
148 Academy Road
Drew, MS 38737   662/756-2547

The Pick of the Crop Two contains 370 pages of the best collection of recipes ever compiled. The Delta, with its unique way of life, brings you a cookbook that is truly, "The Pick of the Crop." Special features: Maids of Cotton, Simply Southern, Rice is Special, Hunters' Delight, The Future Way.

  $20.28 Retail price (includes tax)
   $4.00 Postage and handling
Make check payable to The Pick of the Crop Two
ISBN 0-918544-17-3

The
PILGRIMAGE GARDEN CLUB
Antiques Forum Cookbook

Stanton Hall
NATCHEZ, MISSISSIPPI

PILGRIMAGE GARDEN CLUB ANTIQUES FORUM COOKBOOK
Pilgrimage Garden Club, Inc.
P O Box 347
Natchez, MS 39120   601/446-6631

The Pilgrimage Garden Club sponsors the Antique Forum to help stimulate interest in the field of decorative arts prior to 1865. Each year speakers come to Natchez with valuable historical information and are treated to delicious recipes made in the members' private kitchens. By request, they are shared in this book.

  $7.95 Retail price
Make check payable to Pilgrimage Garden Club

PINEAPPLE GOLD

by Joann Hulett Dobbins
419 Windover Circle
Meridian, MS 39305   601/483-5081

Pineapple Gold represents glorious Mississippi Hospitality and will welcome family and friends into the warmth of your home and hearth. Joann Hulett Dobbins has compiled this 15-chapter collection of southern family favorites. Recipes simple enough for the beginner—or a challenge for the gourmet. Tastemaker Award Nominee, 1983. Honored by Mississippi Legislature, 1985.

$10.95 Retail price
  $1.50 Postage and handling

Make check payable to *Pineapple Gold*
ISBN 0-9610540-0-X

A SALAD A DAY

by Ruth Moorman and Lalla Williams
Quail Ridge Press
P O Box 123   601/825-2063
Brandon, MS 39043   or 800/343-1583

Monday's child is fair of face, Tuesday's child is full of grace . . . Wednesday's woes are brightened by colorful vegetable salads. And since Thursday's child has *far to go,* hearty meat salads provide the necessary protein. A delightful presentation of wholesome, fresh salads and dressings for every day of the week!

$5.95 Retail price
$3.00 Postage and handling

Make check payable to Quail Ridge Press
ISBN 0-937552-02-X

SEASONED WITH LOVE TOO

by Barbara Page
2899 Highway 471   601/829-1652
Brandon, MS 39042   or 601/829-1803

Seasoned With Love Too has over 300 recipes showing the author's love of country cooking, country sayings and country lore. Barbara Page gives the how-to's on country-style recipes that are used in her Fannin Mart Restaurant in Rankin County. It's a cookbook you'll want to read from cover to cover.

$14.95 Retail price
  $5.00 Postage and handling

Make check payable to Barbara Page

THE SEVEN CHOCOLATE SINS

by Ruth Moorman and Lalla Williams
Quail Ridge Press
Brandon, MS

Chocolate lovers readily admit that anything as good as chocolate must be sinful. True chocoholics *lust* for chocolate candy, get *greedy* for one more chocolaty cookie, are as *proud* as "Chocolate Milk Punch," become *slothful* if they eat too much "Sell-Your-Soul Pudding." Debonair devils and heavenly angels abound in this devilishly delicious book! Currently out of print.

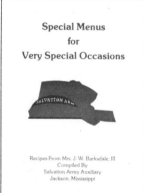

SPECIAL MENUS FOR VERY SPECIAL OCCASIONS

The Salvation Army Auxiliary
c/o Mrs. Andrew Warriner
4636 Meadow Ridge Drive
Jackson, MS 39211   601/366-5831

Have you ever wondered what goes with what? Recipes from *Special Menus for Very Special Occasions* help you plan for these occasions. These are truly gourmet selections, but surprisingly easy to prepare. We say try them, we think you'll like them—and for you and your guests, a very special treat!

$4.50 Retail price
$1.25 Postage and handling

Make check payable to The Salvation Army Auxiliary

SOUTHERN LEGACIES

by Nancy Patty Walker
P. O. Box 1405
Starkville, MS 39760   662/323-2648

A cookbook to cherish. Nancy Patty Walker has compiled a lifetime of cooking in *Southern Legacies,* her cookbook of creative and helpful hints. Outstanding party recipes from unusual hors d'oeuvres to fantastic desserts. 400 recipes in 256 pages with full color cover. A must for every cookbook collector.

$12.95 Retail price
$1.50 Postage and handling

Make check payable to Walker Enterprises

ISBN 0-939-11475-5

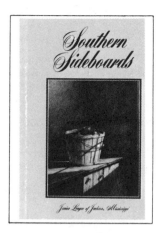

SOUTHERN SIDEBOARDS

JLJ Publications
P O Box 4709
Jackson, MS 39296   601/948-2357

Southern Sideboards is a hard-back, spiral-bound collection of 950 twice-tested recipes. It has been acclaimed by food editors across the United States. It contains two unique chapters: "Rainy Days and Special Days" and "Special Techniques." *Southern Sideboards* is as outstanding as its sales record—150,000 copies in three years!

$16.95 Retail price
$ 2.75 Postage and handling

Make check payable to JLJ Publications
ISBN 0-9606886-0-9

STANDING ROOM ONLY

New Stage Theatre
Jackson, MS

Southern food that's fun to cook; memorable to eat. *SRO's* lively style, explicit instructions, big type, computer cross-referenced index and dazzling theatre-inspired graphics take the stage fright out of connoisseur cooking. Narratives by Pulitzer Prize winners Eudora Welty and Beth Henley. 380 pages. 600 recipes. Currently out of print.

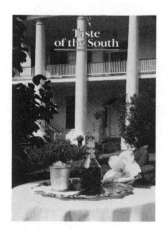

TASTE OF THE SOUTH

Jackson Symphony League
Jackson, MS

The South has always been known for its people, their customs, warmth, graciousness and their unsurpassed mode of entertaining. *Taste of the South* offers 448 pages with 600 triple-tested recipes, 65 menus for every time of day, exquisite color photographs and section introductions by internationally acclaimed Mississippians. Currently out of print.

TASTING TEA TREASURES
Greenville Junior Woman's Club
Greenville, MS

The Greenville Junior Woman's Club hosts an annual Tasting Tea for members, associates and guests. Each member prepares a favorite dish to be judged. The recipes in this cookbook are favorites from past Tasting Teas, and it is our sincere desire that they will become your favorites as well.

TEMPTATIONS
Presbyterian Day School
West Sunflower Road   662/843-8698
Cleveland, MS 38732   Fax: 662/843-6600

Temptations represents a new dimension in Delta dining and Southern hospitality, featuring 450 new recipes and 13 exciting sections including a special section from the talented men cooks of the area, and a special "gifts from your kitchen" section. This attractive spiral-bound hard-cover edition is as appealing to the eye as the recipes are to the palate.

$14.95 Retail price
$3.00 Postage and handling

Make check payable to *Temptations*

ISBN 0-9617154-0-5

TOP RANKIN' RECIPES
Rankin General Hospital Auxiliary
Brandon, MS

Top Rankin Recipes is 88 pages, featuring over 250 of the best recipes from Rankin County and Central Mississippi. Many of the recipes featured are "family" recipes handed down from generation to generation. Currently out of print.

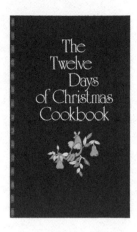

THE TWELVE DAYS OF CHRISTMAS COOKBOOK

by Ruth Moorman and Lalla Williams
Quail Ridge Press
P O Box 123   601/825-2063
Brandon, MS 39043   or 800/343-1583

Ten lords a-leaping will relish "Lord Ney's Bean Soup," the first course in a lordly dinner . . . and piping hot tea for the *eleven pipers piping* along with "Scotch Lace Wafers" and "Dundee Cake." Colorful Christmas illustrations lend a warm holiday spirit to scrumptious recipes in suggested menus for coffees, luncheons, buffets, midnight breakfasts, etc.

$5.95 Retail price
$3.00 Postage and handling

Make check payable to Quail Ridge Press

ISBN 0-937552-00-3

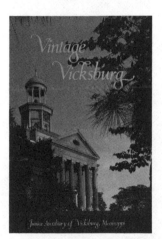

VINTAGE VICKSBURG

Vicksburg Junior Auxiliary
P O Box 86
Vicksburg, MS 39181   601/634-1084

Vintage Vicksburg is a cookbook sure to make history. Compiled by the Vicksburg Junior Auxiliary, this hardcover book features 21 sections with over 900 twice-tested recipes and eight beautiful color photographs of tempting dishes in historical scenes. This unique collectors' volume truly reflects southern history with southern food at its finest.

$19.95 Retail price
$3.00 Postage and handling

Make check payable to JAV Publications

ISBN 0-9614988-0-3

WADDAD'S KITCHEN

by Waddad Habeeb Buttross
P O Box 1506
Natchez, MS 39121   601/445-8584

Waddad's Kitchen is a mother's attempt to preserve for her (six) children what she has learned of the art of cooking. There is wonderful Southern cooking among the photographs and Lebanese recipes which are easy to prepare. Truly Lebanese Zest and Southern Best!

$7.95 Retail price
$3.50 Postage and handling

Make check payable to Waddad H. Buttross

ISBN 0-939114-36-4

The largest octagon house in the U.S., Longwood in Natchez was never completed.

Special Discount Offers!

Join the Best Club—enjoy the Best discounts!

- You'll receive the entire 30-volume set of the BEST OF THE BEST STATE COOKBOOKS.
- The cost is only $380.00—a 25% discount off the retail price of $508.50.
- The books are shipped immediately, and the shipping cost is only $8.00.
- You'll receive a 25% discount on future BEST cookbooks.
- Members say: "These are the most used books in my collection."
              "I know I can trust these recipes."

Join the Best of the Month Club

- You'll receive a different BEST cookbook each month or every other month.
- You'll enjoy a 20% discount off the price of each book ($16.95 discounted to $13.56).
- You'll automatically become a member of the BEST CLUB once you receive all
  available volumes, which entitles you to a 25% discount on future volumes.
- Members say: "My BEST books are my very favorite cookbooks."
              "I usually buy more than one copy—they have a way of disappearing."
              "Most of my other cookbooks are on the shelf—my BEST books stay on
              the kitchen counter."

Join today! 1-800-343-1583

You will speak directly to one of our friendly customer service representatives.
Most orders can be shipped the same day!

Both books: Paperbound • 7x10

The Recipe Hall of Fame Cookbook
ISBN 1-893062-08-2 • **304 pages** • **$19.95**

The Recipe Hall of Fame Dessert Cookbook
ISBN 1-893062-19-8 • **240 pages** • **$16.95**

More than 400 of the most popular and truly exceptional recipes from the acclaimed Quail Ridge Press BEST OF THE BEST STATE COOKBOOK SERIES (see complete listing on next page) have been collected in *The Recipe Hall of Fame Cookbook.* Chosen from approximately 12,000 outstanding BEST cookbook recipes, the Hall of Fame selections have achieved extra distinction for producing consistently superb dishes that are made over and over again. *The Recipe Hall of Fame Dessert Cookbook* boasts over 300 delectable desserts. These recipes are truly the BEST of the BEST OF THE BEST!

Preserving America's Food Heritage

BEST OF THE BEST STATE COOKBOOK SERIES

Cookbooks listed below have been completed as of December 31, 2000.

Best of the Best from
ALABAMA
288 pages, $16.95

Best of the Best from
ARIZONA
288 pages, $16.95

Best of the Best from
ARKANSAS
288 pages, $16.95

Best of the Best from
CALIFORNIA
384 pages, $16.95

Best of the Best from
COLORADO
288 pages, $16.95

Best of the Best from
FLORIDA
288 pages, $16.95

Best of the Best from
GEORGIA
336 pages, $16.95

Best of the Best from the
GREAT PLAINS
288 pages, $16.95

Best of the Best from
ILLINOIS
288 pages, $16.95

Best of the Best from
INDIANA
288 pages, $16.95

Best of the Best from
IOWA
288 pages, $16.95

Best of the Best from
KENTUCKY
288 pages, $16.95

Best of the Best from
LOUISIANA
288 pages, $16.95

Best of the Best from
LOUISIANA II
288 pages, $16.95

Best of the Best from
MICHIGAN
288 pages, $16.95

Best of the Best from
MINNESOTA
288 pages, $16.95

Best of the Best from
MISSISSIPPI
288 pages, $16.95

Best of the Best from
MISSOURI
304 pages, $16.95

Best of the Best from
NEW ENGLAND
368 pages, $16.95

Best of the Best from
NEW MEXICO
288 pages, $16.95

Best of the Best from
NORTH CAROLINA
288 pages, $16.95

Best of the Best from
OHIO
352 pages, $16.95

Best of the Best from
OKLAHOMA
288 pages, $16.95

Best of the Best from
PENNSYLVANIA
320 pages, $16.95

Best of the Best from
SOUTH CAROLINA
288 pages, $16.95

Best of the Best from
TENNESSEE
288 pages, $16.95

Best of the Best from
TEXAS
352 pages, $16.95

Best of the Best from
TEXAS II
352 pages, $16.95

Best of the Best from
VIRGINIA
320 pages, $16.95

Best of the Best from
WISCONSIN
288 pages, $16.95

Note: All cookbooks are ringbound except California, which is paperbound.

Special discount offers available!
(See previous page for details.)

To order by credit card, call toll-free **1-800-343-1583** or send check or money order to:
QUAIL RIDGE PRESS • P. O. Box 123 • Brandon, MS 39043
Visit our website at **www.quailridge.com** to order online!

- -

Order form

Send completed form and payment to:
QUAIL RIDGE PRESS • P. O. Box 123 • Brandon, MS 39043

❑ Check enclosed

Charge to: ❑ Visa ❑ MasterCard
❑ Discover ❑ American Express

Card #_____

Expiration Date _____

Signature _____

Name _____

Address _____

City/State/Zip_____

Phone # _____

Qty.	Title of Book (State)	Total

Subtotal _____

7% Tax for MS residents _____

Postage ($3.00 any number of books) **+ 3.00**

Total _____